Himmler's Cook

Franz-Olivier Giesbert is a French author, journalist and television presenter. He has worked for *Le Nouvel Observateur*, *Le Figaro* and *Le Point* and he appears on literary and cultural television shows on a range of channels.

Himmler's Cook

Franz-Olivier Giesbert

Translated from the
French by Anthea Bell

Atlantic Books
London

First published as *La cuisinière d'Himmler* in France in 2013
by Éditions Gallimard.

First published in Great Britain in 2015 by Atlantic Books,
an imprint of Atlantic Books Ltd.

10 9 8 7 6 5 4 3 2 1

A CIP catalogue record for this book is available
from the British Library.

Trade Paperback ISBN: 978 1 78239 412 9
E-book ISBN: 978 1 78239 413 6

Printed by ScandBook AB, Sweden

Atlantic Books
An Imprint of Atlantic Books Ltd
Ormond House
26–27 Boswell Street
London
WC1N 3JZ
www.atlantic-books.co.uk

For Elie W., my big brother,
who has given me so much.

Fair maids, believe me, wait not for tomorrow;
Life's roses pluck today, forget its sorrow.

(RONSARD)

Prologue

I can't stand people who are always complaining, but they're the only sort you find on this earth. That's why I have a problem with people in general.

There were plenty of occasions in the past when I might have lamented my fate, but I've always been against turning the world into nothing but a vale of tears.

The one thing that separates us from the animals, after all, is not consciousness, which we so stupidly refuse to admit that they possess, but the tendency to self pity that drags humanity down. How can anyone indulge in it when nature, the sun and the earth are out there calling to us?

To my last breath, and even after it, I shall believe in nothing but the forces of love, laughter and vengeance. They have guided my footsteps through all misfortunes for over a century, and frankly I have never had any reason to regret that, even now that I am about to part company with my old carcase as I prepare to enter the grave.

I might as well tell you straight away that the role of victim doesn't suit me. Of course, like everyone else, I'm not in favour of the death penalty, unless I'm the person carrying it out. I've done just that from time to time in the past, both in the interests of justice and to make me feel good, and I have never regretted it.

Meanwhile I am not about to let anyone walk all over me, not even at home in Marseilles where the scum of the earth think they can lay down the law. The latest to discover it at his own expense is a low-life character who often operates near my restaurant in the summer season, where there are queues waiting to go on boating excursions to the islands of If and Frioul. He picks tourists' pockets and sometimes snatches their handbags. He's a good-looking lad, moves nicely, and he has a turn of speed like an Olympic medallist. I call him the Cheetah. The police would say he's the Maghrebi type, but I wouldn't stake my life on it.

He looks to me like a middle-class boy gone wrong. I was going to buy my fish at the quayside one day when my eyes met his. I may be wrong, but all I saw in them was the despair of someone whose world was turned upside down, once either fatalism or natural indolence had shown him that he couldn't go on being a spoilt child for ever.

One evening he followed me after I'd closed the restaurant. That was my chance, because for once I was going home on foot. It was almost midnight, a wind was blowing almost hard enough to make the boats in harbour take to the air, and no one was out and about in the streets. Perfect conditions for a mugging. I was level with the Place aux Huiles when, glancing over my shoulder, I saw that he was about to overtake me, so I turned abruptly and trained my Glock 17 on him. A 9 mm pistol firing twenty-seven rounds, lovely little handgun. I looked at him over it and shouted, 'Don't you have anything better to do than try fleecing a lady who's over a hundred years old, punk?'

'But I never did anything, m'dame, wasn't going to do a thing, I swear!'

He wouldn't stand still. You'd have thought he was a little girl with a skipping rope.

'There's one certain rule, let me tell you. Someone who swears he's innocent is always guilty.'

'Your mistake, lady. I was taking a little walk, that's all.'

'You listen to me, punk. With a wind like this blowing, no one's going to hear if I pull the trigger. So you've got no choice: if you want to save your life you'd better hand me that bag of yours right away, with all the stuff you've nicked today, and I'll give it to someone in need.'

I pointed the Glock at him like a forefinger.

'And don't let me catch you at it again, or I hate to think what will happen to you. Go on, clear out!'

He dropped the bag and set off at a run, yelling back, once he'd reached a respectful distance, 'Crazy old nutter! You're nothing but a nutter!'

After that I passed on the contents of the bag – the watches, bracelets, mobile phones and wallets – to the down-and-outs sleeping off their hangovers on the nearby Cours d'Estienne-d'Orves pedestrian zone. They said thanks with a mixture of alarm and surprise. One of them called me a nutcase. I told him I'd heard that before.

The manager of the bar next door to the restaurant warned me next day: the evening before, he said, some guy had been held up at gunpoint in the Place aux Huiles. By an old lady, would I believe it? He didn't understand what made me burst out laughing.

I

Under the Sign of the Virgin

MARSEILLES, 2012. I kissed the letter and then I crossed my fingers, my forefinger and my middle finger, hoping it would be good news. I'm very superstitious, it's my little weakness.

The letter had been posted in Cologne, in Germany, as the postmark on the stamp told me, and the sender had written her name on the back: Renate Fröll.

My heart began beating very fast. I was happy and anxious at the same time. At my age, when you've survived everyone else, getting a personal letter is bound to be a great event.

After deciding not to open the letter until later, so as to maintain the excitement of its arrival for as long as possible, I kissed the envelope again. On the back this time.

There are days when I feel like kissing everything, plants and furniture, anything, but I take care not to. I don't want people thinking I'm a daft old biddy and likely to scare children. At the age of nearly 105 I have only a thin little thread of a voice left, three sound teeth, an expression like an owl, and I can't smell violets.

When it comes to cooking, however, I still know my way around. I may even call myself one of the queens of Marseilles, only just behind the other Rose, a slip of a girl aged only eighty-eight who makes wonderful Sicilian dishes in the Rue Glandevès, not far from the Municipal Opera House.

But as soon as I leave my restaurant to walk in the city streets I feel that I'm frightening people. There's only one place where, apparently, my presence does not seem out of place, and that's at the top of the limestone hill from which the gilded statue of Our Lady of the Guard seems to preach love to the universe, the sea and the city of Marseilles.

Mamadou takes me there and brings me home on the back of his motorbike. He's a tall, strapping lad, my right-hand man in the restaurant, where he keeps the place tidy, helps with the cash register, and takes me everywhere on that stinking motorbike of his. I like to feel the nape of his neck against my lips.

During the weekly closing of my restaurant, on Sunday afternoon and all day Monday, I can sit for hours on my bench in the sun as it beats down on my skin. Inside my head, I talk to all the dead whom I have lost and shall soon be seeing again in heaven. A friend I've lost sight of liked to say that they were much better company than the living. She was right: not only are they never in a bad temper, they have all the time in the world. They listen to me. They calm me down.

At my great age, I have discovered that people are much more alive in you once they're dead. So dying does not mean the end; on the contrary, it means rebirth in other people's minds.

At midday, when the sun gets out of control and cuts me under my black widow's garments as if with a knife, or even worse a pickaxe, I get up and go into the shade of the basilica.

I kneel in front of the silver Virgin who dominates the altar and pretend to be praying, and then I sit down and have a little snooze. God knows why, but I sleep better there than anywhere. Perhaps because the loving look of the statue soothes me. The silly shouts and laughter of the tourists don't bother me, and nor do the bells. It's true that I am terribly tired, as if I were always coming back from a long journey. When I have told you my story you will know why, but then again my story is nothing, or nothing to speak of: a tiny splash in the mire of history where we all paddle, as it pulls us down into the depths from century to century.

History is a bitch. She has taken everything from me. My children. My parents. My great, true love. My cats. I don't understand the stupid veneration that the human race feels for her.

I am very glad that History has gone away, after all the damage she's done. But I know she will be back soon; I feel it in the electricity in the air and the dark looks of people's eyes. It's the destiny of the human species to let stupidity and hatred guide its way through the charnel houses that generations before us have never stopped filling.

Human beings are like beasts in the slaughterhouse. They go to meet their fate, eyes cast down, looking neither ahead of them nor behind them. They don't know what awaits them, they don't want to know, although nothing would be easier: the future is a return, a hiccup, it's like heartburn, it's sometimes the vomit of the past coming up again.

For a long time I tried to warn humanity against the three vices of our time: nihilism, cupidity and a good conscience. The three of them have turned our brains. I've tried it with my neighbours, particularly the butcher's apprentice on the same floor as me, a pale and puny lad with the hands of a pianist, but I can see that I'm only annoying him with the drivel I talk, and when I meet him on the stairs I have more than once grabbed hold of his sleeve to keep him from getting away. He always claims to agree with me, but I know very well he agrees only so that I'll leave him alone.

It's the same with everyone. Over the last fifty years I've never found anyone who will listen to me. I realized I was fighting a losing battle, and ended up keeping my mouth shut until the day when I broke my mirror. All my life I'd managed never to break a mirror, but that morning, as I looked at the splintered glass on the bathroom tiles, I realized that I'd attracted bad luck. I even thought I wouldn't last the summer, which would be only normal at my age.

When you tell yourself that you're going to die, and there's no one to keep you company, not even a dog or a cat, there's only one thing to be done: you have to make yourself interesting. I decided to write my memoirs, and I went to buy four spiral-bound notebooks at Madame Mandonato's bookshop and stationer's. Madame Mandonato is a well-preserved sixty-year-old, I call her 'the old lady', and she is one of the most cultured women in Marseilles. When I was about to pay her for the notebooks, I could see that something was bothering her, so I pretended to be looking for change to give her time to decide how to put her question.

'What are you going to do with those?'

'Well, write a book, of course!'

'Yes, but what kind of book?'

I hesitated, and then I said, 'All kinds of books at once, my dear. A book in celebration of love, a book to warn mankind of the dangers we're running. So that we will never live through what I have lived through again.'

'There are a great many books on that subject already.'

'Then we must assume that they haven't been very convincing. Mine will be the story of my life. I already have a title: *One Hundred Years Old and Going Strong*.'

'That's a good title, Rose. People love anything to do with centenarians. It's a market growing very fast just now – there will soon be millions of them. The thing about such books is that they're written by people who laugh at themselves.'

'Well, in my own memoirs I shall try to show that we're not dead while we're still alive, and we still have something to say.'

So I write in the morning, but also in the evening, in front of a small glass of red wine. I moisten my lips with the wine from time to time, just for the pleasure of it, and when I'm short of inspiration I drink a mouthful to get my ideas back.

That evening it was after midnight when I decided to interrupt my writing. I didn't wait to be in bed, ready for my night's rest, before opening the missive I had found in the letter box in the morning. I don't know whether it was age or emotion, but my hands were shaking so much that I tore the envelope in several places while I was opening it. And when I'd read what the contents said I felt faint and my brain stopped short.

2

Samir the Mouse

MARSEILLES, 2012. A few seconds after I came back to my senses, a song began running through my head: 'Can You Feel It' by the Jackson 5. Michael at his best, with a true pure child's voice, not yet the tone of a self-satisfied castrato. My favourite song.

I was feeling fine, as I always do when I hum it. They say that after a certain age, if you wake up and you don't hurt all over it means you're dead. I have evidence to the contrary.

Coming back to myself after my fainting fit, I didn't hurt anywhere and I wasn't dead or even injured.

Like everyone of my age, I dread breaking something that might condemn me to a wheelchair. I particularly dread breaking my hip. But I hadn't done it this time.

I had foreseen what might happen: before reading the letter I had sat down on the sofa. When I lost consciousness I had, naturally, fallen backwards with my head on a soft cushion.

Once again I glanced at the card that I was still holding before swearing, 'Fucking filthy bloody shit of a brothel!'

The card announced the death of Renate Fröll, who therefore couldn't have sent it. She had died four months ago and had been cremated in Cologne. There were no further details on the card, and no address or telephone number.

I began crying. I think I must have cried all night, because next morning I woke up drenched with tears, my sheets, my pillow and my nightdress all making a kind of soup. It was time for me to go into action.

I had an intuition, and I wanted to confirm it. I called one of my young neighbours on his mobile: Samir the Mouse. Samir is the son of a septuagenarian who, they say, has spent his entire professional life unemployed. He's done very well at it, he's a very handsome man, neat and clean and immaculately dressed. His wife, the family cashier and cleaning lady, is twenty years younger than him and looks at least ten years older: she's crippled with arthritis and limps up and down the stairs. But it's true that she has always worked hard enough for the two of them.

Samir the Mouse is thirteen, and he already has the keen eye of someone hunting down the big bonuses of life. Nothing escapes him. It's as if he has eyes everywhere, even in his back and his bottom. Not that he makes much use of them. He spends his time in front of his computer, where he can find out anything you want in record time for a consideration, cash down. A price, a name, a number.

Scenting good business, Samir arrived at once, even though he's not a morning person. I handed him the death announcement.

'I'd like you to find out all the information you can about this Renate Fröll for me.'

'What kind of information?'

'Anything, from her birth to her death. Her family, what she did for a living, her little secrets. Her life, if you see what I mean.'

'How much?'

As Samir the Mouse is neither a poet nor a philanthropist, I offered him the little cabinet from the sitting room. He inspected it and asked, 'Is this thing really old?'

'Nineteenth century.'

'I'll look on the Internet and see what something like that's worth, and I'll come back to you if it doesn't work out right. But I guess it will be okay.'

I offered him chocolate biscuits and a drink with one of my own favourite flavourings – barley water, mint or grenadine – but he turned them down, as if those were not for him at his age, whereas they are more to my own taste then ever.

Samir the Mouse always has good reasons to leave me high and dry. He's snowed under with work and doesn't know how to take his time. If I've never managed to keep him with me for more than a few minutes, then that is also, I think, because he has some idea of what I feel for him: in spite of the difference in our ages I'm mad about him.

In two or three years' time, or whenever the man has emerged from the child he is now, he'll be all hair and mixed-up desires, I'll wish he would take me in his arms and hug me close, say crude things to me, shake me up a little, that's all I ask. At my age, I know it's incongruous, even stupid, but if we had to rid our heads of all our fantasies, there wouldn't be much left inside them. A few of the Ten Commandments swimming in brain-juice, that would be about it. Life would be on the point of dying out. It's our follies that keep us going.

My principle is to live every moment as if it were my last. Every gesture, every word. I intend to die with my mind at rest, no regrets, no remorse.

Next evening, I was in my nightdress and ready to go to bed when the doorbell rang. It was Samir the Mouse. I thought he was going to ask me for more money, but no; he'd been working all day and wanted to tell me the first results of his inquiries face-to-face.

'Renate Fröll,' he said, 'was a pharmacist in Neuwied near Cologne. A spinster, nothing known about her parents. No family. That's all I could find out. I suppose you don't have a lead for me to follow?'

I thought I detected irony in his glance as it went through me.

'Think about it,' I replied in a neutral voice. 'If I knew who this woman was, I wouldn't have asked you to look into it for me.'

'But if you didn't have some idea at the back of your mind, you wouldn't care about knowing who she was.'

I didn't reply. Samir the Mouse was happy to have guessed right; an expression of satisfaction crossed his face. With increasing age I have more and more difficulty in hiding my feelings, and he had noticed the emotion that overcame me when he told me the first results of his enquiries. They bore out my intuition. I was like the earth waiting for a quake or some such upheaval.

When he had left I was so excited that I couldn't get to

sleep. It was as if all my memories had come back to me. I felt caught in a whirlpool of images and sensations from the past.

I decided to go back to my book. Up to this point I had been the one who was writing it. But now, suddenly, a voice entered my mind, and it dictated what will follow.

3

The Girl Born in the Cherry Tree

THE BLACK SEA, 1907. I was born in a tree on 18 July, seven years after the birth of the century, which in principle ought to have been a sign of good fortune. It was a cherry tree a hundred years old, with branches like heavy, weary arms. I was born on a market day. Papa had gone to sell his oranges and vegetables in Trebizond, the old capital of the empire of the same name on the shores of the Black Sea, a few kilometres from our home in Kovata, the pear-growing capital and piss-pot of the world.

Before leaving for town, he had told my mother that he didn't think he'd be able to get home that evening, and he was very sorry, because Mama seemed to be on the point of giving birth, but he had no choice: he had to get a bad tooth drawn, and he was also going to collect some money that an uncle owed him. After that, evening would soon come on, and the roads were not safe at night.

I think he was also planning a drinking session with some friends, but he had nothing to worry about anyway. Mama was like those sheep who go on grazing as they give birth to their lambs. They hardly stop eating and chewing the cud, even to lick clean the lambs that have just emerged from their backsides. When they give birth you'd think they were merely obeying a call of nature, and indeed it sometimes looks as if the latter process gives them more trouble.

My mother was a robust woman with big bones and a pelvis wide enough to let any number of children out. She gave birth easily, never taking more than a few seconds about it, and then, once the baby was out, Mama went back to whatever she had been doing. At the age of twenty-eight she'd already had four children, not counting the two who had died very young.

On the day of my birth, the three men who were to ravage the human race were already in this world: Hitler was eighteen years old, Stalin was twenty-eight and Mao was thirteen. I had fallen into the wrong century – theirs.

Fall was the word for it. One of our cats had climbed the cherry tree and couldn't get down again. Perched on a broken branch, it mewed pitifully all day long. Just before sunset, when Mama realized that my father wouldn't be back that night, she decided to rescue the cat.

After climbing the tree and reaching out her arm to pick the cat up, my mother, so the family legend goes, felt her first contraction. She took hold of the animal by the scruff of the neck, let it go a few branches lower down, and then suddenly, seized by a presentiment, lay down in the crook of the cherry tree where the branches intersected. And that was how I came into the world, tumbling out of her.

For the fact is that, before I fell, I had also been ejected from my mother's womb. She might have been farting or defecating, I think it would have come to much the same thing. Except that then Mama caressed me and lavished endearments on me. She was a woman overflowing with love, even for her daughters.

Forgive me for this image, but it's the first thing that comes to my mind and I can't get rid of it: her maternal glance was like a sun lighting us all up. It warmed our winters. My mother's face wore the same sweet expression as the face of the gilded Virgin enthroned on her altar in the little church of Kovata. The expression on the faces of all the mothers in the world as they look at their children.

It is thanks to Mama that my first eight years were the happiest of my life. She made sure that nothing bad happened to us, and indeed nothing at all ever did happen except for the passing of the seasons. No cries, no tragedies, not even any mourning. At the risk of seeming simple, which is probably my real nature, I will call that real happiness: when day follows day in a kind of torpor, when time stretches out to infinity, when incidents are repeated without any surprises, when everyone loves everyone else, and there's no shouting indoors or out of doors when you go to sleep beside your cat.

Behind the hill above our farm, there was a small stone house where a Muslim family lived. The father, a tall beanpole of a man with eyebrows as thick as moustaches, could do anything and hired himself out by the day to the farms round about. While his wife or children looked after their own goats and sheep, he lent everyone else a hand, including us when Papa was overworked at harvest time.

His name was Mehmed Ali Efendi. I think he was my father's best friend. As we did not share the same religion, we never spent festival days together, but our two families often met on Sundays to share meals that went on and on. On these occasions my eyes devoured young Mustapha, one of the neighbouring family's sons, who was four years older than me. I had decided to marry him one day, and I foresaw myself converting to Islam for his sake.

He had a body that I dreamed of holding close to mine, very long eyelashes and a way of looking at you deeply that seemed to be in sympathy with the whole world. His was a proud, dark beauty like the beauty of those who drink in the sun.

I told myself that I could spend the rest of my life looking at Mustapha, which in my eyes is the best definition of love. Since then, my long experience has taught me that it consists of melting into the one you love, rather than forgetting yourself in the mirror he offers you.

I knew my love was returned when, one day, Mustapha took me to the sea and gave me a copper bracelet before running away. I called to him, but he didn't turn back. He was like me, afraid of what was growing inside him.

Our story still leaves a strange taste in my mind, the taste of the kiss that we never exchanged. The more the years pass, the more that regret weighs on me.

Almost a century later, I still wear his bracelet on my arm. I have had it enlarged, and I look at it as I search for words in writing these lines. It is all that remains of my childhood now that History, that damn bitch, has swallowed it bones and all.

I'm not too sure when History began her death-dealing work, but at Friday prayers the imams began preaching the murder of Armenians, after which Sheikh ul-Islam, a bearded and disgustingly dirty figure, spiritual leader of the Sunni Muslims, proclaimed a jihad on 14 November 1914. It was on that day, with great splendour and in front of a row of solemn men with moustaches, that the signal for a holy war was given outside the Fatih Mosque, in the historic quarter of Constantinople.

As for us, the Armenians, we got used to it in the end. We weren't going to spoil our lives for such idiocy. However, some weeks before the genocide of my people I did notice that Papa was in a bad temper, and I put it down to his falling out with Mehmed, Mustapha's father, who never set foot in our house these days.

When I asked Mama why they weren't speaking to each other, she shook her head gravely.

'Such things are too stupid for children to understand.'

Late one afternoon, when I was walking at the top of the hill, I heard my father's voice. I went closer, approaching him from behind and cautiously so as not to attract his attention, before crouching down to hide behind a thicket. Papa was on his own, making a speech to the sea as it rolled before him and raising his long arms:

'My dear sisters, my dear brothers, let me tell you that we are your friends. I realize, of course, that you may feel surprised after all you have done to us, but we have decided to forget everything, let me assure you, so that we do not all of us enter that infernal spiral when blood calls for blood, to the great misfortune of our descendants.'

He stopped short and, with a gesture of impatience, asked the sea please to stop applauding and let him go on. As the sea did not comply with this request, he continued at the top of his voice:

'I have come to tell you that we want peace, and it is not too late, it is never too late to shake hands!'

He bowed to the swell of marine applause, then mopped his brow on his shirtsleeve before setting off for home.

I followed. At one point he stopped in the middle of the path and then yelled, 'Bastards!'

I have often thought of that rather ridiculous scene. Papa was preparing to play the role of political peacemaker, and at the same time he didn't believe in it. In fact he was going out of his mind.

Over the following evenings, my father whispered to my mother for hours on end. Sometimes he raised his voice. From the little room that I shared with two sisters and my cat, I couldn't catch much of what he said, but it seemed to me that Papa had taken a dislike to the world in general and the Turks in particular.

Once both my parents raised their voices, and what I heard through the walls sent a cold shiver down my spine.

'If you believe what you're saying, Hagop,' cried Mama, 'then we must leave at once!'

'First I want to give us all a chance by offering to make peace with them, as Christ did, but I don't believe in it all that much. You know how Christ ended up? If they won't listen to us then I'm not in favour of turning the other check. However, I don't want to leave them what we've spent a lifetime building up without a fight!'

'And suppose they end up killing us, us and the children too?'

'We'll fight, Vart.'

'What with?'

'With anything we can find!' shouted Papa. 'Guns, axes, knives, stones!'

Mama shouted back, 'Do you know what you're saying, Hagop? If they put their threats into practice we're condemned to death already. Let's leave while there's still time!'

'I couldn't live anywhere else.'

There was a long silence, then groans and sighs as if they were hurting each other, but I wasn't worried, far from it. When I heard those sounds, interrupted now and then by laughter or chuckling, I knew that what they were really doing was making each other feel good.

4

The First Time I Died

THE BLACK SEA, 1915. My grandmother smelled of onions all over: her feet, her armpits, her mouth. Although I don't eat nearly so many onions myself, it's from her that I've inherited the sweetish aroma that follows me from morning to evening, and then right under my sheets: the smell of Armenia.

In the height of the season, she would make plaki to last a week. Just writing that word starts my mouth watering. It's a poor-man's dish based on celeriac, carrots and large haricot beans, to which she added all kinds of other vegetables, depending on the day and what she felt like. Sometimes she put in hazelnuts or raisins as well. My grandmother was an inventive cook.

I loved peeling vegetables and making cakes under her benevolent eyes. She took her chance to philosophize or tell me about life. Often, when we were cooking, she would deplore the gluttony of the human species; it's greed, she used to tell me, that gives us all our vital spark, but when, sad to say, we listen to nothing but our innards we are digging our own graves.

No doubt she would find her own grave before very long, judging by the big behind that she could hardly squeeze through doorways, not to mention her legs with their varicose veins, but she was worried about other people, not herself. Ever since the death of her husband she had considered herself dead, and she dreamed only of joining him in heaven. My grandmother often quoted proverbs that she claimed to have made up. She had proverbs for all situations.

When times were hard:

'If I were rich I'd be eating all the time, so I'd die very young. That's why I did well to be poor.'

When people talked about the politics of the day:

'There's never as much to eat in heaven as in your own kitchen garden. The stars have never fed anyone.'

When the subject of conversation was the Turkish nationalists:

'When the wolf is left to guard the flocks, there won't be a single sheep left on earth.'

However, the Ottoman Empire had failed to understand that, and I saw it crumble during the early years of my life. In a manner of speaking, that is; where I lived at the back of beyond, of course I didn't literally see anything. History always walks in without knocking at the door, and sometimes you hardly notice her passing by. Except when she rolls over you, which is what happened to us in the end.

*

We Armenians were sure of our rights. We thought that to survive, we had only to be kind and good. Not to bother anyone. To keep close to the walls.

We found out what came of that. It's a lesson that I've remembered all my life. I owe my malicious disposition to that lesson; it made me a nasty piece of work without mercy or remorse, always ready to return evil for evil.

Let me sum it up. When two sets of people are living in the same country, and one wants to kill the other, it's because the latter has only just arrived. Or then again, maybe because they were there first. Armenians had been living in our part of the world since the dawn of time: that was their fault, that was their crime.

Having arrived in the second century BC on the ruins of the kingdom of Urartu, for a long time their own realm stretched from the Black Sea to the Caspian Sea. After becoming the first Christian nation in history, there in the heart of the Orient, Armenia resisted most invasions – Arab, Mongol, Tartar – before yielding to the tide of Ottoman Turks flooding in during the second millennium AD.

My grandmother, alluding to remarks by the British poet Lord Byron, liked to say that the satraps of Persia and the pashas of Turkey alike ravaged the country where God had created man in his own image. It was the first time I ever heard her mention a writer by name.

If we are to believe Lord Byron and a great many others, Adam was born from the dust of Armenia, and the Paradise of the Bible should be located on the same soil. That would account for the melancholy tinged with nostalgia that could be read in the eyes of Armenians over the centuries, and of all my family at the time, but not mine today. Gravity isn't my strong point.

But you needn't think me uneducated because I spend my life in front of my stoves wearing clogs, or tennis shoes the rest of the time. I have read nearly all the books ever written about the Armenian genocide of 1915 and 1916. Not to mention other books as well. My intellect may leave something to be desired, but there's one thing I can never understand: why was it necessary to liquidate a population that was no threat to anyone?

I asked Elie Wiesel that question one day, when he came to dine at my restaurant with his wife Marion. Wiesel, a fine man who survived the Holocaust and has written one of the greatest books of the twentieth century, told me that you have to believe in mankind in spite of men.

He is right, and I applaud him. Even if History doesn't agree, we must also believe in the future in spite of the past, and in God in spite of his absence, or life wouldn't be worth the trouble of living.

So I won't blame my ancestors. After their conquest by the Muslims, Armenians were forbidden to carry weapons, and were left at the mercy of their new masters, who could thus exterminate them from time to time with complete immunity and the consent of the sultan.

In between raids the Armenians went about their business in banking, commerce or farming. Until the final solution.

It was the success of the Ottoman Empire that paved the way for its downfall. With eyes bigger than its stomach, it died at the beginning of the twentieth century, my own, of a mixture of stupidity, greed and obesity. It no longer had enough hands to make the Armenian people obey its laws, or the people of Greece, Bulgaria, Bosnia, Serbia, Iraq, Syria, and goodness knows how many other nations who just wanted to get on with living their lives. They ended up being left to stew in their own juice by Turkey, which set about purifying its territory in both ethnic and religious terms by eradicating the Greeks and Armenians. I don't need to tell you that Turkey didn't neglect to appropriate their goods.

As Christians in any population were supposed to be separatists, they had to be eradicated. Since Armenians were found from the Caucasus to the Mediterranean coast, they allegedly constituted the most dangerous threat of all, in the very heart of Muslim Turkey. Tired of persecution, they sometimes thought of setting up an independent state in Anatolia. They even managed to hold demonstrations, although my parents took no part in one.

Talaat and Enver, who were basically two murderers with satisfied expressions on their faces, came to put down this unrest and restore order. Under the revolutionary party of the Young Turks and the Committee of Union and Progress, Turkification had begun, and now there was no stopping it.

But the Armenians didn't know that. Nor did I. They'd forgotten to tell us, and we would have to remember next time. So I wasn't expecting a gang of thugs, eyes bulging with hatred, to turn up outside our house one afternoon armed with clubs and guns. Fanatics of the Special Organization backed up by the police. State assassins.

*

After knocking on the door, the local head of the Special Organization, a one-armed fat man with a moustache, made everyone come out. Except for me: I had run out of the back door and no one had seen me get away.

The leader told my father to join a convoy of Armenian workers, saying he was taking them to Erzerum. With courage that did not surprise me in him, Papa refused to do as he was told. 'We need to talk,' he said.

'We can talk later.'

'It's not too late to try coming to an agreement and avoid the worst. It's never too late.'

'But there's nothing for you to fear. Our intentions are peaceful.'

'What, with all those weapons?'

By way of reply the leader of the killers hit my father with a club. Papa grunted and then, with the bowed head of all History's losers, he joined the back of the convoy.

My mother, my grandmother, my brothers and my sisters had set off in the opposite direction, with another group who, carrying suitcases and bundles, seemed to be going on a long journey.

After ransacking our house, bringing out the furniture and tools and taking all our animals, even the chickens, the killers set fire to the farm, as if they were purifying the place after an epidemic of the plague.

I saw all this from where I was hiding behind the raspberry canes. I didn't know who to follow. In the end I opted for my father, because I thought he was in more danger than the others. I was right.

On the road to Erzerum, the armed men lined up their

prisoners, about twenty of them, in a dip in the ground where a field of oats was growing. Forming an execution squad, they fired at the Armenian men. Papa tried to run for it, but the bullets hit him. He staggered slightly, and then fell to the ground. The one-armed man finished him off.

After that the killers of the Special Organization calmly walked away, looking like men who had done their duty, and meanwhile a mixture of grief and fury was rising inside me like a huge spasm cutting off my breath.

When the killers had gone away I went to look at Papa. He was lying on the ground with his arms crossed, and he had what Mama called eyes of the other world; they were looking at something that wasn't there, something behind me and beyond the blue of the sky. Goats are the same when their throats have been cut.

I couldn't see any other details, because my vision was blurred by floods of tears. After kissing my father and then making the sign of the cross, or perhaps it was the other way around, I thought it would be best to go away. A small pack of stray dogs was on its way towards me, barking.

When I got back to our house it was still burning here and there, and smoke was rising. You'd have thought it had been struck by lightning. I called to my cat for a long time, but there was no response, and I thought he must have died in the fire. Unless he had run away as well, because he hated noise and disturbance.

Since I didn't know where else to go, of course I set off for the Efendi family's farm, but when I arrived there something told me it would be better not to show myself.

I hid in a thicket, waiting for a sight of Mustapha. He had taught me how to cluck like a hen who has just laid an egg. I still had progress to make, but it was our way of saying hello to each other.

As soon as I saw him, I clucked like a hen, and he came towards me looking upset.

'Don't let anyone see you,' he murmured when he was close to me. 'My father is with the Young Turks. They've gone crazy, they want to kill all unbelievers.'

'They've killed my father.' I burst into tears, and next moment so did he.

'And if they catch you,' he said, choking, 'the same will happen to you. Unless they enslave you. You must get away from this part of the country at once. Here you're an Armenian girl, anywhere else you'll be Turkish.'

'I want to find my mother and the rest of the family.'

'Don't think about that. Something bad is sure to have happened to them. I told you, everyone's gone crazy, even Papa!'

His father had told him to deliver some sheep dung to a market gardener who lived ten kilometres away. That was how Mustapha thought up the ruse that must surely have saved my life.

With a spade, he dug a big hole in the heap of black, damp dung on the cart that the mule was going to pull. After telling me to curl up in the hole, he gave me two hollow reeds to hold in my mouth, so that I could still breathe, and covered me with warm pellets of sheep droppings, crawling with living creatures, under which I felt like a corpse already.

Gravediggers say it takes forty days to kill a dead body entirely. In other words, if it's to mingle with the soil, with all the life gone out of it and no smell left. I felt like a corpse at the beginning of that process, a corpse still teeming with life, and I'm sure that I smelled like death.

Dung thou art, and unto dung shalt thou return, that's what the priests ought to have told us instead of talking about dust. Dust doesn't smell of anything. They always have to prettify whatever they say.

I had dung in my ears and my nostrils. Not to mention maggots, although they didn't make me itch too badly, probably because they didn't know if I was a pig or already bacon.

That was the first time in my life I died.

5

The Princess of Trebizond

THE BLACK SEA, 1915. You can get used to anything. Even
slurry. I could have spent days on end doing nothing in my
dung heap if the sheep pee hadn't turned me from head
to feet into a huge itch. After some time I'd have accepted
eternal damnation in return for the right to scratch.

I'd been told not to move. Before we left, Mustapha had
warned me that, stupid as they might be, the state assassins
would be quick to check what was in that pile of dung if
they felt the urge. A bayonet thrust is quick, and not always
forgiving. There could be no question of my putting his life
in danger, or mine either, particularly as it now seemed to
me inevitable, after what had just happened, that we were
going to be married. It was fate.

At a certain moment the cart had left the road and
stopped. I thought that the itching would die down, but
it didn't. Now that the potholes were no longer shaking
me about in my coffin of sheep droppings, I felt that they
were making their way into my body to merge with it. The
sensation of rotting alive was worse than ever.

And since the cart hadn't begun to move again, I decided
to emerge from my dung heap. Not all at once; these things
happen of themselves. I set about it slowly, like a butterfly
coming out of its chrysalis: a dirty, disgusting butterfly. It

was night, and the starry sky arching above spread over the earth that mixture of light and silence that, as I saw it, was the way the Lord expresses himself here below, to which I would later add the music of Bach, Mozart and Mendelssohn, which God seems to have written himself through human intermediaries.

The mule was nowhere to be seen, and nor, at first, was Mustapha. It was when I got out of the cart that I found him in the moonlight, lying full length on the verge of the road in the middle of a pool of dark blood, his arms crossed and his throat cut.

I kissed his forehead and then his mouth, before bursting into sobs over his face, which showed that astonishment usual when death takes someone by surprise. I didn't know that anyone could have as many tears to shed as I did.

I supposed that Mustapha had been stopped at a checkpoint by Turkish policemen like those who had taken my family away, and that he had answered them back, which was just like him. Unless they had taken him, swarthy and hairy as he was, for the Armenian he may in fact have been without knowing it.

My grief was even worse when I realized that he would have no decent burial, any more than Papa did, and would finally be torn apart by the pestilential jaws of the slavering dogs who, since the previous day, had been having the time of their lives in these parts. It was impossible to bury him; his murderers had stolen not only the mule but also the spade and fork that had been in the cart.

After dragging him off the road and covering him with grass, I walked over the fields for a long way until I reached the Black Sea, where I threw myself into the water to wash. It was summer, and the sea was warm. I stayed there until early in the morning, cleaning and rubbing my skin.

When I came out of the sea I still seemed to smell of dirt, death and unhappiness. I walked for hours, and the smell kept pursuing me. It caught up with me again in the afternoon when I was hiding beside a river, and saw that it was carrying human corpses downstream.

That smell has never left me, and even when I get out of my bath I feel dirty. Outside, but inside as well. It is what they call the guilt of the survivor. Except that in my case there were aggravating circumstances; instead of thinking of my loved ones and praying for them, I spent the following hours stuffing myself with food. I don't think I ever ate so much in my life. Mostly apricots. By evening I had the belly of a fat woman.

Psychologists would say that it was a way of killing my fear. I'd like to think they were right, but I think that my love of life was stronger than anything else, as it always has been, stronger than the tragedy that had felled my family and the fear of dying myself. I'm like those indestructible flowers that take root even on cement walls.

Of all the warring feelings inside me, hatred was the only one that did not drown out that vital impulse, probably because they were mixed up together: I wanted to live to get my revenge some day. It's an ambition as good as any other, and judging by my great age it has stood me in good stead.

It was that afternoon that I met the person who was about to change my destiny and keep me company all the way over the following years. My friend, my sister, my confidante. If our paths had not crossed, I might have ended up dead, gnawed away by my resentment as if by lice.

It was a salamander. I had trodden on the little creature, which had particularly bright yellow blotches, and I concluded that the salamander must be very young and decided it was female. We got on well at first sight. After what I'd done to the salamander, she was quivering, and I saw in her eyes that she needed me. But I needed her, too.

I closed my hand on her little body and went on walking. The sun was still high in the sky when I lay down under a tree. I dug a hole for the salamander and put a stone on top of it, and then sleep overcame me.

'Get up!'

A mounted police officer had awoken me. He had a moustache and a face like the face of a pig, but a stupid pig who was pleased with himself, which is less usual in pigs than in human beings.

'Are you Armenian?' he asked.

I shook my head.

'I know you're Armenian!' he exclaimed, with the knowing look of idiots when they're pretending to be well informed.

He told me that I had been spotted by a Turkish farmer's wife stealing apricots in her orchard. I wanted to run away, but decided not to. He was threatening me with his gun, and he was the kind to use it. I could see that in his blank eyes.

'I'm Turkish,' I tried. 'Allah akbar!'

He shrugged his shoulders.

'Recite the first verse of the Koran to me, then.'

'I haven't learned it yet.'

'There, you see, you *are* Armenian!'

The policeman told me to get up in front of him on his horse, and after retrieving my salamander I did what he said. So we went off at a trot to the headquarters of the CUP, the Committee for Union and Progress. Once outside it, he shouted:

'Salim Bey, I've got a present for you!'

When a tall, smiling man with a gap between his front teeth came out, evidently in response to this name, the police officer threw me at his feet, saying, 'Look what I brought you. I wasn't making fun of you, was I, may God be with you! You wanted a princess – here's your princess!'

That was the day when I found out I was beautiful. I thought it would be better not to stay long here; now that Mustapha was dead, it would be no more use. Moreover, I told myself it would only get me into trouble.

6

Welcome to the Little Harem

TREBIZOND, 1915. Salim Bey took me home with him when night fell. There was great excitement in the streets of Trebizond. You'd have thought everyone was moving house.

We saw an old lady struggling with a little sideboard too heavy for her, so much so that she stopped every two paces to get her breath back; also a couple carrying a wardrobe, followed by their five children, with a bed, a table and some chairs; a young man wheeling a lot of odds and ends along – sheets, rugs, statues and children's toys. It was the first time I'd been confronted by the ugly face of human greed, its bent back, twisted mouth and furtive or sometimes elated expression.

A few weeks earlier, my new master had been only an ordinary, scrawny teacher who gave history lessons at the Koranic school where it seems that the pupils played him up. Since becoming one of the leading members of the Committee for Union and Progress, he had gained a good fifteen kilos and plenty of self-confidence. Tall, with gentle eyes that didn't suit his firm chin, he was an imposing figure.

I thought he was handsome, and it was not without pride that I held his hand on the way to his house, as if I were his daughter. If one were to quibble, purists might find fault with the many little warts round his eyes, but beauty always needs flaws to set it off to good effect.

He lived in a stone house on top of a small hill overlooking the city, at the far end of luxuriant grounds planted with date palms, orange trees, cherry laurels and Bohemian olives, and ornamented with busts of reddish stone with silver hair on their heads. Years later, I found out that the property had once belonged to the biggest jeweller in Trebizond – an Armenian who, two years earlier, had been 'deported' to a wood five kilometres from the city, to be murdered there with several others of his race. Salim Bey had bought the house from his wife for nothing before she herself was 'deported' to the bottom of the sea, along with her four children.

He took me into a large room on the ground floor, where six girls, all older than me, were dining on black-cabbage soup with beans. I refused the soup bowl offered to me by Fatima, a toothless woman with a harelip who acted as our minder, confidante and nanny all at once. She didn't talk much, but her eyes told us that she was on our side. I loved her at once.

She gave me a tin box for my salamander. Even if the little creature had to coil her tail to fit into the box, she was happy there at once, and even more so when, after the evening bath, I put some earth in the box so that she could settle down in comfort.

Fatima advised me to feed my salamander on insects or earthworms, which I did over the next few days, adding to her diet slugs and tiny snails, which she loved. She also liked spiders and moths.

After that, Fatima warned me against the venomous liquid called samandarin that, as I knew later, could be secreted by the skin glands of a salamander when it thought it was in danger. But I never felt any ill effects after handling mine, so I assume that she felt she was safe with me.

I made several holes in the lid of the box, so that she could get fresh air, and I gave her a name: Theo, short for Theodora Comnena, the Christian princess of Trebizond whose beauty has been famous ever since her lifetime in the fifteenth century.

My salamander's box went everywhere with me, even to the lavatory. I couldn't do without Theo: she was my homeland, my family, my conscience and my alter ego all at once. She often lectured me, and I was very ready to answer back. We had plenty of time to talk.

The work wasn't very tiring at Salim Bey's house. I couldn't stand the verses of the Koran that were dinned into our ears, nor the rest of it, but I can hardly complain when I think of the children who were poisoned in Trebizond Hospital by Dr Ali Saib, Inspector of Health Services, and the others who were roped together in groups of twelve to fourteen before being taken away with their mothers and grandparents on forced marches to Aleppo to die on the way of thirst, starvation, or under the blows of their guards. Not to mention those thrown into the middle of the sea from boats.

Several days a week Salim Bey and his friends, often comrades from his political party, came to take advantage of the bodies of what he called his 'little harem'. I know it was no fun for the older girls, who went from one man to the other to be used in all possible ways, several times an evening. They had to put their hearts into the performance, sweating and straining, until late into the night. In fact they were beasts of burden, and were often left dull-eyed, at least in the morning. They were cows, too. They hated me because of the special treatment I had because of my age; I was reserved for the master, and his morals were not so depraved that he would force his prick on me. He simply expected me to do certain things to him – to spoil him, as Fatima said, having taught me that art, which is also a science.

'Go carefully with your teeth,' she told me. 'It's your job for men to forget them. They hate being scratched or bitten down there. You must use only your lips and your tongue to suck and lick with all the passion you can manage. That's the way to make them happy.'

He would take me into his study, sit in a leather armchair and tell me to go down on my knees and put my head between his thighs, open his flies, take out his prick and pleasure him by licking it. His desire quickly rose, his gasps became groans, and I'll leave out the rest of it.

As I aroused him I offered all kinds of insults in my heart: notably *salak* (stupid bastard in Turkish) or *kounem qez* (fuck you in Armenian). Even if I couldn't for obvious reasons read his thoughts in his eyes, I am sure he knew that he was hurting me. But at the same time he did me a great deal of good. It was he who, making me submit to these sessions, nourished that violence in me that has allowed me to survive.

7

The Sheep and the Kebabs

TREBIZOND, 1916. One morning Salim Bey sent for the imam, so that I could say the ritual words of conversion to Islam in front of him: 'I bear witness that there is no god but God, and Muhammad is His messenger.'

His messenger, fine, but not his only messenger. There is also Jesus, to whom I shall go on praying until my last breath, as well as Moses, Mary, the Archangel Gabriel and many others. No one has a monopoly on God.

When the imam asked whether my conversion was free and voluntary, I lied as Salim Bey had told me to do. I even claimed that I was happy to renounce Christianity, and I had hated it since early childhood.

'I always thought that Christ was a coward and a cry-baby,' I said. 'If he was the son of God, I'm sorry for God, he didn't do his father much credit.'

As I write these lines I am overcome by shame, but not as badly as on that day, which I then spent on my knees praying, before walking barefoot over pebbles to mortify the flesh and do penance for my blasphemy.

I was ready to do anything in order to live, and my master had told me that conversion was the best protection for me. After that, if he was to be believed, I risked nothing; among Muslims, unlike Christians, it was a rule not to kill each other, so at least there was that to be said for Islam.

Even though he had rescued me, Salim Bey felt guilty towards me, and I turned that to good account. One day, when I asked him who the fat one-armed man with the moustache was, the man who had taken my father away to have him murdered in a field, he unhesitatingly replied, 'Fat and one-armed, that can only have been Ali Recep Ankrun. I hate the man. He'd kill his mother, his father, even his own children. I'll check and find out if it was really him at Kovata.'

He checked, and discovered that it was true. He also tried to get news of my mother and the others. It was very complicated, and he had to wait at least six weeks before he got answers to his inquiries.

Salim Bey looked genuinely upset when he told me one day, his eyes lowered and with a lump in his throat, 'Your mother, your brothers and your sisters were attacked by Kurdish brigands who cut all their throats. I don't know what became of your grandmother; no one was able to tell me.'

I burst into sobs. Salim Bey shed tears himself, and it wasn't just for show; they left damp spots on his shirt. From then on I waited for my grandmother every day that God made; I hoped she had been taken in by the Syrians of Aleppo, or some other place where so many Armenians had found shelter. For years, until quite recently when I was really in mourning, I thought we would find one another in the end, and spend our old age together at the stoves of my restaurant. I tried everything: private detectives, appeals to the Armenian community, but nothing was any good.

I cannot remember Salim Bey without feeling a certain uneasiness. What he did to my body disgusted me, but at the same time I appreciated the fact that he disapproved of his counterparts in the Committee for Union and Progress. He spoke to me, with horror, of the tortures inflicted on Armenians in the prisons of the CUP, to make them say where they were hiding their savings. Fingernails and toenails pulled out with pincers, the hairs of their eyebrows and beards removed one by one. Their feet and hands nailed to planks so that they could be mocked for the crucifixion: 'You see, you're just like Jesus Christ. Your God has abandoned you.'

One day he also told me about the death marches, columns of zombies that the Turkish police led into the deserts or the mountains, where they walked round and round until no one was left. He told me about women raped, girls abducted, babies abandoned by the roadside, old men who lagged behind thrown over precipices or ridges.

Salim Bey was very sentimental, as one could tell from his love for Madame Arslanian, a subject on which he dwelt at length during those sessions when I was pleasuring his prick. She was a very beautiful and very rich woman who, he thought, would change her way of life and bring him her fortune. She was free to do so, since her husband, an Armenian doctor, had unfortunately died in the course of his 'deportation'.

Mme Arslanian was elegance personified. She also had a mouth that invited kisses, generous breasts, hips made for childbearing, and luxuriant hair that no brush or comb could subdue. And I must not forget her deep and loving gaze.

The first time Salim Bey saw her it was a case of love at first sight for him. It is true that his feelings were not reciprocated, but he felt sure that she would return them in the end. That, as he knew, meant that danger from his own political party, which was violently anti-Armenian, threatened him morning, noon and night, but he would have left everything in Turkey and gone to live with his great love in the United States if she had asked him to.

Although she had repelled his advances, understandably in the circumstances, Mme Arslanian said she would agree to flee the country with him when she had her children back. She had even found a good place for them to go, Boston. She dreamed of the east coast of the United States.

But his hopes were disappointed. Mme Arslanian inspired too much love and lust in the hearts of men. Her tragic fate was to show that, contrary to legend, beauty and money never protect anyone when History is on the march.

In fact, there were too many men involved in her case, handsome and powerful men at that: Dr Ali Saib, his friend Imamzad Mustafa, manager of a number of shops, and Nail Bey himself. Nail Bey, chairman of the Committee for Union and Progress, had become the real master of Trebizond. There was also Ali Recep Ankrun, my father's murderer. Four nasty pieces of work, with the marks of hatred and cupidity writ large on their faces.

Mme Arslanian, or more precisely her wealth, had turned their heads, and to get what they wanted they had blackmailed her through her two missing children, a boy of ten and a girl of seven. She was ready to do anything to find them – and she was the only person unaware that they had been murdered.

God alone knows whether she told one of the miscreants who were hanging around her about her fortune of 1,200 pounds in gold, or whether she kept it a secret. But one day Cemal Emzi, governor of the province, decided to call an end to the game they were playing. He had Mme Arslanian taken out to sea in a boat and thrown overboard, in line with the method of deportation that the authorities of Trebizond seemed to prefer.

Salim Bey often told me that he didn't understand how the purification of Turkey could have been derailed in such a way; he had never, he kept repeating, never wanted it 'to go as far as that'.

'I am so sorry,' he said one day when I had played my part particularly well, eliciting from him a cry of delight that might have come from the world beyond. 'None of us foresaw what would happen.'

'Nor did we.'

'Everyone has gone mad, you see. People had had enough...'

'Enough of what?'

'Enough of the Armenians, as you know. Merchants who exploited them for centuries, bloodsuckers. Very selfish people, and not just on the religious plane. They systematically refused to behave like everyone else, they thought only of themselves.'

'No reason to massacre them like that, all the same.'

'You must understand, my little princess, that we Young Turks are good Muslims and good Freemasons, not barbarians or murderers, we simply wanted to begin again at the beginning, with a pure race and a modern nation.'

'Weren't there any less terrible ways of getting what you wanted?'

'The sheep must always have its throat cut before you make kebabs, but yes, I agree, you don't have to slaughter the whole flock, and we went too far. Our programme of modernization isn't to blame, only mankind itself.'

I nodded my head. I knew who the real culprits were: the men whose names I had written on a small sheet of paper that never left me.

I would have liked to stay with Salim Bey for years to continue my inquiries, but as the months went by I felt that my power over him was waning. His eyes were not fixed on me any longer, they avoided me. He had the craven expression of a man who would like to be seeing something else.

After that, while I was pleasuring him, Salim Bey read a book and closed it only at the last moment, when he came all over my face or in my mouth. That was how I opened books in my own turn, finding out what was between the covers of the Koran, Robert Louis Stevenson's *Treasure Island* and Victor Hugo's *Les Misérables*. Moreover, he was in a hurry, and came to the point more and more quickly.

I no longer interested him, but he still felt protective towards me. Having noticed that I was fascinated by what he was reading, he gave me *Les Misérables* for the Eid al-Fitr festival of 1916. After that he gave me *David Copperfield*, *Huckleberry Finn* and other books of the same kind that I read in the evening before going to sleep, identifying with all those adventurers of stories large and small.

I had been living in Salim Bey's house for nearly two years when, one morning, Fatima packed my things. It didn't take long, because I didn't own much. Then she took me to see our master, who was finishing his breakfast. With the kind of false joviality that one assumes when breaking bad news, he told me that he was sending me to a friend of his, a wholesaler trading in tea, rice, tobacco and hazelnuts who had visited him the previous evening, and although he had seen me only from a distance, said Salim Bey, he had liked me very much.

'He isn't handsome, but he is kind,' said Salim Bey.

'No one will ever be as kind as you, master.'

'He thought you looked appetizing and asked whether you kept your promises. I said that you did.'

'I will always do as you ask.'

'Well, I'm asking you to give him the kind of pleasure you have given me. But don't worry, little princess, I'm lending you, not giving you away. You'll be back.'

'I'll most certainly be back,' I agreed. 'I have a great many things yet to do here.'

8

The Ants and the Sea Rocket

THE MEDITERRANEAN, 1917. Nâzim Enver, my new master, was not a poet. Fifty years old, and fat, he was living proof that man is not so much descended from the monkey as the pig. In his case, not just any pig but the stud boar who, precariously balancing on his hind legs, could hardly support the weight of his wobbly hams.

He hardly made my mouth water, but I dreamed of butchering him, salting him down, or turning his head into brawn. I worked out that if I'd had to eat him at the rate of two hundred grams a day, it would have taken me more than a year to get through so much pork.

When I arrived on his ship, a freighter lying at anchor in Trebizond harbour, I was taken to his cabin. I stayed there for a long time at a loss, sitting on his bed. I had Theo's box in my hands, and at my feet my bundle containing my clothes and the list of the people I hated. I passed the time praying to Jesus in heaven, asking him to get a move on, kill some Young Turks and find my grandmother for me.

After an hour, when Nâzim Enver turned up, sweating and now not just a boar but a boar in rut, he told me to undress and lie down on the bed. After parting my legs and then crushing me under his folds of tenderized meat, he went straight to the sexual act without asking my opinion or even saying a single word, if only for the sake of civility.

At the moment when Nâzim Enver was relieving himself in me after penetration, he howled as if I had just murdered him. I expect boars howl like that when they come to orgasm.

Then he stayed on top of me, as if prostrated. Terrified by the idea that I hadn't done my job well, I stayed put without saying a word or moving under his chest, which resembled that of a big fat woman, with a woman's nipples at that, and I would have suffocated if he hadn't finally got off me to sit on the bed. He turned and looked at me, but without seeing me. His face bore the traces of savage rapture.

When I rose from the sheets, I found that they were soaked with blood, but I knew what that meant; my grandmother had told me. So had Fatima, and despite my disgust I couldn't help feeling a certain pride.

Nâzim Enver didn't give me time to dress again. He led me, naked, my thighs covered with blood and my belongings in my hand, to a little cabin that he locked behind him. After washing myself, I stayed there all that day and then for the following days, looking out at the sea through the porthole, thinking of the past, and uttering all sorts of prayers, none of which were answered, as if the Almighty wanted me to pay for my trip.

Every evening, my master came to fetch me before going to bed, and it was in his bed that I spent all the nights on our crossing from Trebizond to Barcelona. Apart from the moments when he was on top of me, I didn't exist so far as he was concerned, and on the rare occasions when he spoke to me it was to tell me I didn't do enough to stimulate his desire. 'Concentrate, you must take more trouble than that. One stone doesn't build a wall.'

In the daytime, when I was locked in my cabin, the man with the head of an ox who brought my meals hardly ever opened his mouth either, and when he deigned to look at me it was with a mixture of indifference and lassitude. I might have been a piece of furniture, I think it would have come to the same thing.

Thank God, I had someone to talk to in the shape of Theo. My salamander didn't enjoy our Mediterranean crossing, no doubt because I was feeding her exclusively on spiders and flies, but there wasn't anything else for her to eat on this ship. She was also shocked by the fate reserved for me, that of sex slave subservient to her master's pleasure and treated as the lowest of the low. I spent my days trying to calm her down.

'You can't go on putting up with this,' protested Theo.

'That's sweet of you, but what else can I do?'

'Rebel.'

'Oh yes? How?'

Theo didn't reply, because there *was* no reply to that. Even if she pretended not to know, morality always has its limits, fixed by reason.

I dreaded getting pregnant by Nâzim Enver. In spite of appearances, he had taken nothing from me. Not my dignity, not my self-esteem or anything else. I was unaware that as I had not yet begun to menstruate I wasn't old enough to conceive a child. But I knew from the farm how animals make babies. The same way as us.

I couldn't stand the idea that my lecherous fat boar would give me a pig-headed baby. I knew what to do if that happened. Fatima had explained when I was in the little harem. If you could catch it in time, soapy water was all you needed. I smeared my pussy with it every time he had penetrated me.

I felt like the larva stolen by one colony of ants from another to be enslaved. It's all very well for human beings to put ourselves forward and dress up in all our finery; in the last resort we're nothing but ants like those I used to watch on my parents' farm who were obsessed by the idea of extending their territory and spent their time going to war with other ants.

Always ready to eradicate the neighbouring colony, they were impelled only by their wish for power. When one million, several hundred thousand Armenians were massacred in 1914 and 1916, it was simple to see how and why: they were less numerous and aggressive than the Turks, like the large black ants whose nests I had seen devastated by armies of tiny mechanical red warriors.

I learned later that at the time of the Armenian massacres, children of under twelve were sometimes taken from their parents to be put into 'orphanages' that in reality were bands of more-or-less uneducated dervishes, who brought them up in the Muslim faith.

That is exactly what the ants do when they go on raids to steal eggs, larvae and nymphs which, when they reach maturity, will be at the service of the conqueror. Nothing except the way we look makes us any different, and one might well think that ants are the future of the world.

Belligerent plunderers who are ready to enslave their enemies, they have all the requisite qualities to replace the human species when its obsessive greed has wiped it off the face of the earth.

Science teaches us that certain plants willingly restrict the development of their roots when they are surrounded by members of the same family; they do not want to give the others trouble, and they know how to share water and mineral salts. This has been observed in particular in the case of sea rocket, which grows on the sandy beaches of cold countries.

I'm ready to admit that sea rocket doesn't look like anything much, and has never done anything to further the cause of thought or philosophy. In my humble opinion, however, it outdoes us by far in altruism and fraternity. If the Armenians had been dealing with sea rocket they wouldn't have been exterminated.

It was during this voyage that I truly discovered the art of dissimulation. I pretended to be madly in love with that fat pig Nâzim Enver. When I found him between the sheets I covered him with kisses and caresses, I told him that I couldn't live without him, '*hayatim*', and that I'd die if he left me. Male vanity is the strength of women. He gave way to his baser instincts.

And so it was that at the end of the voyage, as we were sailing along the coast of Italy, Nâzim Enver decided that I wouldn't be locked up any more and could come out of my cabin. Spending hours on deck, looking at the soft pallor of the horizon, I melted into it and travelled a long way, far beyond the world.

9

Chapacan I

MARSEILLES, 1917. I don't know what day exactly our freighter, the *Ottoman*, entered the port of Marseilles, but it was spring, and the failing empire whose flag she was flying was still officially at war with France.

Before making a present of my small self to Nâzim Enver, Salim Bey had told me that our final destination would be Barcelona, but I suspect my new master of organizing the change of route before we left Trebizond; he did not seem annoyed, indeed far from it, when the ship came into Marseilles harbour.

Such research as I have been able to do has shown me that Nâzim Enver was a good businessman who, at the end of the 1930s, became one of the richest men in Turkey, lord of the market for tobacco and hazelnuts, and he also had dealings in oil and the press. But so far as the mystery of our change of destination in 1917 is concerned, I am reduced to conjecture.

Although I have no proof of it, I suspect that, anticipating the defeat of Germany and the disarray into which the Ottoman Empire would fall, he had decided to look for new business connections with the future winners of the war, even before the end of hostilities. With other ornaments of his fleet, which was growing all the time, the *Ottoman*

53

became a familiar sight in the port of Marseilles, to which it regularly brought products from the Black Sea.

On the first night after our arrival in Marseilles, there was no sign of Nâzim Enver. At five in the morning, when I hadn't slept a wink all night, I went up on deck with Theo. I had taken her out of her box, and I let my eyes wander for a long time over the city, from which came the aromas of salt, debauchery and fish.

There was a sense of greatness about Marseilles, well summarized by the Latin inscription that could once be seen, as I learned later, on the facade of the City Hall.

'Marseilles is the daughter of the Phocaeans, the sister of Rome; she was the rival of Carthage; she opened her gates to Julius Caesar and defended herself victoriously against Charles the Fifth.'

That was the kind of city for me. Seditious and independent, she had always held her head up in facing everyone, including Louis XIV. Legend had it that on 6 January 1659, she sent the king two envoys, Niozelles and Cuges, who in defiance of all custom, and to the great displeasure of the Count of Brienne, refused to kneel to him.

The Sun King bore the city a grudge for that. The next year, after seizing the city, he had the Fort Saint-Nicolas build above the port on a limestone headland. The Fort had its cannon turned in the direction of the city to keep the people of Marseilles at bay.

As if I already knew about all that, I was in a state of great agitation. Open to all winds and all human beings, Marseilles is a city that holds out its arms, and you have only to let it take you in them. I was spellbound, and wanted nothing more than to go to it without a moment's waiting.

I didn't wait a moment. It would have been too risky to go down the gangway; the crew members would soon have brought me back. A better idea, I thought, was to open one of the hundreds of crates piled in the hold and slip into it. It was full of hazelnuts, and I had to throw quite a lot of them away to make room for me, my bundle and Theo's box.

In the morning, when the cranes began unloading the cargo, I felt myself being raised from the hold, jolted around in the air, and then a moment later I was dumped on the quayside. A docker spotted me getting out of the crate, but he went on his way after giving me a broad smile, along with a friendly little nod of his head.

I lived on my wits for two weeks in the dockside quarter of Marseilles, La Joliette, but I was visibly wasting away. Discovering from my body, against my will, that freedom has never fed anyone, I nostalgically thought of the cakes and Turkish delight that I had feasted on, not long before, in Nâzim Enver's cabin on the *Ottoman*.

In the end I moved to the Old Port area, where I searched dustbins after the restaurants had closed. On lucky days I feasted on lobster and crab, followed by pineapple and leftovers of tarts. Not forgetting bread crusts. I did well, and so did Theo.

But it was a way of life subject to stiff competition, and one night I was picked up for questioning by the internal policing system of the down-and-outs of Marseilles and taken unceremoniously to a dive near Saint-Victor, where I faced a very elegant little man with patent leather shoes and a twisted mouth. He seemed to have a grudge against the whole world in general and me in particular.

To all appearances, he was a successful man, but he was full of hatred. If you had pricked him, venom would have flowed out of him, black, mephitic venom. His eyes were bloodshot, and his cracked thread of a voice seemed to be making its way through gravel.

I didn't understand anything he was saying, but I could see that he was not pleased. I listened with my head bowed, my back bent, the living incarnation of total submission, as I had learned to do with my previous masters. Servility is a profession; I agreed to everything. If necessary I would even have consented to make love to him, although he had bad breath and I have always had a horror of stinking mouths. But I can't have been the kind of girl he liked, and I wasn't sorry. That meant one trial less.

People called him Chapacan the First. It was not a nice name; in the local slang, *chapacan* meant dog-stealer. All the same, his name was spoken with a mixture of respect and terror.

In his own way he was a king, and he had the power of life and death over his subjects, of whom I was now one. But he was also a businessman, head of a company, good at management through stress, and he knew how to get the best out of his employees. He made a living from six specialist branches of his trade: begging, gleaning, theft, prostitution, gambling and drug trafficking.

At first I was assigned, after training, to the begging department of his empire, and I worked outside churches and public buildings.

Begging is tiring work. You have to be on the watch all the time, often under a leaden sky, if you are not to let good business get away, in the shape of the kind of person who inopportunely meets your eye, slows down, and then you can latch on to him, your body bowed in supplication, uttering the first words I ever said in French.

'Pleeeease, I'm so hungry!'

I was often at the end of my tether when I went to give my day's takings to Chapacan I's underlings, who with expressive gestures had threatened me with the worst disciplinary measures, if I cheated him by keeping anything back. The penalties ran from the removal of a finger to the putting out of an eye, or both eyes, and might end, with persistent offenders, with the amputation of one arm, both arms, or having your throat cut in a back alley.

Chapacan I himself did not seem displeased with my performance, judging by his smile when he summoned me, several months after I had joined the company, for what would now be called, in business jargon, a job appraisal.

I had my bed and board, if I may so put it, in the attic of a ruinous apartment building that I shared with two old ladies who always seemed to be keeping close to the walls for safety's sake, even when there weren't any walls. By dint of carrying all the woes in the world on their frail, bowed shoulders, they had backs so bent that they would clearly end up walking on their noses one of these days.

For a long time I thought of them as princesses in exile, so far as their class was concerned, until the day when I learned that they had both been abandoned at the same time by their respective husbands, a boilermaker and a fishmonger, both of whom had decided, as their fiftieth birthdays approached, to return to their old nocturnal habit of picking up girls of easy virtue.

In the evenings the two ladies taught me to speak French, and I was beginning to do quite well at it. The more progress I made, the more I felt at ease in this life of pretence, groaning and shedding tears all day to earn three francs six sous. Chapacan I understood that. It was why he intended to move me to the gleaning branch of his organization, a promotion that I unhesitatingly accepted.

After that Chapacan I, who always liked to be in charge of his workers, gave me a new first name. 'I don't like Rouzane.'

'I do. It was my grandmother's name.'

'I don't like the sound of it. From now on you will be called Rose.'

IO

The Art of Gleaning

MARSEILLES, 1917. As a gleaner, you don't improvise. You need a technique, special equipment, and training, which I had from one of Chapacan I's barons. The man had a large head – I almost called it pot-bellied – on top of a frail body; he was known as the Bastard, a nickname that he well deserved. This conceited fellow assumed great dignity in everything he said and did, even when he was answering a call of nature.

The Bastard spent three days initiating me into my new profession, in which I used a pick to investigate dustbins, a hook to fish out my finds while keeping my hands clean if they had been searching in anything dirty, a baby's stroller to hold my loot and a knife to protect it, if necessary, against any troublemakers. He also taught me the few rules to be strictly observed if you wanted to become a first-rate gleaner.

'Discretion. People don't like to see you poking about in their rubbish – you only have to think of the black looks they give gleaners at work.

'Speed. If there's treasure in a dustbin, you want to get it out as quickly as possible without attracting attention before you walk nonchalantly away, unseen and unknown, without going to the trouble of explaining yourself.

'Discernment. It's important to be good at choosing your finds instead of falling into the habit of what I will call compulsive collection. Unskilled gleaners fill their little cart without stopping to think, and end up with a lot of useless stuff, which is a waste of time and energy.'

I found old iron, of course, but also toys, clothes and shoes. One day I found some kittens in a cardboard box; another day I found an old hen, a kind of living ulcer, with her claws tied together, apparently too ugly to be worth the trouble of killing her. Some people will throw anything away, starting with their problems. If I'd carried on gleaning, I'm sure I'd have ended up finding a bedridden old man lying at the bottom of his dustbin on top of rabbit guts and potato peelings.

I owe a lot to the art of gleaning. It gave me my philosophy of life. My fatalism. My aptitude for living one day at a time. My obsession with recycling everything: the dishes I cook, my rubbish, my joys, my sorrows.

It was also thanks to gleaning that I met the couple who changed my life: the Bartavelles. Barnabé was a ruddy-cheeked, rustic giant with a big belly that always seemed to be on the point of exploding, which no doubt explains why he so often placed both hands on it with a worried kind of look. He ate his words and talked about his intestines.

Honorade, his wife, seemed to be the result of a marriage between a biliary calculation and a bottle of vinegar. She never smiled: everything annoyed her, the sun, the rain, the cold, the heat, and she always had good reasons to complain.

They ran a restaurant called Le Galavard in the Panier or Old Town quarter of Marseilles. Before they took me on I don't think I ever found anything interesting in their dustbin, although I conscientiously searched it every day; these people never wasted anything. Last night's fish made a second appearance in the day after tomorrow's stuffing, before ending up in mixed fish soup over the following days.

One day, when one of their staff had done something wrong, Barnabé Bartavelle, whose kitchen looked out on the street, called to me out of the window as I was passing with my stroller to say he had work for me.

'Make yourself useful instead of lounging about.'

I realized, later, that my predecessor in the restaurant had run away after receiving one of those memorable hidings regularly inflicted on his employees by the heavy hand of Barnabé Bartavelle, the tyrant of the kitchen. As assistant in charge of washing dishes and peeling and cleaning vegetables, I had plenty of blows myself, unpaid at that, since the restaurant gave me only the day's leftovers collected in a tin dish for my services.

In all my life, I've seldom met such a pair of skinflints The Bartavelles counted everything, and were always checking that the level of liquid in bottles or stocks of flour didn't go down after they had gone out. They distrusted everyone, including, I think, themselves.

I would have been wrong to complain. I owe Barnabé Bartavelle thanks for allowing me to discover my vocation and initiating me into my future profession. He was always saying that one of these days he would settle his accounts with Theo: 'No animals allowed here.' He spoke to me roughly and kicked my backside when I was working too slowly, as well as calling me names, but something told me that I was in his good books. Now and then, when he was snowed under with work, he let me do some of the cooking. He even taught me how to prepare aubergines Provençal style before the restaurant opened, a dish that was to be one of my great specialities later, although I fear their supremacy may have been ousted by the aubergine recipe of that other Rose in Marseilles, my Sicilian rival.

He let me sleep in a shed behind the restaurant, a kind of broom cupboard looking out on the courtyard. Honorade Bartavelle didn't like that; thinking that her husband was too weak and was letting me get a foothold in their place, she made me pay for every sign of relative humanity that he showed me, reducing my daily helping of food or slapping me on the pretext that I was getting in her way.

Doing my best to escape being picked up by the henchmen of Chapacan I, I had done my hair in a different way, and went nowhere at all except from the storeroom to the kitchen and vice versa. They found me, all the same. One day Honorade Bartavelle came into the kitchen, which she never usually did after the restaurant was opened because it annoyed her husband, planted herself in front of me with the one and only smile that I ever saw crossing her face during my stay with them, and said, 'Hey, you, there's someone asking for you.'

I could guess who that was, but all the same I tried to check by glancing at the dining room. The Bastard was standing in the doorway, with a tall, gangling, short-haired fellow who had the face of a boxer. I listened to my instinct; I jumped out of the window and ran for two hours without any idea where I was going, and then I walked on until evening fell. All I had taken with me was Theo's box in one hand, and my list of the executioners of Trebizond in the other.

11

Happiness in Sainte-Tulle

HAUTE-PROVENCE, 1918. A warm little wind was blowing over the fields, running through the bushes, dancing in the treetops. It was at home everywhere. When it had entered into me it carried me far away, all the way to my own people. I heard them talking in it.

The song of earthly happiness was in that wind, the infinite murmur of minuscule copulations, and a mixture of seeds and particles in which I heard, very distinctly, the psalmody of the world beyond.

After eating some maggoty apples at the edge of an olive grove, I fell asleep in a ditch full of dry grasses, with my head full of familiar voices. Summer was drawing to a close, and nature had had enough of it. Bitten for weeks by the fangs of the sun, bleeding as a result, the season seemed to be in the state that often precedes death when, after a long death agony, the sufferer ends up, arms lowered, by drifting away into gentle torpor.

It did so in order to recover its strength all the better when the great storms of September came charging up from the horizon, felling everything here to the ground, when happiness would spring from the fertile soil again, in a kind of general resurrection, to last until All Souls' Day. As they waited, the trees, plants and grasses suffered with all their drained fibres: their cracking assailed my ears like little howls of pain.

When I woke up again, the wind had died down, and after helping myself from the apple trees once more I went on my way. At the beginning of the afternoon, I was near Aix when I was hailed by an old man wearing a straw hat, in charge of a cart drawn by a large white horse.

'Would you like a lift, mademoiselle?'

At the age of eleven I was not afraid of men, and I accepted the old man's invitation without any misgivings. He reached out his hand to help me climb up into his cart. When he asked where I was going, I said, 'Further on.'

'Where have you come from?'

'Marseilles.'

'But your accent comes from somewhere else. What country are you from?'

'I'm from Armenia, but that country and its people are all gone.'

'If you don't know where to go, you can sleep at our place.'

He gave me the smile of a farmer, that long-suffering smile accompanied by a wrinkling up of his eyes and a mischievous look. His face was dark as a vine shoot, and he made me think of a branch that has lost its vital spark and is turning into firewood on the tree.

I did not reply. I thought his invitation was rather hasty, but something in his face told me that it came from the heart, with no ulterior motives.

His name was Scipion Lempereur, and he was a farmer from Sainte-Tulle, near Manosque, who reared sheep and grew melons and courgettes. Until now he had succeeded in everything – his marriage, his children, his work and the harvests. Everything, until that terrible year 1918.

'Happiness makes a man blind,' he said, 'blind and deaf. I didn't see anything coming. Life is a bitch and you must never trust it. It gives you everything and then, one day, it takes everything away again without warning, absolutely everything.'

Scipion Lempereur had just lost three sons to the war, and the fourth was lying between life and death in the military hospital at Amiens. A piece of shrapnel in his head; generally you didn't recover from that, but all the same, he said, God couldn't take all his children at the same time, it would be too inhuman.

'God he may be, but he has no right to do that to me,' he said. 'I've always tried to do my best. I don't know what he wanted to punish me for.'

He uttered a strained, nervous laugh, then began shedding tears, and I cried as well. It was a long time since that had happened to me, and it did me good; tears often take your grief away, or at least it doesn't seem so bad after you've shed them. This was the first time I had met someone turned into a living corpse by the death of his loved ones. He didn't get over it.

I did. I felt bad about not being crushed by sorrow as he was, and I asked my family to forgive me for having survived them so easily.

'Why?' asked Scipion Lempereur, looking up at the heavens.

'Why?' I repeated.

After that I told him the story of my life. I left out Salim Bey and Nâzim Enver, and talked at length about my adventures in Marseilles, which held him spellbound. When I had finished, he repeated his invitation to me to stay for at least a few days with him and his wife at their farm in Sainte-Tulle.

'You won't be in our way at all,' he insisted. 'Stay a while for our sake – it will do us good, I assure you. We need someone to take our minds off things.'

This time I accepted. And so later that evening I found myself in the Lempereurs' farmhouse at the top of a steep hill standing above a river hardly worth the name, a ridiculous slimy little stream waiting for rain to come to make it look like the real thing. All around us a huge, living, teeming carpet of wool was grazing the gilded grass.

Emma the farmer's wife had a jaw like a horse, with matching teeth, and shoulders like a labourer's bowed by working in the fields. However, that had not tarnished her proud face; furrowed by wrinkles, it called to mind dry ravines after raging torrents had gone tumbling down them in the rainy season.

She had never travelled further afield than to Manosque, but thanks to the books she read she had lived a full life. It was she who introduced me, among other writers, to the poet Keats, who wrote: 'A thing of beauty is a joy for ever'.

Where Mme Lempereur is concerned, I must add the words *intelligence* and *culture* to *beauty*. Seen from those three points of view, she was the kind of beauty that you seldom meet in a whole lifetime.

She accepted me at first glance, and then embraced me as if I were her daughter. And one day I was to become her daughter in reality: after years of legal proceedings, I ended up bearing her surname. Three of her sons had died on the field of honour during the 1914–18 War, and after the death of the fourth, I was named in the Lempereurs' will, signed by them and deposited with a notary, as their sole heir.

Emma also adopted Theo, who spent the best years of her life at Sainte-Tulle. My salamander was happy, and stopped telling me off as she used to in the past.

I too was happy, if the word has any meaning. Scipion and Emma Lempereur gave me everything. A family, values, and an abundance of love. My adoptive mother also taught me the art of cookery; it was she, for instance, who gave me the recipe for the caramel flan which did so much to make me famous.

Another recipe contributed just as much to my renown. That was the parmesan vegetable dish of Mamie Jo, a pretty woman who lived nearby and often used to bring cooked dishes round to the Lempereurs, until one day, much to our regret, she left for the United States to begin a new life with a gentleman in the shipping business.

In the off season, when there was less work to be done in the fields, Emma Lempereur regularly organized large country lunch parties for a hundred guests, inviting her neighbours, as well as guests who sometimes came from very far away. One day, when I asked her why she went to so much trouble, she told me, 'The presents you give yourself take the form of acts of generosity. There's nothing like it to make you feel good.'

She left me many such sayings, now imprinted on my mind for ever. Following in the footsteps of Salim Bey, Emma introduced me to many books, in particular the works of George Sand, and such love stories as Colette's *Chéri* and *Le Blé en herbe*, which I must admit are so lightweight that, these days, they don't hurt me at all if they fall from my hands and drop on my feet.

I feel ashamed, writing that, as if I were betraying the memory of Emma Lempereur, who in spite of all her love for her husband used to say that one day 'men must stop making doormats of women.' That was why she liked Colette, and all other women who make much of their pride in being women.

She was a feminist, and liked to make ironic remarks such as, 'It's still a well-kept secret, but the fact is that one man in two is a woman. But all women are men, although, thank God, all men are not women.'

Between the ages of eleven and seventeen I lived many indulgent seasons with the Lempereurs, a time when one day followed hard on the heels of another, but nothing really changed, everything knew its place, the swallows in the sky, the sheep in their fold, the haze on the horizon, while simply by breathing I inhaled a mixture of joy and intoxication.

You will tell me that I am being silly, but happiness is always silly. Moreover, having known it before on my parents' farm, I didn't trust it. All that intoxication frightened me. Experience had told me that it never lasts.

It's when everything is going well that History comes along to make a nuisance of herself.

12

The Man Who Was Shot

HAUTE-PROVENCE, 1920. It was in the year when I had my thirteenth birthday and my first periods that the world began going mad. Perhaps there were signs and portents saying so, in the sky or somewhere else, but I must admit that I never noticed anything like that at Sainte-Tulle.

I never looked further than one day ahead. I was too busy making preserves, bringing in the hay, doing my household duties, playing with the dogs, stroking my cat, maturing cheeses, praying to the Lord, cooking, feeding the chickens, picking tomatoes, shearing sheep and dreaming of boys.

In the evening, before going to sleep with my cat, I used to read books as I had in Salim Bey's house, and the book that made the deepest impression on me was Pascal's *Pensées*. Emma Lempereur had told me that, of all such works, it came closest to the truth, because it traced all contradictions to the very end: God, science, negation and doubt.

The friendliness of the world, the trees, the animals and books prevented me from seeing beyond the horizon. If History went off the rails within a few months, it took me a long time to realize it, and then to understand that it was the fault of several people, not least Georges Clemenceau, a nasty piece of work although brilliant, a great man, master of amusing sayings such as, 'When you are young, you're young for life.' I have made that my own motto.

At this time Clemenceau was President of the Council. He was the hero of Sainte-Tulle and indeed of all France. The man who had broken the Boche and brought him low. The Father of Victory, the Tiger whose eyes were never cold. He had won the war, but he was going to lose the peace. 'Never humiliate the donkey you have defeated,' my grandmother used to say. 'Or if you do, kill him.'

Imposed on Germany by Clemenceau and the victors of the 1914–18 War, the Treaty of Versailles came into force on 10 January 1920, and it did indeed create an Armenian Republic, but apart from that it was incredibly stupid. It humiliated the German Reich, dismembered it and in economic terms bled it dry, sowing the seeds of the war that was yet to come.

A month after it was promulgated, a man with bad breath and a toothbrush moustache called Adolf Hitler took control of Germany's labour party. After giving it the new name of the National Socialist German Workers' Party, he endowed it with a logo in the shape of a swastika, and a programme nationalizing cartels, confiscating the profits of major industrialists, and abolishing revenues that were not the fruit of honest labour. At the same time a popular army of several tens of thousands of militant communists occupied the Ruhr, and workers' governments, maintained by proletarian units, took control of Thuringia.

It was chaos against a background of social destitution, like the state of affairs in Russia, where the Bolsheviks and the monarchist White Russians were killing each other while the star of Stalin rose. In 1922 he was to become General Secretary of the Communist Party.

God knows I had nothing to do with all that. Happiness does not like bad news, and it was as if it did not reach us there in Haute-Provence; the aromas of our cookery had discouraged it. I think I never heard of Hitler until long afterwards, in the 1930s.

Armenia ought to have taught me otherwise, but I was unaware that you don't escape History when her millstone has begun to grind. Whatever you do, you are always reduced to the fate of those ants who scuttle away before the rising waters on stormy days: sooner or later, their fate catches up with them.

I was like them, and indeed like the whole world. I didn't want to know, and I didn't see anything coming. Even today, when half my carcase seems to have left for the next world already, I do not hear Death knocking on my door to take me away. I have too much to do in the kitchen with my pots and pans in front of me to waste time letting Death in.

*

It was also in 1920 that an old soldier who, during the war, had fought in the same section as Jules, the third of the Lempereur sons, came to see us. A tall, strapping fellow with a pale complexion and panic in his eyes, he went about with a dirty corduroy coat hanging off him. He always seemed as if he were about to apologize, as if he felt he was in the way merely by speaking, breathing or living.

Although he was not strictly speaking ugly, I felt a kind of repugnance for him. Two large, hairy warts on his right cheek emerged from his collar. A froth of white saliva was always dribbling from the corners of his mouth and the tip of his tongue. And then there were his hands, which were the size of shovels, gnarled and purple in places. He never seemed to know what to do with them.

His name was Raymond Bruniol. Up in the north he had been a cowman. He had lost that job now, but had found another, to start in two months' time at a farm nearby. While he waited he had decided to see something of the country. He stayed in Sainte-Tulle for several days. A good sort, hand on heart, always trying to help out. I soon realized that he had come to say something to his friend's parents, but couldn't manage to bring it out.

An hour after his arrival, as we were about to dine, he took the watch that had belonged to Jules out of his pocket and put it on the kitchen table. Emma wept, and Scipion said, 'We thought that had been stolen.'

'He gave it to me to return it to you,' the man replied. 'He didn't trust the army.'

'I wouldn't say he was wrong,' remarked Scipion.

Emma gave him a black look, and the soldier opened his mouth to speak again before suddenly closing it. His glottis was trembling.

'Was he brave to the end?' asked Scipion in a casual tone, as if he knew the answer.

'To the very end.'

When Emma asked what his last words had been, there was a long silence. We had given him wine, and he drank a great gulp of it to give himself the courage to go on. Then he said, 'Mother.'

We all looked at him, dumbfounded, while Emma sobbed more than ever.

'You know,' said Bruniol, 'that's what most soldiers say when they're dying. You mustn't forget those were just children being killed. Boys whose voices had hardly broken.'

As if to make the incident seem relative, so as to comfort my adoptive mother, Raymond Bruniol added, 'He did say something after that, but it was a kind of gurgle and I didn't understand it.'

The day before the man left, he and I had both gone to fill crates with apples. Red, chubby apples, like little girls' bottoms after a spanking.

We were on our way back to the farmhouse when I turned round in the middle of the road and asked, 'What happened that you haven't told us about?'

He lowered his eyes, and when he raised them again there was a stunned expression in them. 'It's kind of delicate.'

There was a silence, during which he looked at the little hill nearby as if in search of inspiration, and then, in a strangled voice, he said, 'Jules came up before a military tribunal and was condemned to be shot, that's all there is to be said about it.'

'What had he done?'

'Nothing.'

'That's not possible.'

'No, that's the way it is in war. You weren't doing anything, but still you found yourself in front of the firing squad.'

'But what did they condemn him to death for?'

'For idleness. The year before he'd talked a little too big when a mutiny looked like starting, but it came to nothing, and his superior officers had pardoned him. In the end they got tired of the way he was always dragging his feet. General Pétain, the louse at the back, the runt of the Great War, he wasn't a man to joke with, you know. He had a commander at his heel, a man called Morlinier who presided over the military tribunal. If you came up in front of him you were sure to be executed. That's what happened to poor Jules.'

'So his last word wasn't Mother at all?'

'How would I know? I wasn't there when he died. I improvised. You see, everyone's supposed to have said that at the front as they breathed their last.'

After dinner that evening, I wrote the name of Morlinier on the little sheet of paper I had kept ever since I was in Trebizond. I called it the list of my hates.

I kept it in my copy of Pascal's *Pensées*.

I read it over and over again, and whenever I did, I felt the same internal tremor as I did at the name of the diabolical one-armed man who had killed my father.

Like Raymond Bruniol, I never had the heart to tell the parents of Jules Lempereur that he had been one of the six hundred soldiers condemned to death and executed in the name of France, in the cause of victory, by chance, and for no apparent reason.

13

The Cookery of Love

MARSEILLES, 2012. Decades later, Emma Lempereur lives on as much as ever in my mind. I have many occasions to think of her in my restaurant. Sometimes, while a fried dish is sizzling, I think I hear her giving me the gastronomic advice that she repeated over and over again, so that it would be imprinted on my mind as we stood at the stove preparing her wonderful meals.

'Don't salt the food too much. Don't add too much sugar to sweet dishes either. You can always skimp on oil, butter and sauces – what matters is the product, the product again, and finally the product.'

It is thanks to her and my grandmother that I became a cook, a successful cook, even if I have never been honoured by the Michelin Guide. I owe Emma so much that, when I think of her, nostalgia comes over me as I write these lines at the little desk with the cash register presiding over it where, in the normal way, I calculate the bills. But I am never sad for very long; at the same time a sense of fruition rises in me, while Mamadou and Leila finish tidying up the room, lit as it is with morning sunlight. I feel rich, very rich; there's gold everywhere, gold on the glasses and gold on the place settings.

The temptation is too strong. I can't help eyeing Mamadou and Leila as they lay the tables. I specially like

Mamadou's arms and legs, which remind me of his mother. In Leila I am fascinated by her bottom, the most beautiful in Marseilles, like a ripe tomato in its firm skin. You may say that such thoughts are inappropriate for someone over a hundred years old, but never mind, I wriggle inside as I watch those two provocations to love.

I still find love on the Internet sites that I visit at night. It's only virtual love, to be sure, but it does me good. At least, until the day when, having caught my prey, I reluctantly agree to reveal myself. You should see the expressions on men's faces when at last I condescend to meet them, after keeping them on the hook for some time.

The last was an alcoholic and paunchy septuagenarian, divorced, an insurance agent, the father of seven children, and I met him on a site frequented by those who appreciate olive oil. The very opposite of an affair. We got on well on the Internet. We had the same culinary tastes. We used the familiar *tu* pronoun to each other.

I was disappointed. He'd lied about his age. So, to be honest, had I. Once he was sitting opposite me in the café where we had arranged to meet, he addressed me by the formal *vous* pronoun, frowning, after he had flicked some imaginary flies off his face.

'So this is you?'

'Well, yes, it's me.'

'You don't look much like your photograph.'

'I could say the same of you.'

'How old exactly are you?'

'That's impossible to say exactly,' I replied calmly. 'You see, my age changes all the time.'

'So what else?'

'I'm the age that I am, and I keep it to myself, that's all.'

'Excuse me, but you look much older in real life.'

I exploded. 'Just you listen to me, punk. If you don't like the look of my face, then let me inform you, in case you don't know, that nature did you no favours, not by any means! Have you ever seen yourself for real, you nasty piece of work?'

The more I see of men, the more I appreciate women. But with them, too, I've found failures like my overweight insurance agent. I know it's better to leave love before love leaves you, but I can't manage it. That's why I carry on surfing the Internet under the name of *rose-heartfree*.

A daily crowd of surfers visits the site where I say what I think of today's celebrities, or the difficulty of being a woman on her own, getting nothing back but stupid remarks suggesting a cat on heat. I am careful to use expressions of the current generation, like *I'm gutted* or *that's cool*. I'm a woman of my time.

*

In La Petite Provence, my restaurant on the Quai des Belges in Marseilles, facing the Vieux-Port, there are no photographs of Emma Lempereur, or of all those who, later, shared *rose-heartfree*'s bed. All the same, my restaurant sums up my life. I see it passing before my mind's eye if I only smell the aroma of the dishes or look at the menus, which among other items feature my grandmother's plaki, Barnabé Bartavelle's aubergines à la Provençale, and Emma

Lempereur's caramel flan. Ultimately, I owe a great many of my recipes to my adoptive mother. She added medicinal herbs to them, and I sometimes do the same.

She took her inspiration from an old book that she often consulted, *Le Petit Albert*, published in the eighteenth century, in which Albertus Magnus claimed to reveal 'all the marvellous secrets of natural and cabbalistic magic.' I always keep a copy in the restaurant, and I follow its more-or-less scatty directions to suit the wishes of my customers, particularly where matters to do with love are concerned.

The old book concentrated on those to such an extent that a *Modern Albertus* was published to set the record right, since the old one, so the authors of its modern rival claim, dealt with 'subjects of rather too free a nature, and in a way not conducive to the decency that should be preserved in a work for the general public.' They also disparaged its leaning towards astrology and mystical spells to open the doors of love.

In order to seduce the person you love, the original Albertus recommends getting him or her to swallow extracts of hippomania, a piece of flesh measuring ten to fifteen centimetres and found in the amniotic fluid of mares, not, as Aristotle claimed, on the foreheads of colts. Nor should you forget to add the hearts of swallows or sparrows, the testicles of hares and the livers of doves. Personally I confine myself to using such medicinal plants as elecampane or *Inula helenium*, which grows in ditches and can reach up to two metres in height. In the form of a powder or a decoction, it is very good for anaemia, lack of appetite, digestive trouble, diarrhoea and chronic coldness of the heart.

I add it to my dishes if required, as well as rocket, marjoram, verbena, fennel roots and poplar leaves. Every time, I feel as if I am bringing Emma Lempereur back to life. 'We are what we eat,' she used to say. 'So we should eat dishes made with the cookery of love.'

She also frequently consulted another book, *Les Plantes médicinales et usuelles* by a certain Rodin, published by Les Éditions Rothschild, of which I have found a copy dated 1876, which praises the mollifying qualities of mallow and verbena, and the use of rosemary and wild mint as stimulants. We also owe the rehabilitation of the nettle to this work; it is good for cattle, turkeys and human beings, and I often serve nettles in soup.

Nettle soup is a favourite dish of Jacky Valtamore, a former gangland boss of my acquaintance who, along with the procurator and the president of the regional council, has become one of my restaurant's regular guests. He is a handsome man with the blue eyes of the Mediterranean, and he knows and can sing many Italian operatic arias. A romantic of the kind I like; the ideal lover who, contrary to all expectations, survived an attempted assassination that left him for dead. A shame that he's too old for me. After their sixties, neither men nor women attract me, and he became an octogenarian some time ago.

I like it when his protective gaze rests on me. It's my life insurance. It makes me stronger. The other evening two shifty characters with a lot of hair gel came to see me in the kitchen. They suggested my paying them a monthly sum in exchange for what they called 'security'.

'You mean a racket!' I protested.

'No, no, we're going to help you.'

'You'd better discuss it with my authorized representative. He deals with all that.'

I made them an appointment with Jacky Valtamore, and I never heard a squeak out of them again. His mere presence put them to flight.

Once, when Jacky had told me that he felt he had wasted his life, I asked him what kind of man he would have liked to be. He said, without a moment's hesitation, 'A woman.'

Coming from a macho man like that, it was the kind of reply that Emma Lempereur would have liked. In my adolescence I went through a phrase when I read nothing but novels in which the central character was a woman: Maupassant's *Une Vie*; Flaubert's *Madame Bovary*; Ernest Péruchon's *Nêne* and Louis Hémon's *Maria Chapdelaine*. The heroines of these books were all victimized by men and the society that men had built up for their exclusive benefit. One day, when I told my adoptive mother that I would have liked to be a man, she dissuaded me, with an expression of horror.

'Don't even think of it, dear! You wait and see; life will teach you that woman is descended from monkeys, but conversely monkeys are descended from men.'

Then she laughed, and added, 'Mind you, I don't mean Scipion. He's my husband, he's not a man like the rest of them.'

14

The Queen of Bowing and Scraping

HAUTE-PROVENCE, 1924. One day when Emma Lempereur and I were picking apricots she fell off the ladder. It was the year of my baccalaureate examination and my seventeenth birthday.

It was also the year when, after the death of Lenin, Stalin set out to gain absolute power. And the year when Hitler began writing *Mein Kampf* in Landsberg jail, where he was imprisoned after a failed coup d'état against the Weimar Republic so ridiculous that it was known as the Beer Hall Putsch.

My adoptive mother died a couple of weeks later in Manosque hospital, after an abscess had formed in her spinal column. When we got back from her funeral, Scipion Lempereur told me, before going up to his room, 'I'm going to die too.'

I protested, but he replied, 'I could try to go on living, but it wouldn't make any difference. There's something flowing inside me. I don't know what it is – grief, weariness or death – but it's flowing so strongly that I won't be able to stop it. I'm finished.'

He lay down fully dressed beside the wall, with his straw hat over his face cutting him off from the world. I didn't worry too much; I was sure you couldn't decide to die of your own accord, and it was God who decided on the date, but next morning he had dried air-bubbles on his lips and he wasn't moving. He was in a coma.

While I went to fetch a doctor, Scipion Lempereur died. He hadn't shivered, he hadn't made a move or said anything, he died as he had lived, quietly. And so now I was orphaned for the second time in my life.

My adoptive parents had foreseen everything except that they would die only a few days apart, and before I had come of age. So I had to have a guardian, Justin, a cousin of Scipion Lempereur who arrived from Barceloneta two weeks later with his wife, Anaïs, a handcart and two large, black, unruly dogs.

The winter before, Emma Lempereur had introduced me to the study of physiognomy as taught by Pythagoras and Aristotle, a science that claims to be able to tell what people are like from their features. In the two new arrivals, whom I had never met before, I immediately detected a mixture of violence, greed and cunning in their truffle-dog noses, vicious and hopeful beady eyes, and the fat that had accumulated on their heads from their lower lips upwards. I wasn't wrong.

On the first evening they told me that they were going to take me in hand, and gave me their orders, which I may sum up as follows:

'You'll stop going to school, that's no use, particularly for a girl.'

'You will never look your masters in the eyes if you want to keep your own.'

'You will not use your masters' earth closet. You can do

83

your business behind the house in a hole that you will dig for yourself.'

'When we speak to you, you will keep your back bent, your head lowered, and your hands behind your back. You will never complain and you will always do as you are told.'

'If you answer back or question your orders, what you say will be regarded as insolence and suitably punished.'

'You will leave your old room, which will now be given to the dogs; they always want to sleep close to us. From tonight on you will spend the night in the stable with the horses.'

'There'll be no more airs and graces from you, no more dresses and shoes and all that. You will wear a smock and your hair will be cut short so that it doesn't fall into the dishes you cook. We hate finding hairs in our food.'

And so, eating enough for four as they did, even getting up in the night, after a substantial dinner, to find more nourishment, Justin and Anaïs turned me into a household drudge on the very day that they moved in, treating me as less than dirt and showing no consideration for anyone except their two dogs, who had appetites as voracious as their own and no more sense than a bluebottle.

As it happened, the favourite food of Justin and Anaïs was meat, preferably very rare steak, although they didn't turn up their noses at stews, ragouts, fricassees and the local dish of stuffed offal and sheep's feet known as *pieds paquets*. Living most of the time in the kitchen as I did, cooking dishes to fill their bellies, I felt that I was swimming in blood.

After several days in their service, I smelled of grilled meat, charred dead flesh and burnt, bleeding sores. I couldn't get rid of the smell, which followed me everywhere, even into the straw of the stable at night.

It wasn't long before Justin and Anaïs made their intentions clear. By the time they had been on the farm three weeks they had already sold the Lempereurs' horse and some of their furniture, a sideboard, a table, a clock, two cupboards and several armchairs. They were plucking me alive. When I expressed my concern, Justin sighed.

'We have to meet expenses.'

'What expenses?'

'We have to feed you.'

'I don't cost you anything.'

'More than you think.'

'You know that there's plenty to eat on a farm. That's what farms are for.'

'There are expenses, all the same,' Anaïs insisted. 'I think you're too young to understand.'

After this conversation Anaïs told me to go out of the room, and listening at the door, I them heard murmuring. When they had finished talking to each other, they told me they had decided that, as my punishment for answering back, they were going to give my cat to their two dogs to eat.

My cat was a big white Angora tom, who followed me everywhere like a dog when he wasn't chasing females on heat. Realizing as soon as they arrived that their mastiffs would never get on with him, I had put him in the granary, and let him out only at night, when those two dirty brutes were asleep in my old room.

Justin climbed to the loft of the granary, caught him and threw him to the dogs as if he was throwing them leftover scraps of chicken. I would rather not describe the cry he uttered as they killed him, a cry of rage and revolt that echoed in my skull for a long time. I sometimes still hear it, almost a hundred years later.

'That'll teach you,' said Justin, having carried out his threat. 'And I hope that now you'll think twice before saying anything stupid.'

I was told just as firmly not to try escaping; the dogs, who followed me everywhere when I was out in the farmyard, wouldn't fail to track me down, and according to Justin would drag me straight back to them by the scruff of my neck. Dead or alive, or somewhere in between.

I might as well admit that after their first lesson I knuckled under, although I didn't omit to hide Theo and her box in the barn at once. I went on feeding my salamander, but I took good care not to be caught doing it, or she would die too.

She was very indignant. Every evening, when I came to see her with her day's supply of worms and insects, she told me off. 'Why don't you do something? What are you waiting for? Take the initiative, child!'

'There's nothing I can do. I don't hold the right cards.'

As usual, Theo was scratching the place where it itched. Even as I hatched plots that never came to anything against my new masters, I behaved from now on as a docile, indeed deferential servant. Immersing myself in the almost enjoyable depths of mortification, I had become the queen of bowing and scraping. And

I might have gone on in the same way for several more years if love hadn't suddenly fallen on me like a day of heavy rain.

15

A Bad Attack of Love

HAUTE-PROVENCE, 1925. Meeting your great love is like suffering a bad attack of flu. The first time I saw Gabriel I felt myself trembling all over, and the trembling went right through me from top to toe, all the way into the marrow of my bones. It was a seismic earthquake in my spinal column and it left me devastated, with my legs shaking.

Furthermore, it was the right weather for flu. It had been raining for months on end. The sky had fallen flat on the ground and wouldn't get up again. The world was like a dishcloth in the middle of a rising river, in the act of flowing away.

Gabriel had had enough of that rain. True, he worked in the shelter of the sheepfold, but the rain was getting him down, and he couldn't work as fast as usual. Since arriving at the Sainte-Tulle farm late that morning he had dealt with only 123 sheep. The animals were nervous, and he had twice that number to castrate.

Justin Lempereur didn't want to help the gelder; he didn't like the job, and he was also very tired. He had eaten too much the evening before; my fricassee of chicken livers hadn't agreed with him. So he had sent Gabriel the old shepherd from the farm next door, a decrepit character who went by the nickname of Guenillou or rags-and-tatters, and who gave up after twenty minutes on the pretext that one of his sheep was having trouble giving birth, which as it happened was quite true.

'Giving birth at this time of year?' said Gabriel in surprise. 'Anyway, that's not an illness.'

'No, it's a lamb.'

It was unusual for Gabriel to fail to work neatly, but now here was a young male pissing blood and bleating in agony, its little prick dripping like a piece of red meat. After that the sheep lay on its side with the look of an animal that had gone under the knife. Its muzzle was open wide, showing its teeth, like a sheep about to die.

Gabriel needed string to stop the bleeding, and on finding that he had none left in his toolbox he ran to the farmhouse and hammered on the door. When I opened it he was scarcely visible. He was swamped by his farm labourer's garments, which were soaking wet, and the cap on his head had softened like a sponge saturated with water.

He was a rather small young man with curly chestnut hair that was to remind me, later, of Michelangelo's Apollo. Not that day, of course, because of the rain flattening everything under people's caps, even their skulls.

I'm afraid of not doing his features justice if I try to describe them. Beauty is obvious and needs no description. Anyway, I could see at first glance that he was a loving, sensuous and considerate person. His moist, open lips made me feel such love that I wanted to kiss him at once. My heart was on the point of exploding, like an over-ripe tomato in the vegetable garden feeling the sharp bite of the midsummer sun.

If I'd been a purist, I might have found fault with his large feet or his face, which looked as if it had been carved in a hurry by a blind man vigorously wielding a sickle. But when you were in front of him, you were instantly captivated by his piercing brown eyes as their gaze went right through you. Something was cutting me apart. I felt a mixture of vertigo, rapturous emotion and panic.

What did he think of me? I was a shameful puddle, and I felt terrible in my washed-out red-check smock, with my muddy clogs and my farm-hand's sunburnt complexion. Love gives no advance warning, and I hadn't even had time to prettify myself. I wasn't up to coping with this.

'String!' he cried. 'I need string, right away!'

I didn't ask why, I immediately ran to the scullery and came back with a ball of string. Later, Gabriel told me it was at the moment when I put it into his hand that he decided I was the woman for him.

But I hadn't reached that point yet. I didn't understand what was happening to me. I felt sensations that I had never known before. My heart was pitching and tossing. My mouth was dry, and my lips were quivering as if worms were burrowing into them. I was like the Israelites in the Book of Exodus, chapter 9, verse 24, at the time of the seventh plague of Egypt, suffering deluges of 'hail, and fire mingled with the hail, very grievous.' I was shivering with cold, and at the same time so hot that sweat was coming out of all the pores of my skin. I wanted to shout out loud with joy, and at the same time I wanted to lie down. I had fallen in love.

He had already run off again with his ball of string, on the way back to his sheep, when I called after him, offering to bring some mulled wine out to the sheepfold for him.

'I wouldn't say no,' he called, without turning back.

A few minutes later, when he had saved the sheep's life, I brought him a steaming mug held in my shaking hand.

'This will warm you up, monsieur.'

'Call me Gabriel.'

'My name is Rose.'

There was a silence. He didn't know what to say, and nor did I. I was overcome by panic when I thought that our conversation might peter out there, and I'd miss out on my chance of a great love.

In the end he said, 'Talk about flaming June! I've never seen anything like this weather!'

'You're right about that.'

'There's still plenty of work for me to do here. I won't be able to get it all done today. I'll be staying overnight.'

'What, in the sheepfold? It smells bad.'

'No, there are good smells of milk and wool too. It smells of childhood.'

'You're right about that,' I repeated.

I was in an emotional state, trying not to fall down in a faint, my breath coming short, my gaze desperate. I made a great effort to pull myself together before stammering, 'Will you be dining with us?'

'That's the idea.'

I was glad he'd be staying for dinner, but at the same time I dreaded the moment when he would discover that I was only the skivvy. The girl who cleaned vegetables, spread liquid manure, dealt with trimmings and leftovers, emptied earth closets, polished floors, furniture and shoes and massaged her bosses' egos.

I didn't eat at the family table, but in the kitchen once the Lempereurs' dinner had been served.

'Next course!' bellowed Justin after the starter, when it was time for the main dish.

'How much longer are you going to take?' grumbled Anaïs, annoyed that I was being so slow.

I had cooked chicken in garlic and artichoke sauce, a recipe of my own invention and, I may say in passing, a real hit. After serving Gabriel and the Lempereurs, I waited to hear their opinion of it with my heart thudding.

'I've never tasted anything so good in my life,' said Gabriel.

'Yes, it's not bad,' Justin conceded.

'Except that it needs more salt,' commented Anaïs.

As a reward, Justin said I could stay with them to hear Gabriel talk about his job. I sat down on a stool near the window and drank in his words with delight. I am sure that the expression on my face was that of St Teresa of Avila in Ecstasy as carved by Bernini, a sculpture that I saw one day in the Cornaro chapel of the church of Santa Maria della Vittoria in Rome, and that to my mind is one of the finest depictions of love in its pure state.

16

The King of the Burdizzo Clamp

HAUTE-PROVENCE, 1925. Gabriel Beaucaire was a professional gelder. He had been known to castrate up to four hundred animals in a single day. He was skilful, quick and muscular, because the job calls for strength, particularly in the arms.

He was also an artist, for castration is an art as well as a science. You have to be both firm and gentle in handling the animals, so that they don't make panic-stricken movements. Gabriel had a steady, reassuring hand.

He could geld anything. Mainly sheep, but also calves, donkey foals, piglets and even young rabbits. He was a master of the most up-to-date method, castration using the Burdizzo clamp to crush the spermatic cords bringing blood to the testicles.

Gelding was a seasonal job, beginning at the end of one winter and finishing when the next begins. By Gabriel's calculations, he castrated nearly eighty thousand animals a year. He was the king of the Burdizzo clamp, taking care not to wound the animals and to cause as little pain as possible.

Since the dawn of time human beings, not content with beating animals until they bleed and eating their dead flesh, have humiliated them throughout their lives. While female creatures are subjected to unnatural rhythms of fertility to keep them producing more young, as well as milk and eggs, the males of the various species have had their testicles ruthlessly removed in a kind of permanent genital hecatomb on the grand scale.

For a long time castration was a danger to male animals bred for their meat, since they sometimes died as a result of the operation. It was systematically carried out, all the same; otherwise they would have been like human males, always chasing sexual satisfaction, climbing on the backs of the females, penetrating them again and again and sending them crazy. It wouldn't have done the males any good or fattened them up.

So for a long time farmers cut off the penises of wethers, or destroyed the testicular cords of bullocks by wedging them between two pieces of wood that were then struck with a mallet. The arrival of castration pincers made the process more humane, if I may put it like that. And Gabriel was in the forefront of this testicular revolution.

It was begun by a Frenchman, Victor Even (1852–1936), who invented the first castration pincers. By crushing the testicular cords of animals without breaking the skin, they blocked the blood supply to the testicles and allowed them to atrophy naturally, without leaving a wound or risking haemorrhage or infection.

A few years later an Italian, Napoleone Burdizzo de La Morra (1868–1951), perfected the tool, superseding Even's pincers. His own version, a clamp with wide jaws and shortened handles, was lighter and easier to manipulate, but the principle remained the same: the crushing of a part of the blood vessels interrupted the circulation of blood to the testicles, leading to the death of the tissues affected.

Gabriel first felt the scrotum of the animal to locate one of the two spermatic cords above the testicles. When he had found it, he pulled on the side of the scrotum to pinch it, then placed it between the jaws of the Burdizzo clamp, closing them on the cord before stretching it in a back-and-forth movement. The operation took about ten seconds, and was carried out four times running, since he clamped the two spermatic cords in two places each, on the second occasion crushing the cord lightly just below the first place.

In the following days the testicles of the animals swelled before shrinking and gradually turning into rachitic and useless scraps of skin. Gabriel did not exactly love his job, but he was proud of doing it well. As he explained that evening with an ambiguous smile, he felt that his was the work of a peacemaker. 'When there are fewer balls on a farm there's less violence and conflict. Every peasant knows that.'

'Perhaps we should think of applying the same principle to human society,' suggested Anaïs.

'There wouldn't be so many wars,' added Justin.

'We'll be counting on you to prevent the next,' I concluded.

Everyone laughed, Gabriel most of all. He confessed that it was not without a certain exhilaration that he used his clamp to eliminate so many future lives. And he added that he could well see himself gelding certain generals and marshals who had commanded troops in the Great War. I thought at once of Morlinier, who had condemned Jules to death, but it didn't seem to me that the clamp was a sufficient punishment for his crime.

When Gabriel had left, the Lempereurs went up to bed, along with their dogs. I washed the dishes and cleaned the kitchen in less time than it takes to say so. My hands were shaking, I was unable to keep my mind on anything, I was trembling from head to foot, I had lost my wits, and I knew that I'd never find them again except in Gabriel's arms.

It would have been too dangerous to go in search of him before finishing all my work; I would have aroused the suspicions of the Lempereurs, and they wouldn't have stopped short at spoiling everything, since their one purpose in this world seemed to be to ruin my life until death released me.

But I couldn't have been mistaken about the way that Gabriel looked at me, and I knew what was going to happen. Sure enough, as soon as I left the kitchen he was waiting for me outside the door.

I didn't see him at once because the night was too dark, but as soon as I had closed the door he struck a match, and there he was, two or three metres away from the steps up to the house.

The rain had stopped some time ago, but the farmyard was like a large drain. He took several squelching steps towards me and then said, 'I want to spend the rest of my life with you.'

If he'd hit me over the head with a mallet it would have had the same effect. I didn't know what to say.

'Are you ready to spend what time God is pleased to grant us with me?'

I opened my mouth, but no sound came out. I felt so stupid that I wanted to run away in tears, but finally I managed to nod my head, not that he could see it, because the match had gone out.

I coughed, as if to clear my throat, so that he wouldn't take my silence to mean No, and then, in a strangled voice, said something that might be taken to mean Yes.

I thought he would kiss me, or take my hand, but no, he stayed there in front of me as if he didn't know what to say. He was in the same state as me.

He suggested I follow him to the sheepfold. I'd have preferred him to ask me to meet him in the stable. The smells there are so much nicer; you might think the horses had honey in their dung, and its odour tickles the lungs so exquisitely that I'm carried away, but never mind, I wasn't about to make a fuss.

Gabriel and I spent much of the night in the middle of the flock of sheep expressing our love, without touching each other, even lightly, but looking at one another although we couldn't see a thing in the dark. I dare not tell you what we talked about, it was so foolish and incoherent.

'We always have to go back to the spirit of childhood,' my grandmother used to say. 'That's where we find everything again. God, love, happiness.' All the same, it's odd that love makes you so stupid and at the same time so happy.

17

Seventy-Five Days of Kissing

SISTERON, 1925. Gabriel had a heavy workload for the next few days: three hundred sheep to castrate at a sheepfold in Sisteron, more sheep in Les Mées and La Motte-du-Caire.

As for ourselves, he had made arrangements even before telling me he loved me. He was a man who never doubted anything – me, himself, our love.

He had told my masters that he would be leaving very early in the morning, long before they woke and let out their dogs. He had no intention of making it difficult for us to leave.

In order to keep them asleep while we got away, Gabriel had left his mule and his cart some way from the farmhouse, in a field of clover lower down, on the banks of the river. My lover thought of everything.

I took nothing with me but Theo's box, Pascal's *Pensées* with the list of my hates inside it, some clothes and a kitchen knife for defending myself against those mastiffs if necessary.

On the way, as flocks of rooks soared in the air overhead, we kissed so much that when we reached our journey's end I couldn't feel my mouth or my tongue, and indeed I could hardly speak. Our conversation went round in circles. He asked if I would marry him, I said I would, he begged me once again to give him my hand in marriage, I accepted once more, and so on. I had to keep reassuring him with a gesture, a kiss, a caress.

No true love is free of fear. Fear that it will all stop at any moment. Fear that life will suddenly take back what it has given you. That was why Gabriel sweated so much, and so did I. The perspiration was pouring off me, my eyes stung, my vision was blurred.

We stayed in this condition for several days on end, clinging together except when Gabriel was using his clamp on the little pricks of the male lambs, who always seemed to feel it was a humiliating experience, and they emerged limping, heads down, looking like punished children.

On the day of our arrival in Sisteron, the home of Gabriel's friend Aubin, who bred and reared sheep on a large scale, I felt a pang; I feared, wrongly, that this would put an end to all our kissing.

Aubin was a confirmed bachelor about sixty years old, with little yellowish eyes under the fat creases of his eyelids. When he opened the door to us he looked briefly taken aback, before saying something that couldn't be made out because of the wind howling in the mountains that stood behind Sisteron in a semicircle. He inspected us with disapproval, gestured to us to come in, and then, addressing himself to Gabriel, growled, 'I didn't think you'd dare come here, not after what you've done, or I'd have told the police.'

'So what have I done, then? Can you tell me?'

Aubin went in search of a newspaper in his kitchen and held it under Gabriel's nose. The front page of the previous day's *Le Petit Provençal* bore a large headline:

Sensation In Sainte-Tulle
Under-age Girl Abducted By Dangerous Maniac

The news story under this headline quoted Justin and Anaïs Lempereur at length. They dwelt on the naivety of their cousin Rose, a simple soul who, to the sorrow of her family, had never been quite right in the head. According to them, it wasn't the first time she had run away from home. 'She has the Devil in her,' wrote the reporter, who also described Gabriel as a malefactor obsessed with sex who had been up in court several times charged with offences against decency, in fact a reprobate who seemed to illustrate the very worst features of the human race.

'This is grotesque,' Gabriel exploded when he had read the article. 'Grotesque and ridiculous. I can explain, Aubin.'

'Don't bother,' said his friend. 'I understand it all.'

But Gabriel insisted, and together we told the story of our adventures. When we had finished, Aubin said, 'Well, I'd like to, but...' And he went to find a bottle of gentian spirit and three glasses from his glass-and-china cupboard. When he had filled our glasses, he said, 'I can see only one thing for it: you'll have to tell the police what you've just told me.'

'We can't,' I said. 'My masters are such liars that they'll still be saying the same thing in ten years' time. I'd rather let them have the farm and go on to something else.'

'In that case, if you two need a bolthole you can stay here until the hue and cry has died down.'

Then he invited us to join him at the table. There were hard-boiled eggs, vegetable soup with basil, and goat cheeses in a pot of olive oil. We ate it with large slices of bread dipped into the soup or spread with pesto. It was his daily diet, and he never seemed to get tired of it.

I remember Aubin rolling his eyes at Gabriel as the latter – for my lover was a conversational virtuoso – set off a pyrotechnic display of anecdotes and funny stories, moving from one to the other without stopping for breath.

That night, when I asked Gabriel where he had learnt all that, he said, 'From books. In these parts there's nothing but life, as well as books to teach us how to live it better. My father told me that; he's a teacher. My mother is a market gardener and I take after them both. Heaven and earth.'

'You know so much, Gabriel. Forgive me for asking, but why do you work gelding animals?'

'There wasn't anything else for me to do.'

'You can do anything.'

'I was expelled from school in Cavaillon when I was sixteen for biting the philosophy teacher's ear so hard that he lost a bit of it. There was a great fuss, and the story's pursued me ever since.'

'Why did you bite him?'

'Because he said Spinoza was a degenerate philosopher.'

'Perhaps he was right.'

'Spinoza is my favourite philosopher. It was he who taught us that God is everything and vice versa. When he wrote 'God is nature' there was no more to add. We can see how right he was every day, simply by watching a blade of grass turning to the sun.'

Theo, naturally, loved Gabriel as much as me. Every time I brought her her food, my salamander told me, as she munched her worms, spiders and snails, 'Marry him, Rose, marry him right away. You've found the very man for you.'

I don't think I'd ever been as happy as I was for the two and a half months that we spent at Sisteron. I'd never been so frightened before, either. I did all I could to hide my joy, even from Gabriel, for fear of attracting the attention of those evil spirits who, at the first signs of happiness, come running to disillusion us.

That stay in Sisteron was one long and almost uninterrupted kiss. A kiss lasting seventy-five days. It wasn't just that we could no longer live without each other; our lips could not bear to be parted, however briefly. Like those snails who merge with each other so entirely that you can't separate them, we were kissing all the time. When we were keeping Aubin's sheep on the sloping sides of the Alpine foothills. When we were taken by surprise in a storm that, having caught up with us, drenched us in buckets of water. When we went gathering mountain herbs for the dishes I cooked in the evening. When we made the baby who, one day, began to grow inside me.

18

Uncle Alfred's Countless Bellies

CAVAILLON, 1925. Gabriel lived in a small stone apartment block in Cavaillon, a little town that lies in the shadow of the Cathedral of St Véran. The cathedral is one of the great sights of Provence, with its pictures by Nicolas Mignard, a fine seventeenth-century painter who was mad about the building.

In the old days towns hid away from the heat, or from invaders. The whole district around the cathedral dwelt in twilight, even at noon, because of the heat of the sun. Its topography was laid out so cunningly that the two-storey building where Gabriel lived never saw the light of day.

When he turned the key in his door, his neighbour on the floor above, an old lady with a moustache and a limp, came hurrying down as fast as the limp allowed, crying out, 'I'm glad to see you, laddie, but you mustn't hang around here too long. The police are after you. They've been here several times, saying you've committed a terrible crime.' She gave us a toothless smile, and went on, 'So this is the girl you abducted? Well, congratulations, my boy. You have good taste.'

Whereupon she kissed me, leaving the odour of piss on my face, before predicting, with the gravity of a fortune teller, 'I feel it in my bones that you will love one another deeply, and quite right too. People are always right when they're in love.'

Gabriel's apartment was inundated with books flowing all the way through it to the kitchen cupboards: novels, stories, philosophical works.

'Have you read them all?' I asked.

'I hope to have read them all before I die.'

'What's the point of dying an educated man?'

'The point is not to die an idiot.'

After asking the old lady to see that his parents in Cheval-Blanc, a village near Cavaillon, got the mule and cart back, Gabriel threw a few things into a cardboard suitcase, and an hour later we were on a train bound for Paris.

He had decided that we would take refuge there in the capital with his Uncle Alfred, whose first wife, now dead, had been Gabriel's mother's sister. Gabriel described his uncle as a first-rate writer, one of the classic authors of the twentieth century. His works included essays, novels, plays and collections of poetry.

When we arrived in Paris the next morning, we went straight to the imposing apartment building where Alfred Bournissard lived in the Rue Fabert, near Les Invalides. He was just finishing his breakfast, his lips shining and covered with croissant crumbs. When the maid showed us in, he rose to his feet and embraced Gabriel warmly.

He knew our story, and immediately called us 'Romeo and Juliet'. There was something impressive about him, a liveliness of the mind, a gift for repartee and a benevolent sense of humour. He also had a clear look in his eyes that inspired one with confidence. He had been a handsome man in his youth, there was no denying it, and that had allowed him to marry a rich heiress after the death in childbirth of his first wife, Gabriel's aunt.

However, Alfred Bournissard had also reached the age where, after fifty, a man is responsible for his own face, and his did not suggest that he would be let off lightly on the Day of Judgement, marked as it also was by hatred, apathy and avarice.

Rotundity was a word that sprang to mind in connection with his physical appearance. You'd have thought he had countless bellies. He bulged all over: his chin, his cheeks, even his fists bulged, and it all contributed to the look of self-satisfaction that his enemies couldn't stand, and that had twice prevented him from being accepted into the Académie Française when he stood for election. On both occasions he had received more votes against him than in favour of his becoming a member.

Without asking our opinion, Uncle Alfred, a man whose nature it was to act fast, decided that Gabriel would be assistant to his personal secretary, while I was sent to work in the kitchen, beginning by cleaning and trimming vegetables and washing dishes; he was waiting for me to show what I could do.

*

Uncle Alfred was working on a major project, and intended to co-opt our services as ghost writers. He called it 'The Drumont Event'. He was writing an essay, a biography and a play, all to come out at the same time in

1927, commemorating the tenth anniversary of the death of that eccentrically loquacious writer Édouard Drumont. Uncle Alfred had worked with Drumont at the end of the latter's life.

That was why Gabriel and I read and annotated all the works of Drumont: journalist, parliamentary deputy, founder of the Anti-Semitic League of France, a man who cast his spell over Charles Maurras, Alphonse Daudet and Georges Bernanos. Not forgetting Maurice Barrès, so well described as 'the nightingale of carnage'.

It felt as if we had set up in a literary *ménage à trois* with Drumont. I can't count the times when Gabriel and I kissed or made love in the middle of his works, and in spite of the care we took our playfulness sometimes still managed to crease their pages or cover them with suspicious marks. My pregnancy made Gabriel desire me even more.

And so I gained a certain intimacy, in every sense of the term, with Édouard Drumont, that child of the century of Romanticism who, in his book *Jewish France*, one of the great publishing successes of the end of the nineteenth century, was happy to imitate Victor Hugo in a style that flows like lava, or I almost said saliva.

It's ridden with maggots, too. Before dying in 1917, half-ruined and affected by cataracts, Édouard Drumont asked Maurice Barrès, who noted it down, 'Can you understand how God can have done this to me – me, Drumont! – after all that I have done for him?'

In *Jewish France* Drumont also describes the main characteristics by which Jews can be recognized. 'That notorious hooked nose, the blinking eyes, the clenched teeth, the jug ears, the nails cut square instead of rounded to an almond shape! The upper body is too long, Jews have flat feet, round knees, extraordinarily jutting ankles, and offer the soft, limp hand of a hypocrite and traitor. They often have one arm shorter than the other.'

After reading this passage, Gabriel said, laughing, 'You might say that's the spitting image of me.'

In his anti-Semitic manual, Drumont made a note of other features: 'The Jew has a wonderful way of adapting to all climates.' Or as he also says, 'A phenomenon confirmed many times in the Middle Ages, and still to be seen today in times of cholera, is that the Jew seems to enjoy particular immunity to epidemics. He appears to suffer from a chronic case of plague, and thus is not affected by ordinary plague.'

He also noted that, 'the Jew smells bad... the most privileged of them have an odour, *fetor judaïca*, a disagreeable aroma, Zola would say, which is an indication of their race and helps them to recognize one another [...]. This fact has been verified again and again; "All Jews stink," Victor Hugo has said.'

Finally, according to Drumont, 'Neurosis is the typical Jewish malady. Among this race, subjected to persecution over so long a period, always living in the midst of constant anxiety and incessant conspiracies, practising only professions that involve solely mental activity, the nervous system has changed. In Prussia, the numbers of the mentally disturbed are much greater among Jews than Catholics.'

Édouard Drumont gives some striking figures to support this assertion: out of 10,000 Prussians, 24.1 Protestants are mentally disturbed; the number of Catholics is 23.7; and the number of Jews is 38.9. 'In Italy,' he adds, 'we find one mentally disturbed person in 384 Jews and one in 778 Catholics.'

From book to book, Édouard Drumont pursued the same point: the Jews had come down 'like a plague of locusts' on the unfortunate land of France, which they had 'ruined, bled dry, and reduced to poverty' by organizing 'the most appalling financial exploitation ever known in the world.' I quote these passages from his book *Jewish France in the Face of Public Opinion*, published in 1886, in which he returns to the triumph of his famous essay, published in the same year.

I cannot force you to read the quotations that follow. A Hitler before his time, Drumont writes good French. You should know, however, that what he says sums up the ideological gallimaufry that did duty for thought among such patriots as Uncle Alfred, before reaching its zenith in Nazi Germany.

'French society of the old days, being Christian,' writes Édouard Drumont in *Jewish France*, 'took as its motto "Work, Sacrifice, Devotion". Today's society, being Jewish, takes as its motto "Parasitism, Idleness, Egotism". The predominant idea is not to work for the community – for our country, as it used to be – but to force the community and the country to work for you.'

Édouard Drumont was not a conservative. The evidence, so he predicted, was that 'all France will follow the leader who is a lawmaker and, instead of striking down the unhappy French workers like the men of 1871, will strike down the Jews who are stuffed with gold.' For a while Jules

Guesde, one of the great figures of the Socialist left, thought it proper to participate in public meetings at his side. No doubt he shared Drumont's analysis of the capitalism that was then emerging everywhere in the West.

'It is on the ruins of the Church alone that this ravenous idol of capitalism stands like an Ashtoreth, a monstrous goddess fertilizing herself and constantly reproducing, giving birth without a qualm, so to speak, while we sleep, while we make love, while we work, while we fight, stifling all that is not capitalism in her terrible act of increasing and multiplying.'

Whatever we may say about Édouard Drumont, no one can deny his extraordinary gift for prophecy when, suggesting that an end must be put to the 'Jewish system', he writes, over fifty years before the time of the seismic upheavals that would ravage the old continent of Europe: 'The great organizer who stockpiles weapons such as rancour, anger and suffering, will have accomplished something with repercussions that will be heard all over the earth. He will have given Europe equilibrium to last two hundred years. Who is to say that he is not already at work?'

Adolf Hitler had not yet been born. The world would have to wait until 1889, still three years hence, before that spiritual son of Édouard Drumont came into the world, and, like the archangel, would announce what was to come.

19

La Petite Provence

PARIS, 1926. My relationship with Theo had deteriorated a good deal during the months when we were working for Uncle Alfred. When I took my salamander (who from now on had an aquarium to live in) her flies or spiders, I often found myself deluged with accusations.

'What's the matter with you, Rose? What have you done to your soul?'

'Like everyone else, I'm trying to survive, Theo.'

'Couldn't you have survived in a better cause?'

'I'm doing my best, but I'm going to get out of here. Trust me.'

'Look at yourself. Spineless, that's what you've become. You've fallen into the lavatory pan, so pull yourself together before someone flushes it and you go down the drain.'

I heard what Theo said, but I wasn't really listening. Uncle Alfred was so pleased with our work on Édouard Drumont that he paid us a substantial sum of money, which allowed me to open my restaurant a few months later.

I couldn't set the business up myself; I was nineteen, and in those days you were still a minor at that age. Gabriel was wanted by the police after my 'abduction' from Sainte-Tulle, but for my sake he took the risk of opening the restaurant in his own name.

'I can tell that we shall go on to do great things together,' said Uncle Alfred, patting his paunch with satisfaction. 'You two have everything – talent, passion, convictions. All you lack is success, and I'm going to give you that. It will come, children, you just wait and see, it will come.'

He had asked us to clear the ground by preparing him some notes on the author of *Jewish France*. But carried away as we were, and writing all the time, we completed the whole first drafts of the play, the essay and the biography, and he used them more or less as they were, not forgetting to give us credit for our help in the introduction to the two books.

'You're living proof of the fact that ghost writers can be intelligent,' laughed Uncle Alfred, with a nauseatingly self-satisfied look on his face.

His many stomachs quivering with enthusiasm, he next wanted us to draw up a list of French Jews, but we declined. Apart from the fact that I had decided to spend my life in kitchens and not with books, I didn't like the idea, and nor did Gabriel, as I could tell from the expression on his face when Uncle Alfred told us his plan.

Being as clever as he was, Gabriel managed to turn the offer down tactfully and without offending his uncle.

'It's a titanic work, and I don't feel equal to it,' he said. 'What's more, the baby will be here very soon, and we won't be available all the time. I wouldn't want to disappoint you.'

'As you like, children.'

Uncle Alfred didn't press the point. He had alternative ideas for us. A biography of Charlemagne, an essay on Napoleon and the Jews, a history of the various European mentalities, an atlas of the races of the world and I don't know what else.

'I've always liked Charlemagne,' said Gabriel.

'Mind you tread carefully,' said Uncle Alfred. 'He employed a lot of Jews, in fact he stuffed his government with them. That's something you'd have to look into when you're investigating his origins.'

'Charlemagne was Jewish?'

'I don't know, but very likely; you can tell a Jew by the way he gives work to other Jews. People like that stick together, it's an obsession of theirs. Let them have their way and there'd be nothing left for anyone else. I may add that Charlemagne was a cosmopolitan, a kind of militant stateless person, and that's one of the salient characteristics of the Jewish mind. They never owe allegiance to any one place, they make themselves at home everywhere... particularly here in France, I'm sorry to say!'

'We'd need to be historians to write a work like that,' said Gabriel. 'I'm afraid you'd be disappointed.'

But Uncle Alfred never owned himself defeated. Always full of ideas, he then suggested that we could write him the screenplay of a film – he already had the plot and the title, *Moloch*. He opened his desk drawer and took out a copy of the scientific journal *Cosmos*, dating from 30 March 1885 and featuring an engraving by an artist called Sadler. It showed 'the torture of a child in Munich, whose death led to the massacre of the Jews there in 1285.'

The child, said the text that accompanied this engraving, 'was found through information from the woman who supplied victims for ritual sacrifice; the child had been tied to a table in the synagogue, where he was stabbed with stilettos and had his eyes put out. Children collected his blood. The indignant townspeople rose violently against the Jews of Munich, and it took all the bishop's authority to calm popular anger and put an end to the massacre.'

'Those are the fundamental points of the plot,' said Uncle Alfred. 'The film could be a great success, setting off discussion of something that people refuse to acknowledge: the Jews love blood, and that's a fact. Édouard Drumont found a Talmud published in 1646 where we can read, in black and white, that shedding the blood of young non-Jewish girls is a means whereby the Jews are reconciled to God. Moloch, who must always be fed with bleeding human flesh, is the typical Semitic deity. Nothing satisfies his hunger and quenches his thirst. Sacrifices such as the murder of the child in Munich were carried out everywhere in the past, in Constantinople and Ratisbon alike, and I am sure they are still going on. It is time to say so, to cry it from the rooftops: the Jews adore hot blood. If they didn't, the Pentateuch wouldn't forbid them to drink it.'

I was horrified by his sharp tone of voice, and at the same time affected by the sad benevolence that his words suggested. Uncle Alfred, a man who wanted only our good, was both despicable and touching. I was always at a loss with him, and took refuge in a stupid smile, leaving him to Gabriel, who knew better than anyone how to confuse his ideas.

This is not something I'm proud of, but we called our son Édouard after Drumont, our late benefactor, and to please Uncle Alfred, who also stood godfather to our child, a baby conceived and born in sin.

We still had two years to wait before we could get married. Until I came of age, I'd have had to ask my guardians at Sainte-Tulle to give their permission for the wedding, and I might just as well have handed myself in to the police right away.

The birth of Édouard was the best day in my life. With due respect, Chateaubriand must have been very obtuse to say in his autobiography, *Memoirs from Beyond the Grave*, that, 'After the misfortune of being born, I know of no greater unhappiness than that of bringing a man into the world.'

If Chateaubriand had been a woman, he would have known about the terrible joy of giving birth, that internal sense of sublimity, bloodshed mingling with delight and going hand in hand with a religious awe. After the birth, when Édouard was asleep on my stomach, I wept with happiness before Gabriel's eyes. It was as if I were outside and above myself. I could have stayed in that position until I died.

But the world was waiting for me. I had to earn my living and produce milk. I breastfed Édouard until he was six months old, when I handed him over to a wet nurse, a fat neighbour of ours who lived on the sixth floor, and was still producing a litre of milk a day, seven years after she last had a baby.

At the end of the year I had found shabby premises in the Sixth Arrondissement, in the Rue des Saints-Pères. They consisted of a dining room measuring sixteen square metres, with a tiny kitchen that meant I couldn't serve more than thirty customers a day. The restaurant was called Le Petit Parisien, a name that I changed to La Petite Provence.

I served my specialities there every day: plaki, vegetables with parmesan, and caramel flans, and supplemented the menu with my vegetable soup and pesto, to which I added both garlic and cheese with a generous hand. After a few months I had a delightful clientele of writers, intellectuals, and the middle-class inhabitants of the district.

In order to attract customers, Alfred Bournissard often came to have lunch or dinner at La Petite Provence. I owe it to him that my restaurant was frequented by such people as the singer Lucienne Boyer, and the writers Jean Giraudoux and Marcel Jouhandeau. Nor must I forget a very old gentleman, Louis Andrieux, formerly a prefect of police who had also been a parliamentary deputy, then a senator, and who was also the natural father of the writer Louis Aragon. All these well-known figures made the reputation of my restaurant.

Uncle Alfred did so much for us that I often found excuses for him when he proposed his monstrous notions. I took care not to offend him, but his generosity made me uneasy. After the death of his first wife, he had married the heiress of the Plantin hardware stores, and then she was run over by a train; the engine of her car stalled in the middle of a level crossing, and she didn't get out quickly enough. A widower for the second time, he never got over her death. He shed tears easily, looked for love everywhere, even in the eyes of his dachshund, and suffered from the lack of it. I was cross with myself for being unable either to hate him, or to envisage breaking with him some day.

I consoled myself by reflecting that it is always more difficult to receive than to give.

20

The Art of Revenge

MARSEILLES, 2012. I must interrupt my story briefly here. At about one in the morning, just as I was finishing the last chapter, Samir the Mouse rang my doorbell.

'I hope I'm not disturbing you?' he asked, with the nervous air of those young people of unprepossessing appearance who sit on the pavement outside cafés, giving cheek from behind their dark glasses to old folk like me, those of us who find that putting one foot in front of the other is indescribable torture.

'I was just going to bed,' I told him.

'I have some amazing news for you.'

I didn't like his equivocal smile as he said that.

'It's dynamite,' he insisted. 'I found it in an official register: Renate Fröll was sent to a Lebensborn institution in 1943. You know what those Lebensborn places were?'

'Not really,' I replied in a neutral tone, before asking Samir the Mouse to sit down, which with his usual bad manners he was about to do anyway, uninvited.

He told me about the Lebensborn project, but in fact I knew anyway: Himmler set up SS maternity homes to develop a superior race, using stolen or abandoned children both of whose birth parents were certified Aryan: blue eyes, fair hair, the whole works. Their civil status was removed from the records, and they were adopted by model German families with the idea of regenerating the pure stock of the Third Reich.

After a long silence on my part, intended to make him uneasy, a slight trace of anxiety crossed the face of Samir the Mouse. 'Aren't you going to congratulate me?'

'I'm waiting to hear the rest of it.'

'We'll both have to go to Germany to make inquiries, and it will all come clear.'

'You know I can't travel,' I protested. 'I have a restaurant to run.'

'A few days will be enough.'

'Now that I've found out what I wanted to know I don't feel like digging any deeper. I'll give you the cabinet I promised you for your work, and we'll be quits.'

'No, I want to go on.'

'Why?'

'To identify Renate Fröll's birth parents, and find out about her life after the Lebensborn place. To understand why you were interested in her.'

The mixture of irony and insinuation in his expression gave me the creeps. I felt he knew more than he was saying.

'Bloody hell of a fucking piece of shit,' I suddenly cried, 'what's all this crap you're giving me, you little cunt? If you carry on like this you'll get a punch in the kisser, my lad. Can't you stop bothering me? I mean, do you know how old I am? Don't you think you owe me respect?'

Samir the Mouse had jumped up and was pointing a menacing forefinger at me.

'Stop that this minute, Rose. You've insulted me, you owe me an apology.'

I thought for a moment. I was regretting my bad temper.

'Sorry,' I said, to close the incident. 'I'm busy reviving all sorts of memories while I write the story of my life, and it's not always fun. That's why my nerves are on edge, you see.'

'I see,' he said, 'but don't do it again. Don't ever speak to me like that another time, understand? Not ever, or it'll be the worse for you.'

To make things up, I offered him a mint syrup and iced water, and we drank it on my balcony, looking at the starry sky as it twinkled back at us. It was one of those nights which seems as bright as day, and you sense the presence of God far out in space, in the kind of veiled light that makes everything vibrate.

Samir the Mouse was like a delicious sweet, and it took all my strength of will to resist my wish to pick him up, crunch him and suck him. He felt the fire rising in my centenarian carcase, and judging by his quizzical expression it amused him.

'You're a funny old girl,' he said at last. 'I think I'd better inquire into you.'

'Don't bother. You'll know all about me when you read my memoirs.'

'Are you really going to tell the whole story in your memoirs?'

'Every bit of it.'

'Will you even write about the people you killed?'

He was going too far. I said nothing, but gave him a scornful look to show what I felt and express my disapproval.

'I know you've killed people,' he said after a moment. 'I can see it in your eyes. There's sometimes so much violence in them that you frighten me, you really do.'

'It's the first time I ever heard that.'

Although I'd have liked to stop the conversation then and there, I couldn't. There was another silence, and Samir finally broke it.

'You're always saying that if we're to feel good we have to get our revenge.'

'You're right, I do say so. Revenge is the only justice worth having, and those who say the opposite have never lived. What's more, I don't think you can really forgive until you've taken revenge. That's why you feel so good afterwards. Look at the shape I'm in at my age. I have no regrets and I feel no remorse, because I've observed the principle of retaliation all my life. Tit for tat, that's the thing.'

'Thanks for confirming it.'

'I'm not confirming anything. You can get your revenge perfectly well without killing anyone, Samir. Revenge is an art, and it can be taken slowly, sadistically and craftily, often without spilling a drop of blood.'

He shook his head two or three times, and then sighed, ostentatiously shrugging his shoulders. 'Rose, you can't believe a word of what you've just said. Only blood avenges blood.'

'No, intelligence can do it too.'

I was proud of that reply; there was a good ring to it, and we had to stop the conversation there. To prove my good faith, I told Samir the Mouse he could go back into the sitting room and read the first chapters of my book.

He was a pure product of our era, when ignorance of all that is literary continues to take giant strides. In spite of his protests to the contrary, I don't think he had ever read a book in his life, not even one of those he was supposed to be studying at school; he had looked up the Internet summaries of their contents and simply reproduced them.

It took him over an hour to read my prologue and the first seventeen chapters, often stumbling over the words. When he had finished he was stunned. Not by my genius but by exhaustion, as if he had just made a superhuman effort.

The only comment he made before going home to bed was, in the tone of a blackmailer, 'We'll have to talk about all this again face-to-face.'

I wasn't too sure what he was trying to say, but it kept me awake.

21

A Mushroom Omelette

PARIS, 1930. Everything was going well, almost too well, but I had to upset our everyday happiness and satisfy the baser instincts that were troubling me.

It was a promise I had made myself. Only Theo knew what I was going to do, and she backed me with enthusiasm.

Gabriel and I were like two fish swimming in the warm waters of bliss. We had been married for over a year, and I still loved everything about him, including his parents. I had met them on our wedding day, and they had cast their spell over me. They were two philosophical Provençals like Emma and Scipion Lempereur.

You had to hurry up about appreciating them, because they weren't going to make old bones. That was obvious from their eyes, and it was confirmed in the following months, while for us life was just beginning. Édouard was three, I was twenty-two, and Gabriel was twenty-six when I decided to close my restaurant for the Easter holiday.

I claimed to have personal business to settle in Provence, and he didn't ask what it was. A certain delicacy kept Gabriel from asking me to account to him for the least little thing, but it's true that he could read my mind as easily as a knife cuts through butter. I left him Theo as a pledge that I'd be back.

With Gabriel, I was sure that our love would last a lifetime. In the servants' bedroom we occupied on the sixth floor of the Rue Fabert, no voice was ever raised in anger, even when Édouard had given us a broken night, as he often did when sinusitis was followed by laryngitis and all those other ailments that babies suffer.

Gabriel knew just what my plan was. He was familiar with those outbursts of hatred that sometimes choked me. He and Édouard took me to the Gare de Lyon, and as I was about to get into the train, my foot already on the running-board, he whispered in my ear, 'Go carefully, my love. Think of us.'

Going carefully was not my strong point, but Gabriel wisely made me feel guilty. He wasn't arguing against my plan, he was only weighing up the risks and setting their limits. If he hadn't said that, I don't think I would have stopped off at Marseilles before taking the train to Sainte-Tulle. I would simply have listened to the strong desire urging me to hurry up and satisfy it.

In Marseilles I went to the hairdresser to have my hair cut in the boyish Joan of Arc style, and then I bought a basket, some meat, and clothes to make me look like a man: a pair of trousers, a coat and a shirt, a cap and a scarf to hide part of my face.

When I reached Sainte-Tulle station, I set off for the Lempereurs' farmhouse by walking through a small wood of oak trees. I knew a good place to pick mushrooms there, and I filled my basket. I put a few morels on top of the others, but most important of all, I picked two deadly species whose smell and taste had misled their victims for generation after generation: I picked *Amanita phalloides* and *Inocybe fastigiata*. Enough of them to kill a regiment.

When the two mastiffs came leaping towards me, I threw them some pieces of meat that I had laced with hemlock seeds. They gobbled up the meat with that stupid greed to be found only in dogs, pigs and human beings. It was the best way of killing wolves in the past. Success was guaranteed. After a few minutes the dogs dropped to the ground, shaken by spasms, their eyes popping out, their muzzles foaming. You'd have thought they were perishing with cold, dying over a slow flame, if I may say so.

'I'm sorry for you,' I told them, 'but you shouldn't have killed my cat.'

As they lay in the yard in their death agony, I went to knock at my former masters' door, with the basket of mushrooms over one arm and a revolver in the other hand. An Astra mod. 400, a semi-automatic pistol of Spanish origin that a journalist friend in the Latin Quarter had sold me.

It was Justin who opened the door. Except that his brick-red complexion was turning purple, he hadn't changed. He recognized me at once in spite of my disguise, and offered me his hand while keeping his distance, with an expression of alarm and consternation on his face.

'What's happened to the dogs?' he asked.

'They're not well.'

Pretending not to notice my pistol, he said, 'I'm pleased to see you. What brings you here?'

'I've come because of the cat.'

'The cat?'

Although his mouth was dry and his voice blank, he assumed a falsely jovial voice because of the balance of power between us: my revolver pointing at him, his dogs writhing in agony behind me.

'If that's all, we can give you another cat. Cats are easily replaced, there are so many of...'

'I accepted all you did, all of it except the cat,' I said, making for the kitchen. 'Call your fat wife and we'll have something to eat, it's about the right time of day. I'm going to make you a mushroom omelette like the omelettes I used to cook, remember?'

'Of course I remember! You're the queen of mushroom omelettes...'

'... and of many other things.'

Drawn to us by the noise, Anaïs came in, treading heavily. Her water retention made her ankles look like demijohns. When she saw me in the kitchen with my Astra mod. 400, she let out a shriek of fright, and would have fallen over backwards if her husband hadn't caught her.

'Why have you brought a revolver with you?' asked Justin in a strangled voice, exactly appropriate for his present situation.

'I didn't want to take any risks with you. We've had too many misunderstandings, and I was afraid you might not appreciate the intention of my visit, which I make as a gesture of peace and friendship...'

'It's a shame we didn't understand each other better.'

Justin was so proud of this remark that he repeated it twice.

'Now or never is the time to make up for that,' I said, 'and to begin again with a clean slate.'

I peeled and chopped the mushrooms, before mixing them with the beaten eggs, fifteen eggs in all. When my omelette was just the way they liked it, still soft and runny inside, I helped them to a large portion each, telling them not to gulp it down in haste, as they usually did with their food, but chew it slowly and relish the flavour, in honour of the good old days. They complied, with the professional gluttony of pigs being fattened for the slaughter.

'I loved my cat very much,' I murmured, as they ate their omelette.

'So did we, honest to God.'

'Then why did you kill him?'

'It wasn't us, it was the dogs,' protested Justin, 'but you're right, we shouldn't have let them have him, it was stupid of us. We're sorry.'

When their bellies were full of the omelette I made them coffee. They were just beginning to drink it when, seeing the first sweat break out on their skin, I told them that they were going to die. The process would begin in a few minutes' time and would take several hours.

They seemed surprised. It must have occurred to them that I was planning to pay them out, but they weren't expecting to be trapped by what had always been their weak point, good food.

'I did it for the cat,' I told them. 'I had to avenge him. I kept thinking of it all the time; it was spoiling my life.'

Justin had risen to his feet, but I threatened him with my semi-automatic to make him sit down. I left them to their fate when the nausea, vomiting, diarrhoea and dizziness set in, but before they fell into convulsions and their livers were destroyed. I didn't want to watch that; I am not morbid in taking vengeance.

Before leaving, I emptied some of the remains of the mushroom omelette into the dogs' bowls, before putting the pan, still quarter full, on the kitchen table so as to leave the police in no doubt about the cause of death of the Lempereurs and their dogs.

Two weeks later, I received a summons from the Manosque police station. I went back to Haute-Provence, where I was interrogated by a suspicious inspector who, with one of his colleagues, bombarded me with questions for over four hours, but was unable to find anything in my answers to confirm that I had been involved in the affair.

His name was Claude Mespolet, and his nose was like a pointed chisel jutting out of the face of an embittered old mummy whose head topped the body of a little buffoon. He was barely thirty years old, and wore a greasy waistcoat over a shabby shirt that nonetheless had gilt cufflinks. Sceptical as he was about the story I suggested of an accidental case of mushroom poisoning, he had a grudge against the whole world in general and me in particular.

'When there's a murder,' he told me, 'the first thing to be done is to look for the motive. You have a motive.'

'I may have a motive, but there wasn't any murder.'

'There's no proof of that,' he objected.

'And no proof of the opposite either.'

'Yes, there is, madame. Traces of hemlock have been found in the bodies of the dogs. That makes me think that someone wanted to set the scene after their deaths, and tipped the remains of the poisonous mushrooms into their bowls.'

Inspector Mespelet looked hard at me until I lowered my eyes.

'True, it's only a suspicion on my part,' he concluded, 'but you must agree that there's a worm wriggling under the stone if we lift it.'

Unintentionally, Claude Mespolet had taught me a useful lesson. If he wasn't the most brilliant police officer ever known, then I was no virtuoso criminal either. I wouldn't set the scene another time; it aroused too many suspicions. Improvisation was a better idea.

A few months later, I received a letter from the Manosque notary telling me that 'after the tragic death' of Justin and Anaïs Lempereur, I was the sole heir to the farm at Sainte-Tulle. I replied saying that, now I was of age and wanted no more to do with the property, I would like him to sell it for me as soon as possible.

At the end of the same year, the proceeds of the sale enabled me to buy a three-roomed apartment in Paris, in the Rue du Faubourg-Poissonnière, for Gabriel, Édouard and me. And all the time I lived there, nearly ten years, I was the happiest woman in the world.

22

Return to Trebizond

PARIS, 1933. Happiness, Emma Lempereur used to say, has no story to tell. It's like an apple tart; you eat it to the very last crumb picked up from the table, before licking the golden juice that stains your fingers.

Happiness doesn't advertise itself either. The best way to make enemies of your friends is to show how happy you are. They can't stand it. Happiness is a masterpiece that must remain unknown at all costs; you must keep it to yourself if you don't want to attract hostility or bad luck.

Gabriel and I had reached the peak of happiness when we gave Édouard a little sister, Garance, a blonde with blue eyes, like her mother but with finer features, and she showed her passion for dancing very early. I already saw her as a ballerina at the Paris Opera.

As for Édouard, he wanted to be a policeman, an engine driver or an orchestral conductor. He had no inhibitions about getting into everything; he hated compartments and labels. At a very early age he seemed to me so far from the typical French spirit that I was frightened for him.

Forgive me if I can't tell you any more about Édouard and Garance. I shall avoid the subject of my children in the following pages. You must understand me: simply putting their names down on paper leaves me with tears running down my face and my throat racked by sobs.

As I write these lines, the ink mingles with my tears, turning my words into large bluish blots on the page of my notebook. I didn't begin telling you my story in order to hurt myself. Every time I try to conjure up my children in words, everything is confused, and the ground gives way beneath my feet. Since the tragedy happened I live with them in my head, but it is better for me if they stay there and don't come out.

God knows why, but it's easier for me to remember Gabriel, although they all suffered the same fate. At the time he was hard at work professionally. My husband was now officially Uncle Alfred's secretary, and was also his ghost writer, inundating the anti-Semitic press of the time – *La Libre Parole*, *L'Ordre national* and *L'Antijuif* – with Bournissardian prose.

Even though he never told me so I sensed, and not with displeasure, that he was ashamed of his work. He hardly ever talked about it, and when we happened to mention it by chance he kept his eyes lowered, while his lips twisted in a bitter smile. He was an accomplice in something that I hated, and at the same time I knew that he was worthy of better things. That was why I forgave him, especially as he seemed to be trying to change direction, for instance by writing the music columns of *Le Figaro* when the usual music critic was away.

After the death of Alfred Bournissard in the spring of 1933, at the age of fifty-two and as the result of an apoplectic stroke brought on over a long period by his congested blood vessels, Gabriel tried to free himself from the deplorable extreme right of opinions in which his uncle wallowed. For a short while he worked for Jean Giraudoux, author of *The Madwoman of Chaillot*, who was often accused of anti-Semitism, but much may be forgiven to a man who once wrote that 'the French are a composite race', and that there is no such thing as 'a Frenchman born, only a Frenchman made.' Even if he seems a little suspect, I have never classed him with the rest of them.

A few months later, looking for a permanent position, Gabriel agreed to be editorial secretary to the magazine *La France réelle*, a right-wing journal the mere sight of which nauseated me. But I could not have thrown the first stone at my husband. The clientele of my restaurant consisted mainly of persons of that cast of mind.

The disgust that we felt for it, although we never expressed it, was undoubtedly the only drawback to our happiness, and you always have to make the most of what happiness you have left. I knew that Gabriel had nothing in common with those loud-mouthed brawlers who claimed to be patriotic, and who flourished in the 1930s. I approved of the way Gabriel tried to buy back his soul by working on a biography in praise of Salomon Reinach, whose origins lay in a family of German Jewish bankers, and who was an archaeologist, a humanist, and a specialist in the history of religion, one of the finest minds of his time. He died a year before Uncle Alfred.

Nothing could detract from our harmony as a couple, neither the dark atmosphere of the time, nor Gabriel's professional problems. We understood each other even without words.

He could read my thoughts, as he did in the year when he cheerfully agreed to look after the children during the annual closing of La Petite Provence. From his understanding smile, I saw that he knew what I had in mind when I told him I planned to return to the scenes of my childhood in Trebizond, 'to settle some personal business.'

*

1933 saw the birth of the Third Reich. It came into the world on 30 January, when President Paul von Hindenburg, a hidebound politician in the image of his dying republic, gave Adolf Hitler his blessing by appointing him Chancellor.

A few weeks later, after the Reichstag fire, Hitler assumed full powers in order to protect the country from what he claimed was a great communist plot, and on 20 March Himmler, the Munich chief of police, announced that two days later the first official concentration camp would be opened near Dachau. It would be able to 'accommodate 5,000 persons', and to hold asocial characters whose riotous behaviour endangered their own lives and health.

At school in Manosque I had chosen to study German as my first foreign language. Emma Lempereur, who was fascinated by German culture, had introduced me to it by putting Goethe's *The Sorrows of Young Werther* into my hands, and after that everything else fell into place naturally – Bach, Schubert, Mendelssohn and all the others.

In spite of this Teutonic inclination of mine, however, I had paid no attention to the rise of the Nazi Party, nor did

I think of the millions of dead – five, six or seven million of them – as a result of the great Soviet famines in the same year.

On 22 January 1933 Stalin, one of the worst criminals in the history of mankind, and his henchman Molotov signed a directive ordering a blockade of Ukraine and the northern Caucasus, condemning the inhabitants to die of starvation where they were, and forbidding them to go in search of the bread they needed anywhere else, while the Soviet Union exported eighteen million hundredweight of wheat.

Genocidal fever was on the march, and nothing could stop it now. Under the aegis of Hitler and Stalin it would crush, in turn or simultaneously, the Jews, the Ukrainians, the Byelorussians, the people of the Baltic States, the Poles and many more.

If I had taken the trouble to find out about all this, 1933 would have left a taste of dust and ashes in my mouth. As it was, that year brought me one of the greatest joys in my life. I felt the first vibrant thrill of it in the summer of 1933 when, from the deck of my ship, I saw Istanbul approaching.

And it did not leave me during the three days I stayed in Istanbul, the ancient city of Constantinople that had changed its name in 1930, and where I immediately felt at home. I don't know whether that was because of the aromas drifting through the air or the goodwill in the eyes of those I met, but I had a feeling, as I walked along the streets, that I was finding the part of myself I had lost when I left the Black Sea.

Where were the murderers of my family? Here, the executioners had soon become victims themselves, and the victims had become executioners. The crowd was so well-disposed that I couldn't for a moment imagine it slaughtering my relations. I was Turkish here among the Turks – I almost said, to the Turks; I thought the men were better-looking than the Frenchmen of Paris, but I didn't give way to temptation.

Not quite, but almost. One man followed me into the great bazaar of Istanbul, where I was buying presents for my family. After a while he addressed me, suggesting that we walk together, but I didn't go along with that idea.

I had been to pray in the mosque of Hagia Sophia, the greatest monument in the Christian world for almost ten centuries from 537 to 1453, the date when it fell to Islam. That was the last year when it was a place of worship, before its transformation into a museum. I was carried away. I seemed to see something divine in the luminous white light that came in through the windows, refracted from the interior of the dome.

Several days later my joy was redoubled when our ship arrived off the port of Trebizond, which rose at the far end of a milky sea that joined the low, cream-coloured sky.

However, my joy was tinged with the sense of anxiety that one feels before making love for the first time, on opening the door of the room where a bed of pleasure awaits. Except that on this occasion, it was to be a deathbed.

I knew who I was going to see, but I didn't yet know what I would do to him.

23

A Boating Trip

TREBIZOND, 1933. Ali Recep Ankrun had as many bellies as Uncle Alfred, not to mention another on his nose, which looked like a Caucasian tomato that had been thrown at him and landed in the middle of his face.

He had only one arm, and was one of those maimed people who refuse to admit that they have lost a limb; he made suggestive nudging movements with his elbow from time to time, as a way of emphasizing those of his remarks that he thought most important. It was only with some difficulty that I resisted the temptation to ask him how he had lost the arm.

He sweated profusely, particularly his face, and therefore kept a check handkerchief as big as a duster on him at all times to mop up the perspiration. But he smelled good, with an aroma of Turkish delight, caramel and almond milk which made me feel a little hungry.

The mayor of Trebizond welcomed me by advancing on me with that silly, vulgar cheerfulness typical of politicians, as if he had been just waiting for my visit since the day he was born.

'You're quite right to take an interest in our city,' he said.

'Well, when *Le Figaro* asked me to write a major report on Trebizond I accepted at once.'

'Which goes to show that *Le Figaro* is a very intelligent newspaper, as I already knew.' And lowering his voice, he added, with a sugary smile, 'You speak Turkish very well. Where did you learn the language?'

'At school. My father was fascinated by the Byzantine Empire.'

'I'm sure you know that for over two hundred years our city was the capital of another empire, known as the Empire of Trebizond.'

'Yes, and I also know that your city was founded by the Greeks long before the present era.'

'Ah, the Greeks,' he sighed. 'We didn't get on well with the Greeks. Dull-minded Christians, obsessed by their feeble faith and crazy about crosses. They went putting them up all over the place. Now that the Greeks have gone, frankly, we feel much more at home.'

Although I was itching to tell him that the Turkish government had settled the Greek problem just as it settled the Armenian problem a little earlier, I refrained from doing so. The Turks solved their problems by ethnic cleansing. The genocide of the Greeks between 1916 and 1923 had left 350,000 dead. Christianity had disappeared from the region. Muezzins had drowned out the sound of church bells.

But I hadn't come to argue with Ali Recep Ankrun, I had come for a much more important reason. So I pretended to share his opinions, acting like a meek and fascinated little girl. 'And was it this cleansing,' I conjectured, 'that allowed the city to start again on a sound basis?'

'Starting again doesn't quite describe it. I'd call it more of a renaissance, even an economic explosion. I'm prepared to give you an exclusive interview describing all that, as well as my many plans for development in all fields, industrial, educational and religious.'

He praised the mosques of Trebizond to me – they must at all costs be seen – before going on to talk about fishing, one of the main activities of a city that, in his eyes, was the world capital of just about everything. Anchovies, sprats, red mullet, and also hazelnuts, tobacco, maize and potatoes.

An hour passed, and then another. Ali Recep Ankrum was in no hurry to bring our conversation to an end. A guard regularly put his head round one of the doors of the mayor's office, looking meaningfully at him; there was a delegation of Georgians in the outer room waiting to see him and getting impatient; they had to leave very soon for Erzerum, where they had other meetings.

Before concluding our first encounter, the mayor of Trebizond invited me to dinner that very evening, and I accepted, pretending to feel a pleasurable tingling sensation down my spine, which judging by the dilatation of his pupils put him in great good humour.

I spent the afternoon walking in the streets of Trebizond, particularly Uzun Caddesi, my ears full of the cries of the fishmongers and my nostrils satiated with the good smell of *lavash* bread. After a while I felt so full of fresh air, of odours, perfumes and colours that I ended up forgetting what I had come for.

So many deaths later, nothing had changed in the teeming city, as crowded as ever, at the foot of its mountain. Life had gone its own way, and was carrying me with it through the busy throng. In spite of all my prejudices, I had fallen for the charm of Trebizond. You could have said that I was reconciled to myself.

That evening, when Ali Recep Ankrun invited me to the best restaurant in the city, I had to be tactful about rejecting the advances of the mayor, who seemed to have decided that I would be ready for them as soon as we had finished dessert. Without wishing to boast, I think I managed it pretty well.

'Never on the first day,' I told him, taking his moist hand. 'Forgive me, but well... I always have to think for a little before I say yes. I'm so sentimental, you see, and then again I'm married.'

It was only putting off the moment. When Ali Recep Ankrun suggested a picnic on his boat at lunchtime next day, I accepted without hesitation, fluttering my eyelids and moistening my lips before letting out a moan that, while not exactly subtle, was to say the least very promising. I almost told him that then I would be ready for what he wanted, but it was my lumbar and posterior regions that, with a little light trembling, conveyed that information to him.

'Don't tell anyone my name,' I insisted. 'I'm fond of my husband, and I wouldn't like any scandal.'

'Nor would I. I'll be very discreet, have no fear. That's in my own interests as well.'

'I'd prefer it to be just you and me on the boat, no servants. You know how they like to gossip.'

'Naturally, and I am too modest to have anyone else present when I make you my declaration.'

So saying, he gave me a wink accompanied by a meaning smile. I laid my hand on his and caressed it gently to confirm my intentions.

We began addressing one another by the familiar *you* pronoun.

'I am so keen to show you how I feel,' I said.

'I love you.'

'I think this is the start of something special.'

When I came on board his motorboat next day for our little cruise, I had my semi-automatic Astra mod. 400 at the bottom of my handbag, but I didn't expect to be using it. As I said earlier, I had decided to improvise.

First I asked him to put well out to sea, and the mayor obliged me without any argument when I pointed out that, as I was a very modest woman, I would like to have as much distance as possible between us and the shore before we embarked on the preliminaries.

Then, when we were far from land, and after he had stopped the engine to let the boat drift, I gave him what he wanted. It was nothing to speak of, and was over quickly, in much the same time as a sneeze would take, but I think the mayor was moved by it. So was I, but not for the same reasons. I was in the fevered state where I had found myself before giving birth.

When we had finished, he licked my nipples with the greed of a baby at the breast. Realizing that he wanted to start again, I claimed that making love had given me a good appetite.

'All right,' he said, 'we'll eat, then we'll do it again, and so on.'

Ali Recep Ankrun produced Turkish dishes from his basket, in particular the most delicious *pides* with feta cheese and spinach. It was when we had finished the meal, and he was leaning overboard to have a piss, that I pushed him with an oar kept on board for all contingencies, and he fell into the sea. As he was struggling in the water and panting like a large dog, I told him, 'That's for the death of my father.'

'Your father?'

'A farmer from Kovata.'

'I don't remember.'

'An Armenian. You killed him, just as you had the rest of my family killed: my mother, my grandmother, my brothers and my sisters. You had to pay for it sometime. For my father and all the others.'

His poor health was hampering him, and in any case he hardly knew how to swim. He was out of breath, and he panicked. I couldn't have said whether he was mooing, squealing or whinnying, but in between every word he said, he was letting out terrible cries, like an animal in the slaughterhouse.

'Did you come to orgasm when you thought of throwing all those people into the water, all those women and children?'

'I was obeying orders.'

Judging by the way his lower lip was sticking out, I thought he was shedding tears, but I couldn't have sworn to it.

'If you save my life,' he managed to howl with one final effort, 'you can have all the money you...'

He gurgled something, kicked for a few more seconds, let out some little squeaks like a dying rabbit, was knocked over by a wave and then sank.

I was sorry I hadn't asked whether he had ever managed to lay hands on Madame Arslanian's money. I believe that people always tell the truth when they know they are going to die.

I started the engine of the motorboat again, and when I was back on shore I went to the hotel to collect my things, before returning to the port, where I got on board the next vessel about to leave.

A nice round sum of money was enough to get me a berth as a stowaway. The ship was a freighter with a cargo of raisins, wool and cowhide. Its first port of call was in Romania, and from there I went back to France by rail, as innocent as a newborn lamb.

24

A Jew Without Knowing It

PARIS, 1938. You often don't realize that you have been happy until it's too late. I never made that mistake. I took all the advantage I could of the five years that followed, and I have nothing to say about them except that they were wonderful. Until the tragic moment came that was to change our lives, when a newspaper accused Gabriel of being Jewish.

As the author of the news story said, there were Jews everywhere, not just in the banks and the press, but also 'in the crowd with which they have been allowed to merge' by changing their surnames.

It all began with the Austro-Hungarian Empire. To put an end to the practice whereby Jews used their hereditary names, the authorities gave them, whether they liked it or not, Teutonic surnames with a pleasant sound, such as Morgenstern (morning star), Schoenberg (beautiful mountain), and Freudenberg (mount of joy), or sometimes the names of towns: Bernheim, Brunswick, Weil and Worms.

In France, the Napoleonic decree of 20 July 1808 gave registrars the right to choose the names of Jewish immigrants themselves. Some of these immigrants had the name of Anus imposed on them, but later changed it to

Agnus. Others, as also happened on the other bank of the Rhine, were given the names of towns or villages: Caen, Carcassonne, Millau, Morhange.

Thus the name Picard does not necessarily have anything to do with Picardy, but is a free transliteration of Bickert or Bickhard. That surname is one of those that, like Lambert and Bernard, can cause confusion. As Uncle Alfred once wrote, 'The Jews hide themselves anywhere, even under French names.'

At the end of the 1930s some noted authors took it upon themselves, in the manner of Henry Coston, to track down Jews in the fortifications of the surnames behind which they were concealed. With the enthusiasm of hunters, they unearthed families called Cavaillon, Lunel, Bédarrides and Beaucaire in their burrows.

It was our bad luck that Gabriel's surname was Beaucaire. On 8 January 1938, an article under the name of Jean-André Lavisse appeared in *L'Ami du peuple*, a rag that for a long time had a circulation of a million copies, denouncing my husband's Jewish origins on the front page and three-quarters of a page inside. I was astonished. So was he.

Under the heading 'Find the Jew', the article, as venomous as it was well-informed, revealed that Gabriel came from a long line of Jews on his father's side. It printed a number of names and a family tree. This work traced his genealogy, apparently inexorably, all the way back to the arrival of his ancestors in France in 1815. It was like a police file.

L'Ami du peuple said that Gabriel was secretly preparing a work in praise of the 'Jew and traducer of Christianity

Salomon Reinach'. It also accused him of having 'viciously infiltrated himself' into extreme right-wing circles on behalf of 'Lica', the International League against anti-Semitism, with several of whose leading figures it said he had been secretly associated for a long time.

According to Jean-André Lavisse, Gabriel was an 'informer' who collaborated with the police forces of the former socialist President of the Council Léon Blum, the 'ethnic hybrid and hermaphrodite' to whom he was close, writing memos for him, when he wasn't feeding information to all kinds of well-known enemies of France, headed by the League.

The article gave names, and I have to say that I knew at least one of them, Jean-Pierre Blanchot, one of Gabriel's best friends. My husband had always introduced him to me as a professor of history, rather than as the kingpin of the League that he really was.

On the day when *L'Ami du peuple* came out, Gabriel unexpectedly came to see me at La Petite Provence. I was breaking eggs into a pan of milk for my famous caramel flan when he walked into the kitchen. I could tell at once, from the distress in his face, that the situation was serious.

When he had explained, I said, 'Did you know you were Jewish?'

'Of course not. No one in the family knew. Otherwise do you think Uncle Alfred would have welcomed us so warmly?'

'There's something else intriguing, although I never thought of it before: your first name. Don't you think it's funny that your parents called you Gabriel?'

'Plenty of non-Jewish people are called Gabriel. It's a name you find, like the Archangel Gabriel himself, in Judaism, Christianity and Islam. Rose, I knew you wouldn't mind, but if I'd known I would have told you at once that I was Jewish. So where's the problem, and what do you take me for?'

When I asked him if he had been playing a double game with the extreme right, as *L'Ami du peuple* claimed, Gabriel replied with another question, as he often did. According to Uncle Alfred, that was a notable social characteristic of Jews.

'Do you think I'm capable of playing a double game?'

'Frankly, that would surprise me a little... but all right, I won't hide my preferences from you.'

Gabriel didn't say anything to that; he just dropped a kiss on my face in the usual spot between my temples and my eyes. I hoped that I had interpreted the way he meant that correctly, but I couldn't bring myself to ask him for fear of being disappointed by his answer. Furthermore, I was punch-drunk. I'd just had one of the most important lessons of my life: you never really know people even when you live with them.

If he had managed to hide his real political convictions from me, I wasn't safe from other surprises. I even began to think that Gabriel might be unfaithful to me. While I was perspiring in my kitchen, there was nothing to prevent him from putting his skill in dissimulation to the service of a double love life. Particularly as, after so many years, I began to feel his desire wearing off.

He made love to me less and less frequently, and in addition he was quicker about it. At night, while he slept beside me, I often fantasized about his suspected infidelities, and in my dreams I saw him straddling one of the ladies of easy virtue who clustered around him at receptions, drinking in his words and his glances.

I reached the point where I could bear the sight of their squirming bodies in my mind, but not their groans and orgasmic cries of pleasure in my head. These nocturnal torments always left me in a kind of terrible ecstasy. I had difficulty in recovering from it, and every time I emerged from the sheets looking as if I had risen from the grave.

The more I thought about it, the less I doubted that he was a typical adulterous husband. He never talked about his days, and did not seem to have to spend his time in any particular way, working a great deal but only when he felt like it. Furthermore, he was always even-tempered, which wasn't the case with me, and he never forgot those little attentions, like bouquets of flowers, that brought a blush to my cheeks and that, as we women know, allow straying husbands to buy a clear conscience at little expense. However, the Duluc Détective Agency told me, after a month of investigations, that Gabriel was whiter than white.

After the revelations in *L'Ami du peuple*, Gabriel found himself out of a job overnight: an anti-Semite to the Jews, and a Jew to the anti-Semites. He had lost on all counts. I must confess that finally, and with some difficulty, I persuaded him to come and work with me – mainly so that I could keep an eye on him.

I had parted with the premises in the Rue des Saints-Pères in order to buy a new and much larger restaurant, which

I opened a few weeks later, in the Place du Trocadéro, still named La Petite Provence. It was there that, for a time, Gabriel and I became kings of Paris with our cat Sultan, whom I had bought to keep the mice away, a job that he did with consummate art and unrivalled distinction.

25

Carefree Days

PARIS, 1938. A few days after the publication of the article in *L'Ami du peuple* that changed our lives, Adolf Hitler annexed Austria. It didn't take long for the German troops to enter the Führer's native land, to the applause of the Austrians themselves, and the Anschluss was decreed on 13 March.

While Hitler was proclaiming victory on the balcony of the Hofburg in the Heldenplatz of Vienna, holding forth in front of a rejoicing crowd, Himmler was closing the frontiers, thus trapping inside them the rats, the lice, the Jews and all enemies of the regime, whom he intended to wipe off the surface of the earth.

The event made no particular impression on me. When Gabriel and I talked about the Nazis we couldn't manage to feel very anxious. Berlin was a great cauldron, a cultural melting pot, and we dreamed of tasting its contents some day. German culture, in full creative flow with such writers as Thomas Mann and Bertolt Brecht, seemed likely to protect us from all evils.

I am sure I never even read the newspapers reporting Hitler's latest misdeeds. I was brimming over with confidence. In the restaurant's big register, where I noted everything down, I have found that on the day of the Anschluss I entertained the deputy of the Sixteenth Arrondissement, who had reserved a table for forty – he was Édouard Frédéric-Dupont, well known as a defender of the rights of concierges, whose professional welfare he had very much at heart. It was said of him that he would be a parliamentary deputy until his death, and after that he would be a senator.

He was a man with a head like a hook, the manners of a millipede and ferrety eyes. I was very fond of him, and he liked to visit La Petite Provence, which he assiduously frequented. If I am to believe the note at the foot of the reservation for that day, he ordered a special menu in which the main dish was to be my unique *brandade* of salt cod with garlic and potato. At my age, I think it's about time for me to pass on the secret of the dish: I always add a little chilli pepper to the purée.

On 30 September 1938, the day of the signing of the Munich agreements that allowed Czechoslovakia to be taken apart for the benefit of Nazi Germany, I still had my mind on other things: we were celebrating Garance's birthday at the restaurant, as we did every year, with my unrivalled crab soufflé and lobster sauce, her favourite dish. I still remember that Yvette Guilbert was dining with two old ladies at the next table, and after our daughter had blown out her candles she came over to sing 'Madame Arthur':

Chacun voulait être aimé d'elle,
Chacun la courtisait, pourquoi?
C'est que sans vraiment être belle
Elle avait un je-ne-sais-quoi.

While I was serving customers at La Petite Provence, events were coming thick and fast on the opposite bank of the Rhine. I can't say exactly what I was doing on Kristallnacht, the night of 9 November 1938 when the Nazis began hunting down Jews all over Germany. Probably not making love with Gabriel, since that had become a relatively rare occurrence. The most likely hypothesis is that I was suffering from a severe bout of insomnia and trying to drown it in port.

Apparently that vast pogrom passed right over my head. After synagogues had been burned down, shops looted and 30,000 Jews arrested, I might at least have been anxious on Gabriel's account. Particularly as, in the aftermath, German Jews were obliged to sell all their assets – houses, businesses, works of art – for derisory sums before 1 January of the following year, and furthermore were banned for life from going to swimming baths, cinemas, concerts and museums, and were also forbidden to use the telephone, go to school or hold a driving licence.

Our lives were carefree, and if Gabriel and I had been asked what we would die for, it would have been for our two children or for the restaurant. Since all three were thriving, everything was for the best in the best of all possible worlds, to repeat that stupid expression. I heard it again and again in the mouth of my husband, who, when he saw me finishing work at my stoves, recommended me to relax by reading the great sages of classical antiquity, for instance Epicurus, one of whose sayings he often quoted: 'He who cannot be content with little will never be content with nothing.'

One day I called his bluff by replying with another quotation from Epicurus, one that shut him up for a long time: 'Let us make haste to succumb to temptation before it goes away.'

I succumbed to it one evening when Gabriel was staying at home in our apartment to look after the children. It came in the form of one of the directors of the Félix Potin chain of shops. He was a vigorous man with the shoulders of a woodcutter, he smelled of cigars and eau de Cologne; his looks suggested that he was cut out to play the part of Maupassant on film. He always ate alone, and recently he had seemed to be waiting for the moment when I made my round of the customers just before we closed the restaurant for the night. I had realized that he was after me a week earlier, when he had placed his hand on mine, murmuring something that I thought I understood, although I preferred not to get him to repeat it.

That evening we had finished serving the tables earlier than usual, and I had sent the staff home before midnight, when there was only one customer left in the dining-room, meditatively drinking his Armagnac at a table near the door. Gilbert Jeanson-Brossard was the name of my temptation.

I joined him with my own glass of Armagnac, and finished it in the kitchen after he had taken me from behind as I stood against my working surface. He was not a man to make much ado about the sexual act, but I loved him a great deal, and when he had finished I said, 'Thank you.'

'It's not for the woman to thank the man,' he said, 'it's the man who should thank her, because the woman gives and the man only receives.'

'I'm afraid it's the other way around, if I may say so.'

'No, that may be the case physically, but not in reality, as you well know.'

With his high forehead, regular features and chestnut hair, Gilbert Jeanson-Brossard was a very handsome man, and had the best figure that I ever took in my arms. His large hands, the hands of a manual labourer, excited me enormously; just feeling them on my skin under my blouse gave me gooseflesh.

Apart from horses, Parisian restaurants and the Côte d'Azur, where he went every summer, three subjects on which he could dilate for ever, his conversation was limited. He was far from being an intellectual. There was something rough-hewn and animal about Gilbert Jeanson-Brossard that came as a change after Gabriel's considerate lovemaking. Two or three times he left purple love bites on my neck, thus confirming my suspicions that Gabriel wasn't really looking at me any more, although I concealed them with scarves that looked incongruous at that season.

It became a habit for Gilbert Jeanson-Brossard to eat at the restaurant every Thursday evening, the day that my husband took off to devote himself to the children. My lover too was married, and although he thought me beautiful and increasingly desirable, all he wanted was a little extramarital adventure once a week that also added to my own happiness.

26

War is Declared

PARIS, 1938. Gilbert Jeanson-Broissard not only spiced up our marital relationship, he brought me closer to Gabriel than ever, if possible. Or at least so I thought.

Every time he had taken me in his swift, rough way in the restaurant kitchen, I went home to the conjugal bedroom full of amorous feeling for my husband, and tried to express it at once between the sheets, although my efforts did not always meet with success.

I discovered that guilt can be one of the best stimulants of ardour, so long as you are not giving but only lending yourself to an adulterous connection kept well within bounds: a relationship of convenience with nothing in view but to enjoy the respect of all concerned, as they say in Marseilles. General de Gaulle wrote that 'Man is made to feel guilty', and so is woman. I liked feeling the pangs of conscience.

It was with some annoyance that I listened to Theo's criticism. Her aquarium now had pride of place in the restaurant kitchen, and we fornicated before her eyes.

'What do you think you're doing to me? A woman doesn't cheat on her husband, you bitch! Or anyway not at the age of thirty! What will become of you after this?'

I had nothing to say in my own defence, but I moved the aquarium to spare Theo the sight of our lovemaking. All the same, she kept scolding me, although she did moderate her language a little.

As maître d'hôtel, Gabriel was well acquainted with Gilbert Jeanson-Brossard, who had become one of the regulars at La Petite Provence, and I had often (not without a thrill) seen them talking to each other. You might have thought that there was a secret complicity between them. I feared it might be developing at my expense, but I never heard my husband utter any insinuation or say anything with a double meaning, to lead me to think his suspicions had been aroused.

Until that memorable Thursday when he told me that he would stay with me for that evening's service in the restaurant.

'What about the children?' I asked.

'I've fixed all that. They're sleeping with their nanny. I wanted us to have time to explain ourselves to each other.'

'What do you mean?' I asked, with assumed surprise, which was contradicted by the trembling of my lips.

'You know very well,' he said in a weary tone.

I think I must have served the worst meal of my entire life as a cook that evening, at least so far as the dishes not prepared in advance were concerned. Several customers complained. One of them even sent back his *poulet fermier*, which was almost raw, the thigh and the drumstick swimming in a pool of blood. I went in person to present my apologies to a martinet in a bow tie, who didn't accept them.

'At the price you charge, madame, there's only one word for it: shameful! It's shameful!'

But I knew how to deal with difficult customers like this. He calmed down when I told him that he was the guest of the house, and we were also offering him a bottle of champagne as compensation.

At the end of the evening, when I was making my round of the restaurant, I naturally stopped in front of Gilbert Jeanson-Brossard, who murmured, with his hand hiding his mouth, 'What's he doing here? Can you tell me?'

'I don't know.'

'Does he know about us?'

'I fear the worst.'

'Would you like me to stay?'

'I don't think that would be a good idea.'

When everyone had left, Gabriel closed the tambour door and came to join me in the kitchen, where I was busy clearing up with a glass of pinot noir in my hand. He came over to me without a word, and took me from behind as Gilbert Jeanson-Brossard liked to do.

After that he said, looking me in the eyes as he pulled his trousers up, 'Well?'

'That was good,' I murmured in terror, trying to assume a loving expression.

'Don't you have anything else to tell me?'

'No.'

'Don't you think I have a right to an explanation?'

'First I'd like to know what you're accusing me of.'

'You've been cheating on me, Rose.'

'I don't understand what you're talking about.'

'I'm not about to do you a drawing.'

'You're making things up, Gabriel.'

The best way to get forgiven for your faults is not to admit them. I don't know where I learned that, but it has come in very useful in the course of my life.

He went on. 'Can you say, looking me in the face, that you have never been unfaithful to me?'

'Yes, I can.'

He made me repeat it. I did. He seemed to be astonished.

'You're lying,' he said at last in a toneless voice.

I wasn't lying. He was the only one I loved, since when I did stupid things with Gilbert Jeanson-Brossard they were of no importance to me; making love to him wasn't really love.

Affairs don't destroy love. On the contrary, they revive and feed it, they keep it going. If only cuckolds knew that they wouldn't get so upset.

Men ought to understand that instead of getting on their high horse, like Gabriel, over unimportant adulteries and little adventures that don't matter. Instead of which they spoil their own lives and complicate ours into the bargain.

'I have always been faithful,' I told him, with the purity of good faith in my eyes.

'Yes, faithful to your husband and your lovers alike.'

I don't know who had told him, no doubt an employee whom I had fired, but Gabriel knew what went on between Gilbert Jeanson-Brossard and me on Thursday evenings. He knew the crudest details of it, as he had just shown me, but he never told me how, even after informing me, with an air of outraged dignity, that he was going to leave me and sue for divorce.

'After what you have done to me,' he said, 'you at least owe it to me to let me have the children.'

'You've no right to take them,' I cried.

I was beginning to tremble.

'You have done wrong, you must atone for it,' he persisted.

I was trembling more than ever. 'You have no right!' I repeated.

He looked at me for a long time without a word, and then said, 'You've spent your life making concessions. Can't you make at least one to me, now that you are in the wrong?'

I could no longer control my trembling.

'It's a question of morals,' he said. 'Can't you understand that?'

'I'll do anything you like.'

'I'm leaving you the restaurant and the apartment, but I'm keeping the children.'

I was devastated. I don't remember the precise date of the break between us, but it was early in September 1939, and I might as well tell you that I couldn't have cared less when, on the second of that month, France and Great Britain declared war on Nazi Germany, which had just invaded Poland.

Gabriel had organized everything in advance. He left our conjugal home that very evening, and next day he began working in one of the large restaurants in Montparnasse, Le Dôme. As for me, I cried without stopping for twenty-four hours, and then at intervals for the next few days.

After that I did all I could to occupy my mind. I threw myself into phytotherapy, the science of medicinal plants,

taking my inspiration mainly from the teachings of Emma
Lempereur, my grandmother, Hippocrates and Galen, who
was physician to the Emperor Marcus Aurelius. Under the
brand name of Rose I created my own range of pills for
good health and sound sleep, with a flower logo designed
by myself. I began taking private lessons in German and
English, given to me by a young tutor who was excellent,
but in whom I felt not a spark of personal interest. I also
studied Latin with an old teacher. I spent endless hours in
my restaurant, staying to sleep there on a folding bed in the
dining room.

Nothing worked. The grief of love is like the death of a
mother or a father; you never get over it. All these decades
later, the wound has never closed.

27

Setting an Example

PARIS, 1939. After Gabriel had left home with our children, something like a large lump began rotting away inside me. I gave a name to this flesh-devouring pain. We all suffer from it two or three times in our lives: I called it the cancer of grief.

It left metastases everywhere, first of all in my brain which, refusing to stop or concentrate, was running on idle and going round and round. It also affected my lungs, which were breathing poorly, my gullet, which couldn't swallow anything, and my guts, which often twisted in appalling pain.

When my fits of tears wore off, the lump was still there and my grief went on. Decades later, I can still feel the sharp pain of it in my chest, at a very precise place below my lungs. I'm sure there is a tumour there. Mercifully, it didn't develop, thanks to my love of life, and thanks to Theo who helped me to bear the shock. When I told her what had happened, my salamander said, 'I did warn you, you poor fool.'

'I'll never get over it.'

'I hope you'll listen to me now. Come on, smile, keep smiling all the time, and it will get better, wait and see.'

So I smiled, and it worked a little bit, although for long

afterwards, and indeed to this day, I still feel an itching inside me, a private sense of devastation, a sentimental yearning.

I and my smile went to light a candle to Our Lady twice a week, praying her to make Gabriel come back to me. No luck. Whenever I heard a sound on the landing, I told myself that the Virgin had heard my prayer, and I waited, my heart thudding, to hear the key being put in the lock. But no, it was either the neighbour or a false alarm.

When I saw Gabriel as I was taking the children back to him or collecting them from him, he was as tense as a bowstring. He never raised his voice, but his face was closed to me, and he spoke in a guttural tone that I had never known him to use before, his teeth gritted, like a ventriloquist. That was why I had difficulty in making out what he was saying, and often had to ask him to repeat himself.

Eighteen days after our parting, I felt some hope again. When I cast him a pleading glance, however, he imitated it with a contemptuous look. 'I don't believe in the resurrection,' he said. 'Neither the resurrection of the dead, nor the resurrection of love.'

'There can be rebirth.'

'No. A dead tree may strike root again, but it will never grow really well.'

Yet again, Gabriel had not articulated what he was saying very clearly, and I asked him to repeat it. That made him smile – an indefinable smile in which I thought I saw affection, and it made me think that perhaps not all was over between us.

Now that he was out of my reach I loved him more than ever before; the proof of it was that my mouth was dry all day, as it is when sexual passion is at its height. I couldn't get Gabriel out of my mind, and I was faithful to him again, having broken off any idea of resuming my relationship with Gilbert Jeanson-Brossard overnight. The mere sight of him filled me with horror, and at my request he had stopped coming to my restaurant.

I would have nothing to do with the act of love unless Gabriel returned to me. Whenever any man began making advances to me, I felt nothing but disgust, and to discourage him I would whisper, in a mysterious tone, 'Forgive me, but there's someone else.'

For weeks on end I wrote Gabriel a letter of apology every day, quoting passages from the Gospels to support my pleas. He never replied. Not until the Sunday evening when I was bringing the children back to him, and he took me aside.

'Why do you want me to forgive you as you ask?'

'For the sake of redemption, Gabriel. We all have a duty to redeem ourselves.'

'On condition that the feeling is mutual,' he said. 'The beautiful words of the Gospel are not at all credible, Rose, coming from you. You're cantankerous, an avenger, you have always utterly rejected the idea of forgiveness. How could I forgive someone who herself has never been capable of forgiving?'

'I don't understand what you mean.'

By way of replying, Gabriel heaved a great sigh before quoting from the Book of Deuteronomy: '"And thine eye shall not pity; but life shall go for life, eye for eye, tooth for tooth, hand for hand, foot for foot." That's your philosophy, isn't it?' he asked me.

Gabriel knew me too well. At that moment I had an inspiration. I knew what I must do to make myself feel better. It would take two or three days, no more. My salvation had a name, the name of Morlinier, the army officer who, after ruining the last years of the Lempereurs' lives by condemning their son to death, deserved to be top of the list of the people I hated.

I knew where to find him, so I knew how to relieve the pain of my grief for a while. I had been gathering information about Charles Morlinier for years. The full powers held by Marshal Pétain, another product of the charnel house of the 1914–1918 War, whose comrade in war and in dissipation Morlinier had been, had relaunched his career. When the new head of state appointed him to the Council of State and made him a Commander of the Legion of Honour, he was well on the way to becoming President of the Council of the Administration of Postal Services.

While he was marking time in a junior post at the Office of Waterways and Forests, Charles Morlinier, who had been promoted to general in 1925, had presided for three years over the Association of Friends of Édouard Drumont, and I had met him again several times when, with Gabriel, we were preparing for the Drumont Event. He was a man of upright bearing and a yellowish complexion, he had a nose like the blade of a kitchen knife and jug ears. When he walked around you might have thought he was reviewing his troops. You always heard him coming a long way off;

the iron-studded soles of his boots sounded like a horse's hooves.

To make up for being not an aristocrat but a degenerate nonentity, General Morlinier was always talking about nobility. The nobility of warfare, the nobility of his feelings, the nobility of the French nation. His voice, like a ventriloquist's, came from his belly, and he spoke with a contorted look on his face, as if he had a cluster of vipers wriggling about inside him. And he always wore the same expression, similar to that of the fake classical statues of the nineteenth century.

I made my plans carefully. I had arranged to leave the keys of the restaurant with my second-in-command in the kitchen, Paul Chassagnon, a stout, red-faced man. With him in charge, I was sure that everything would be all right. But it all happened faster than I had intended; I was in such interior turmoil that I couldn't control myself. An hour was enough for me.

Charles Morlinier lived in the Rue Raynouard, in the Sixteenth Arrondissement of Paris. Disguised as a fat old lady, rigged out with a blonde wig, and cushions sewn inside my coat, I took up my position before sunrise outside his apartment building, which was part of Haussmann's renovation of the city of Paris in the previous century. My idea was to observe him for twenty-four hours before beginning my operation. The air was chilly, but I felt warm, and my cheeks were burning as if with rising sensual pleasure.

He stole out of the building like a thief at 7.30 a.m., and I had to quicken my pace to keep up with him. He was walking towards the Rue de Passy, and when we reached the crossroads I drew level with him, taking him by the sleeve and addressing him. 'Do you remember Jules Lempereur, General? The boy from Sainte-Tulle whom you had shot to set an example?'

General Morlinier had no time to answer my question. I had been unable to restrain myself. Looking as if he didn't understand what was happening to him, he let out a strange cry, a kind of bleat, his eyes popped and his mouth stayed open under the influence of surprise, or maybe pain, and then he suddenly fell to the pavement like a package. It seemed to me that he had died even before losing any blood. He had died of fear.

I hesitated to retrieve the knife that I had plunged into his chest and then turned like a gimlet, and finally left it where it was amidst his gurgling blood; I didn't want to get myself dirty.

I went away through the Trocadéro gardens, and dropped my soiled gloves into the Seine. They floated away towards Rouen, and I threw my wig, my coat and the cushions sewn into it after them.

After that, I made my way to the restaurant. I was feeling so good, as if I had been delivered from evil, that when Paul Chassagnon arrived to start work a little later he said, 'I don't know what's happened to you, madame, but it's a pleasure to see you so happy again.'

28

As Pink as a Prawn

PARIS, 1940. On 17 June the German troops marched down the Champs-Élysées as they had done daily since entering Paris three days earlier. The air shook, the streets were deserted, and everyone was desperately anxious.

That was the day when Heinrich Himmler decided to dine at La Petite Provence. I had no idea what made him choose it. The German officer sent to make the reservation and inspect the surroundings said that the Reichsführer-SS wanted a restaurant with a view of the Eiffel Tower, which couldn't really be said of my establishment. You saw the Tower only from a single table on the terrace, and then only if you craned your neck.

On arriving at about 10 p.m., and thus after nightfall, Himmler didn't even try to look at the Eiffel Tower, which from the Esplanade du Trocadéro seemed to emerge like a ship from marine darkness. There was nothing to suggest that the Reichsführer-SS had come to see the tourist sights. Protected by some fifteen soldiers, and accompanied by as many colleagues, not to mention the four military trucks parked in the square in front of my restaurant, he worked until late into the night, unfolding maps and making a lot of noise about it.

For the majority of the French population, traffic in Paris was forbidden between nine in the evening and five in the morning, so most of my suppliers had let me down. I made dinner with what I had available, notably salt cod, which I put to soak, and potatoes.

After an entrée of foie gras with port and a fig-and-onion compote, I gave Himmler and his companions my famous salt cod *brandade*, and then a strawberry charlotte, with my special choice of a medley of tisanes. I had surpassed myself.

Nonetheless, my morale was at rock bottom: at half past noon that day, over the radio, I had heard Marshal Pétain's speech, in which he claimed to have 'made France the gift' of his person 'to alleviate the country's distress', before saying, in the voice of a constipated old man, 'It is with a heavy heart that I must tell you today to stop fighting.' Since many units of the French army had surrendered to the Germans at the same time, that evening the Foreign Minister, Paul Baudouin, had thought it necessary to correct the remarks of the new President of the Council by reminding us that the government had 'neither abandoned the struggle nor laid down its arms.' Not yet, anyway.

At the end of the meal, Heinrich Himmler asked to see me. When I had tidied my hair and put on fresh make-up, I went over to his table. My heart was thumping, and I was trembling like a leaf.

'Bravo,' said Himmler, giving the signal for applause to his companions, who never took their eyes off him.

'*Danke schön*,' I said timidly.

It was the first time I had seen a Nazi dignitary. Before we served dinner, Paul Chassagnon had warned me that

Himmler did Hitler's dirty work for him, and was a terrible character who brought death wherever he went. At first sight, however, the Reichsführer-SS inspired confidence. Apart from his big behind, he seemed perfectly normal, I was going to say human – not that I can say the same today, now that we know all the things he did. Nonetheless, I even thought I saw a mixture of respect and compassion for the ordinary French population in his face.

Speaking through an interpreter, Himmler asked me about my tisanes and then medicinal plants in general. My German was too rudimentary for me to venture to reply in his own language; it took me several months to reach that point. Meanwhile, however, I impressed the Reichsführer-SS with the extent of my knowledge of plant lore.

'You understand it all so well,' he said. 'Plants are the future. They care for us, soothe us, cure us. In the new Reich that we are ushering in, I can already tell you that there will be phytotherapeutic hospitals. Don't you think that's a good idea, madame?'

I nodded my head. His eyes were shining with his internal fervour, and he believed in what he was saying so much that one didn't want to contradict him.

To continue ingratiating myself with the Reichsführer-SS, I told him that I owed much to a great German lady of the twelfth century, St Hildegard of Bingen, who wrote a lot about plants, and whose complete works I owned. To show him that I knew what I was talking about, I added that the *Book of Divine Creatures* was one of my bedside books.

At this he made a strange face, as if he had found himself eating a bad prawn or stepped into cow-dung in his slippers. I didn't yet know that Himmler had four great enemies in his life; in decreasing order of importance they were the Jews, communism, the Church and the Wehrmacht.

'Christianity,' he said with a severe expression, 'is one of the worst scourges of humanity. Especially when it is subject to Asiatic influence. A religion decreeing that woman is a sin leads us to the tomb. We are going to get rid of it, retaining nothing, not even Hildegard of Bingen, who was only a hysterical and frigid Benedictine nun.'

Clutching at straws, I got myself out of this difficulty by quoting the Chinese *Pen Tsao Kang Mu*, a work that listed medicinal plants three thousand years before Jesus Christ, and sang the praises of ginseng which, by stimulating male sexuality, has done so much for the reproduction of the human race.

He laughed, the kind of laugh a father might utter when his daughter had told him a funny story. All his companions imitated him, but with that nervous and artificial tone that I call the laughter of courtiers.

'I for one,' he announced, as if taking all the world to witness, 'don't need any ginseng.'

'You know, it never hurts,' I said.

And I asked the maître d'hôtel to go and find him an assortment of my boxes of pills. In the morning, when you want to tone up the organism, they were made chiefly from garlic, ginseng, ginger, basil and rosemary. In the evening, when you have to soothe the beast within, they were a mixture of hypericum or St John's wort, lemon balm, cherry, *Verbena officinalis* and Californian poppy.

Himmler congratulated me on the beauty of my boxes with their old-fashioned labels.

'*Es ist gemütlich*,' he said, and most of the officers with him, who seemed to be drinking in his words, repeated the last of them.

After telling me that he would like to continue exchanging opinions with me, the Reichsführer-SS asked one of the men with him, a tall, pale beanpole, to make a note of my details.

'I'll be back,' he said as they left. 'I don't care for military dinners in official palaces. I prefer to mix with representatives of the nations, such as yours, with whom we are going to work to make a better world, cleaner, purer, with only beautiful people like you in it.'

I turned as pink as a prawn plunged into boiling water.

29

The Man Who Never Said No

PARIS, 1940. There was no sign of life from Heinrich Himmler for several weeks, until one morning two SS men turned up at my restaurant and commandeered my stock of pills, brand name 'Rose', for keeping fit and sleeping soundly. They punctiliously paid, adding a large bonus.

They came back two months later. The same two: a short, squat man with pendulous cheeks and a tall, thin, angular man. I thought of them as Don Quixote and Sancho Panza. I concluded that Himmler must be taking five times the recommended dose, which didn't seem to be like him so far as I knew his character; he seemed to be well-organized and methodical, taking everything seriously, including, I am sure, the instructions on dosage that I had had printed on the boxes.

Judging by that, I had to acknowledge that with my pills to promote the well-being and sound sleep of one of the top Nazis, I was inadvertently working for the final victory of Germany.

I didn't quite see what I could do about that. I will spare you the recriminations heaped upon me by my salamander: Theo was angry with me, and for once I couldn't blame her. I briefly contemplated adding arsenic or cyanide to my pills, but that would have been stupid; like all who deal with death on an industrial scale, the Reichsführer-SS was paranoid, and it was highly likely that he employed a taster, which could explain, at least in part, what seemed to be his excessive consumption of those pills. The fact was that I could see only one way of eliminating him, and that was to set a honeytrap.

Himmler had taken a fancy to me, that was obvious, at least to me. Women know when they're right about such things. Since love makes men lose their wits, I thought I had only to make myself available to the Reichsführer-SS, hook him at the right moment, take him somewhere quiet and dispose of him. And that would bring Gabriel back to me. He would fall into my arms when I told him breathlessly, after running up to the sixth floor of his building with seventy thousand SS men after me, 'Darling, I've just killed Himmler.'

I was sure he couldn't have resisted me then. Our reunion would have begun with a kiss plucked straight from the tree, going on, once the children had been sent to their room and his own was locked, to a wild embrace that would have ended on the floor or the bed, circumstances leading me to prefer the first alternative, after which he would have whispered in my ear, disturbed by my deliciously excited little cries, 'Don't make any noise. Remember, the children are next door.'

I had tried everything I could think of to get together with Gabriel again. Fits of tears. Pleading with him on my knees. Threatening to kill myself. Asking him to wipe the slate clean and begin again from the beginning. Nothing worked. I had come to think that only the assassination of

Himmler would rekindle his love.

It was stupid, but I had to think something up. I couldn't reconcile myself to the idea that my cause was lost, and I had several reasons to think that it wasn't. For instance, I still called him 'darling', sometimes 'my love', and he didn't take umbrage. A slight flush on his cheeks even betrayed his feelings when I deliberately humiliated myself every time we met, telling him how much I loved him in a tearful voice. 'I miss you every morning of my life. As soon as I wake up my hand, in a reflex action, feels under the sheets for your back, your neck, your arm. It fails to find you, and that goes to my heart.'

One Sunday I decided to stake everything on a single throw of the dice. I had suggested spending the day with the children in the Jardin des Plantes, and we began by visiting the zoo. It was a lovely autumn day when the sun, tired of summer, was basking in a softly golden sky.

We were in the monkey house, and the children were deep in conversation with its inmates when I took Gabriel aside and suggested going on with our story where we had left off. He had a way of protesting that was not entirely convincing.

'I'm not sure that that would be good for us, Rose. Let's not do anything in a hurry, let's wait and see.'

'We don't decide how much time is left to us for ourselves. Destiny does that, and you know very well that destiny isn't to be trusted.'

He didn't say no. It's true that Gabriel never said no for fear of hurting people's feelings. I don't think I ever heard him utter the word.

'Let's think about it,' he said.

'People don't stop to think about love,' I said indignantly. 'They live with it.'

'You're right, but all the same it doesn't start up again just like that, the first time you click your fingers. When it's been wounded, it takes time to recover its strength.'

'You and I ought to stop hurting each other. We were made for one another, let's take the consequences.' I reached for his hand. 'Do you have someone else?' I asked.

'No, I don't.'

'Then I wish you'd give me a second chance.'

'There are never any second chances in life, Rose.'

'Life wouldn't be worth living if there were no second chances.'

'No, and I ask myself more and more often if it's worth living at all.'

I took Gabriel's face in both my hands and kissed him with passion that his restraint made ridiculous. His mouth was dry, and left me with an aftertaste of humus and dead, withering leaves.

'Thank you,' I said, when he withdrew his lips. 'Have you forgiven me?'

He shook his head, and I began to cry. He took a check handkerchief out of his pocket and mopped my face with a sad smile.

I was not a pretty sight. Thank God the children were too busy throwing the monkeys peanuts to notice.

'If I go on rejecting you like this,' he murmured as he finished wiping my tears away, 'I shall be the one who comes to blame himself.'

'Don't turn things inside out, Gabriel. When I think of what I did, I disgust myself. I'm so ashamed. The blame is all mine.'

'No, it will be mine if I refuse to turn the page. And I will, but you must leave me alone for another two or three weeks, and then – I can feel it – we shall be able to love each other again as we did at first.'

We stayed there for a moment in each other's arms. But the children didn't like that, and they set about separating us by tugging at our arms. They wanted to go and see the crocodiles.

That evening, when I went home alone, I felt that the air was singing.

*

Over the following weeks Gabriel continued his policy of avoiding me. It had exasperated me not so long ago, but now I felt that it was touching. His eyes increasingly refused to meet mine. Sometimes, wishing to speak to me, he came close and then stayed silent, his mouth open as if the words would not come out. He claimed never to be free to spend a Sunday with the children and me in the Bois de Boulogne or some such place. But he was a pathetically bad liar.

I saw so many signs that Gabriel was troubled by great internal tremors, and that didn't displease me; he was on the right road. It was the same when he complained of migraines, or I saw that he had been losing a lot of weight. On the day when he told me he had stomach trouble I thought I'd hooked him. Several times I burned my hand or wrist when I was in the kitchen; that was the best way to get him back soon, according to my superstitions, which were that you must suffer to get what you want.

I kept a pebble in my shoe for a whole day, and when I ended my torture by taking it out before going to bed, the innersole of the shoe was soaked in blood.

One evening I dug the prongs of a fork into the back of my hand, damaging one of the metacarpal bones; I am ashamed to say so, but I thought I had heard a voice whispering that if I did that, Gabriel would come back to me.

The voice hadn't told the truth. One Sunday when I went to see the children and spend the day with them, Gabriel told them to go and play in their room, and then, in a low voice, told me that he had decided to take them to Cavaillon and live with them there.

'You can't do this to me,' I protested. 'What will become of me without them?'

'I have no choice, Rose.'

'If they go to Provence I won't see them any more. Imagine what that will be like for me.'

'I repeat, I have to go. There's a press campaign against me.'

'Where?'

'In the newspapers published by our so-called friends of the past. Haven't you kept up to date with all this?'

'I didn't know.'

'They call me a filthy Jew, a sheeny and a swine, for columns on end.'

He went to look for a newspaper in his room, and came back declaiming, 'Édouard Drumont always spoke of "the deceitful and cunning enemy" who has invaded, corrupted and stupefied France to the point of "destroying, with her own hands, all that used to make her powerful, respected and happy." Because he corresponds best to that definition, one of the first figures to come to mind is that of Gabriel Beaucaire, a false friend, a false writer, a false patriot and a false maître d'hôtel, but a real traitor to the Eternal Lord. He has all the characteristics of a Semite: he is greedy, an intriguer, subtle and cunning. It is his unbounded deceitfulness that has allowed this vile man to mingle with us, to spy on us, and then shamelessly pass on what he claims to be his intelligence, to our worst enemies. It is time to break with such people, and in particular this one who has chosen, to the misfortune of his neighbours, to reside at Number 23 in the Rue Rambuteau.'

He waved the newspaper in the air as if it were a cloth soaked with acid burning his hands.

'The whole anti-Semitic press is in it, *Je suis partout* and all the others. It's been like this for three days; they're firing off stuff like this non-stop. I'm surprised no one has told you.'

'I don't read such filth.'

'But do you understand my anxiety now?'

'Of course I do, and you can count on me, darling.'

I was trembling and perspiring like a woman in love before her first kiss, but Gabriel kept his distance from me, with an expression of revulsion on his face, and he took a step back when I myself took one towards him. It's a fact that a smell of urine and vinegar surrounded me. I stood still so as not to spread it any further.

I recognized the smell at once; it was the smell of my fear, the fear I felt for him and the children. The cancer of my grief was stirring again, and would express itself in that way until the end of the war.

'This press campaign has made my bosses uneasy,' said Gabriel. 'They're being nicer than usual; I can tell that they're supporting me, but they won't be able to keep that up indefinitely. I'd rather get in first and leave as soon as possible. I'm sorry.'

'Can I keep the children?' I begged.

'That wouldn't be a good idea, Rose. The divorce court decided otherwise, and you know very well that you wouldn't have time to look after them. A childhood in Provence, in the middle of nature, is the best we can give them.'

I pretended to have had a sudden inspiration. 'I've thought of a solution, darling. I can put you all up and hide you in my apartment, I mean our apartment, in the Rue du Faubourg-Poissonnière, unseen and unsuspected, until better times come.'

'Are you suggesting I come home to the apartment?'

'Never fear, if you don't want me I can control myself. I won't rape you. I won't touch you.'

'I believe you. But I'd be too afraid of succumbing to temptation.'

He had smiled. It was the smile I loved.

'Anyway, you'll have to come back some day.'

'Yes, I will.'

There was a silence. I felt as if my heart were caught up in a whirlwind, and I heard the blood pulsing in my head. Finally he sighed. 'It would be absurd to stay. Paris is a trap.'

'Any crook on the run will tell you that it's better to hide in Paris than the provinces.'

'Not in wartime, Rose. I'm supposed to be a Jew. If I stay in Paris I'll have to wear the yellow star after 7 June.'

'Next week?'

'Yes, the order has just been enacted. With the children we'd be like lambs in the wolf's lair, even though I've no intention of wearing the star.'

'Why not go to the City Hall and explain that you're not Jewish?'

'You know it's not as simple as that. If the authorities have decided that I'm Jewish, because of my name or letters of denunciation, I can't come up with any proof to the contrary. My face and my smile won't be enough to convince anyone. When you're a Jew these days, you're a Jew for life.'

'I'm asking just one favour,' I said, with tears in my eyes. 'Stay until my birthday.'

He nodded with the attractive little smile that had always sent me crazy. 'Your thirty-third. I can't miss that.'

'You're right. It won't come again.'

'The thing is that I must move at once to melt into the crowd. A few days ago I saw a two-roomed apartment to rent in the Rue La Fayette, quite close to you. If it's still free I'll take it and move in under a false name.'

I went over to embrace him, but Gabriel went into his room to leave the newspaper on his bedside table.

30

Lunch in the Country

MARSEILLES, 2012. When Samir the Mouse rang my bell it was a little while after one in the morning, and Mamadou had just left me at my apartment, where I had run myself a bath. Before getting into it, I was undressing and listening to a Patti Smith song, 'People Have the Power'.

If I could live my life over again, I'd have wanted it to be like hers: singer, musician, painter, poet, photographer, activist, writer, mother. I am sure that Patti Smith will leave her name on the history of women – the history that men don't like to see us writing.

One evening when Patti Smith was giving a concert in Marseilles she came to my restaurant after the show, and I had myself photographed with her and her smile, bad teeth and all. She has a prominent position in my pantheon of Great Women.

I made Samir wait while I put on my dressing gown and turned off the bath tap, and by the time I opened the door he was visibly sulking. To the point of caricature, he's one of what I call the everything-right-away generation. The young people who always seem to have trains or planes to catch when the whole day lies before them. The generation who, unlike mine, don't know how to savour every God-given drop of life.

Samir was holding his tablet in one hand, and offered me the other with what he meant to be a menacing look. 'My inquiries are getting somewhere. I have something remarkable to show you.'

'Let's see it.'

'But first I'm going to tell you the latest story I found on the Internet.'

He walked in and sat down, uninvited, in an armchair in the sitting room.

'What happens,' he went on, 'when a fly falls into a cup of coffee during an international meeting?'

He said nothing for a moment, and then added, 'The American won't touch the coffee. The Italian throws away the cup with the coffee still inside it. The Chinese eats the fly and throws away the coffee. The Russian drinks the coffee, fly and all. The Frenchman throws away the fly and drinks the coffee. The Israeli sells his coffee to the Frenchman, his fly to the Chinese, and buys another cup of coffee with the money he makes. The Palestinian accuses the Israeli of putting a fly in his coffee, asks for a loan from the World Bank and uses it to buy explosives to blow up the cafeteria, just as all the others are telling the Israeli to buy the Palestinian another cup of coffee.'

I smiled. 'That's a Jewish story.'

'Thanks, I'd noticed. Funny, isn't it?'

'I didn't say it wasn't.'

Now Patti Smith was singing 'Because the Night', written with Bruce Springsteen and one of her greatest. She put such fire into it that you couldn't be in any doubt: women are men now like anyone else.

Samir the Mouse stood up, came over to me and said, with heavy irony, 'Take a look at this. I've got dynamite for you. It's a photo from the last war I found on an archival site.'

He handed me the tablet, and I recognized myself in the photo. I was standing behind Himmler, who was sitting at a table, and I was holding a large platter. I think that the dish on it was *poulet fermier* with basil purée, a speciality of mine: the Reichsführer-SS loved it. His head was slightly turned towards me, he was looking at me with an almost imperceptible smile tinged with affection. In the background there was a flower bed, and further away a group of trees, many of them conifers. The scene showed lunch in the country at Gmund in Bavaria.

Samir the Mouse was looking at me in the same way as the policeman in a film noir shows the murderer photos of the crime scene to get him to crack up, but I didn't crack up. 'What's this?' I asked.

'It's you.'

'Me? Excuse me, but I was much more beautiful than that.'

'Stop playing games, Rose.'

There was a silence between us. Fortunately it was filled by the Patti Smith song, and I concentrated all my attention on Patti Smith.

Finally I said, 'Is that man Himmler?'

'Looks like it.'

'What would I have been doing with Himmler?'

'That's what I'm wondering myself.'

'This is grotesque,' I objected.

'It's disturbing.'

'I think you should call off your investigations of Renate Fröll.'

'I've no intention of doing so.'

'You won't get anywhere with this,' I said.

I wasn't sure that he was venal enough to stop raking around in my past if I paid him to do so. It might just get him even more excited. I decided to send him packing, and rose to my feet to show that our talk was over.

'It's late, Samir. At my age I should have been in bed long ago, and I still have to take a bath.'

He stayed where he was, and said, 'All the same, you'll have to tell me what you were doing between 1942 and 1943. There's no trace of you anywhere between those two dates. You went right off the radar before disappearing again after that. Odd, don't you think, all those disappearances?'

'It's perfectly normal. I was hiding in Provence.'

'But the police weren't looking for you.'

I sat down again. 'The police were looking for me because they were looking for my former husband, the love of my life, the father of my children, who was Jewish. Is that good enough for you?'

'You're hiding things from me, Rose, and when people hide things it's because they're interesting.'

'I am a very old lady who would like to be left in peace, and to whom, if it's not too much to ask, you ought to show more respect.'

When Samir had left I took my bath. It was very hot, and as usual I topped up the hot water at regular intervals. I soaked in it for a long time, my eyes closed, my ears in the water, letting memories surface in my mind and float above me, mingling with the steam.

When I got out of the bath I was as white as the flesh of a boiled fish.

31

Sparkling White Teeth

PARIS, 1942. Summer always comes early. Everyone knows that it never begins on the official date, which is 21 June, but a few days before. It came even earlier than usual that year, when the oak trees, lazy as they always are, had only just shown their new green leaves.

As my thirty-fifth birthday approached, I was still leading the chaste life that Theo had recommended to me, although I felt a rising desire for orgasm, a flame fanned by the increasingly warm weather, the harbinger of that rush to fornication that would soon take over the natural world.

One morning in June, probably at the end of the first week of the month, the usual two SS officers, Don Quixote and Sancho Panza, came into my restaurant. The staff were just setting the tables, and I was supervising the final stage of baking four large apricot tarts. I had just sprinkled them with almond chips which threatened to burn, and so did my caramelized flaky pastry underneath the fruit. I was beside myself.

Sancho Panza asked me to follow them in a tone of voice that would admit no argument. I asked the SS men to wait two or three minutes until the tarts were baked to just the right point, and after taking them out of the oven I followed the two men. I didn't know where we were going, and I hesitated to ask them, aware as I was that this kind of summons usually bodes no good.

When we were in the car, and I did ask them in German where we were going, they didn't reply. I was imagining the worst, especially where Gabriel was concerned, until Sancho Panza let slip the information that while the matter wasn't serious, it was important.

'You can't tell me any more?'

'Military secret.'

I was speaking German, and he replied in French. I concluded that he felt guilty about the occupation of France, particularly because he looked at me like a beaten dog, unlike his colleague.

They drove me to Number 49, Rue de la Faisanderie in the Sixteenth Arrondissement, where I found Heinrich Himmler enthroned behind a Louis XIV desk in a large panelled room, with three old SS officers in front of him holding documents on their knees. At the age of forty-one, he was in full command of them. They might as well have been pet dogs for all the difference it would have made.

As soon as he saw me Himmler rose to his feet cautiously, as if he had sciatica, thus letting his officers know that the meeting was over. They immediately went away, unasked, leaving behind a strong smell of sweat and tobacco that reminded me of the brothels of Sainte-Tulle. After shaking hands with me, the Reichsführer-SS invited me to join him in the corner of the room where there were comfortable chairs.

My heart was in my boots, and he noticed at once. Accordingly he began by reassuring me, in German, 'I've come to Paris incognito. There's urgent business to be done.

And I also wanted to have a strictly private conversation with you.'

He took a deep breath, and went on. 'You appeal to me very much, and since our first meeting two years ago I have never stopped thinking of you. By night, by day, as soon as I close my eyes I see your face. I would like to live with you.'

I bowed my head, feeling the symptoms of someone about to faint: a slowing of my heartbeat and a fall in my arterial blood pressure. He thought I was nodding agreement.

'I would like to live with you to the end of my days,' he went on. 'I'm never in one place long, you know. I come and go, I'm travelling all the time. What Hitler asks of me is even worse than devotion to the priesthood. I never stop, it's impossible. I don't know what I'd do without your pills. But I need to know that you are mine, all mine, during those rare moments of relaxation that my work allows me.'

His blue-grey eyes were fixed on me – I almost said 'in me', for I felt as if they were biting me. He was waiting for me to say something, but I was frozen to the spot. I felt that I would never be able to move my tongue away from the roof of my mouth again.

'Honesty compels me to say that I wouldn't be able to marry you,' he went on. 'First, Hitler is against divorce. He forbids those of us close to him to get divorced, he has made difficulties for a great many people who, like Hans Frank, would like to start a new life. Secondly, you have Aryan origins, judging by your blue eyes and fair hair, but I am sure that you are of mixed blood.'

'I'm Armenian,' I said, in German that was much better than at our last meeting.

'I know. So you have a good basis, Armenians being one of the purest branches of the Aryan race. The trouble is that, like all the inhabitants of the Caucasus, they have often mingled with the Mongol or Turanian peoples who invaded, violated and enslaved them.'

The Reichsführer-SS inspected me from head to foot, looked me in the eye for a long time, and then said, 'I don't have leisure to read books or visit exhibitions, but I am very susceptible to beauty. I share the opinion of the poet John Keats, who said that "Beauty is truth, truth beauty."'

'My adoptive mother loved the work of Keats.'

'And so do I. Let me tell you that I think you are beautiful, very beautiful. But as always, for beauty to shine at its most dazzling, it needs its flaws. Yours are obvious, as I will tell you frankly; you have certain characteristically Mongol features. High cheekbones, slit eyes, delicate eyebrows, a matt skin.'

I blushed.

'I am sure that you have the Mongolian spot,' he added. 'A blue-grey spot on the skin, often just above the buttocks and close to the coccyx. Am I wrong?'

'No, you are not.'

'There, you see, I have good intuition.' Himmler smiled smoothly. 'Your Mongolian features do not bother me personally. I will even venture to say that I like them, particularly because, I repeat, you are of fundamentally Aryan stock, there's no doubt about that.'

I was horrified by the look in his eyes, that of a butcher assessing a piece of entrecôte or sirloin steak on his bloodstained block, and at the same time I did not dislike the way those eyes reduced me to the state of a mere object at his mercy. It was the first time I had felt anything at all for him: a depraved wish to debase and punish myself for all my sins, not the least of which had been my infidelity with Gilbert Jeanson-Brossard.

Nor was Himmler's receding chin any obstacle. Heaven knows why, but I've always been mad about receding chins. I find them sexually exciting.

Like all timid people trying to seem assured, Himmler coughed slightly before taking off his glasses, which suddenly made him more human. Behind the lenses, his eyes were moist, and I thought I saw a pleading expression in them, a kind of indefinable suffering. Some thirty seconds passed in the deep silence when desire and fear reach their culmination.

After putting his glasses back on, Himmler continued. 'And I have a third reason not to marry you; your first marriage was to a Jew.'

'My first husband has never been Jewish!'

'That's not what I've been told. He is Jewish, even if he's tried to put people off the track of it.'

'Check the facts. It's not true.'

'I will indeed check them, but that won't change anything. What I am asking you is to be my companion.'

'It's very difficult to reply to you in these circumstances,' I said in a hesitant voice, my throat constricted. 'We hardly know each other.'

'Then come and get to know me better in Germany,' he said, jokingly. 'You won't be disappointed.'

'I must think about it.'

'Think fast, or you'll be making me suffer.'

He gave me a business card with the phone number of his office in Berlin. If he had kissed me, I am ashamed to say, I would probably have yielded to him, particularly as his fine white teeth – indeed, they were sparkling white – suggested that he would not have bad breath, although nasty surprises sometimes lurk behind white teeth.

However, that was the end of our interview; the Reichsführer-SS confined himself to shaking hands with me – his hand was limp, and left me with an uneasy feeling that I suppressed, once I was back at the restaurant with my heart thudding, by drinking three-quarters of a bottle of Saint-Julien.

That evening a very nice couple came to dine at the restaurant: Simone de Beauvoir, a beautiful woman working as a presenter on Radio Vichy, the national broadcasting station, and Jean-Paul Sartre, whose novel *La Nausée* I had read and admired before the war. They smoked heavily and talked a lot.

Sartre liked my cooking so much that he said he would write an article about the restaurant in the collaborators' weekly paper *Comoedia*, where he published pieces from time to time. I'm still waiting for his article.

32

My Weight in Tears

PARIS, 1942. The day after my meeting with Heinrich Himmler, I heard banging on the door of the apartment at around six in the morning. A falsetto voice on the landing was shouting, 'Open up! This is the police!'

The voice belonged to a small man with a very large nose and feet, which was a good sign if it is true that a man's feet are in proportion to the size of his reproductive organ. However, in spite of the state of sexual abstention in which I had been languishing so long, I felt not the faintest thrill of desire.

The man looked daggers at me and then shouted, 'Inspector Mespolet!' Such was his way of introducing himself.

'Have we met?' I asked.

'I believe I have had that honour.'

He had hardly changed at all since our last meeting in Manosque. Still the same mummified head with a grimace of a smile above the same buffoon-like body. Not forgetting the same chisel of a nose.

Four policemen entered the apartment to search it thoroughly. I was going to protest, but the inspector showed me his search warrant before asking, in a voice that grated, 'Do you know where we can find your ex-husband?'

'We are no longer in touch.'

'But you have children.'

'I have no news of them either.'

'Allow me to say I don't believe you. An arrest warrant has been issued for your ex-husband; he's wanted by every police force in France. If you refuse to cooperate with us I can accuse you of complicity.'

'I see nothing to prevent me from cooperating with you. You might as well know that Gabriel has not behaved well to me.'

I had already made coffee, and I offered him a cup. We sat in the kitchen while his men emptied drawers and moved wardrobes and chests, I suppose expecting to find secret passages or underground tracts leading to the caverns of Sion in Switzerland.

'What has the idiot done this time?' I asked with assumed exasperation.

He was lumping Gabriel and me together, judging by the accusing expression in his eyes as he ran through his grievances.

'He's a foreign agent who has always tried to pass for a good French citizen. A master of blackmail, a man who assumes false identities, and a professional slanderer who has done a great deal of harm to men of importance to our country.'

'And who might they be?'

'It's a long list.' Inspector Mespolet seemed overwhelmed. He sighed, and finished his coffee in a single gulp. When I poured him more, I stood behind him so that locks of my hair, which I wore long at this time, fell on his shoulders, while my breath caressed the nape of his neck and my arm brushed against his. He suddenly turned more loquacious when I asked him again for the names of those who accused Gabriel.

'First of all there's Jean-André Lavisse, a great writer and journalist of our time, an admirable man who wouldn't hurt a fly. They say he will soon be made a member of the Académie Française, and believe me, he deserves to have had that honour long ago. I have met him several times, and he is a very impressive figure. If all the French were like him, we wouldn't have surrendered to the German army. He is a man of culture, an upright and energetic character. No doubt you have read his book, *Pensées d'amour*.'

I shook my head, my lips twisting slightly in disgust. Lavisse was the man who had launched the press campaign against Gabriel in *L'Ami du peuple*.

'Then you've missed something. That book has done a lot of good,' Claude Mespolet went on. 'At any event, the great integrity of Jean-André Lavisse did not prevent your ex-husband from accusing him of illicitly laying hand on the possessions of Jews. Such pretended trafficking never existed except in the head of that malicious Jew himself. It was defamation pure and simple, madame. His wife Germaine could not bear such attacks on her husband, and tried to gas herself. Her attempted suicide has left its mark on her, and they say that she will not live long.'

'How terrible!' I exclaimed.

'Terrible indeed,' he agreed. 'And you have yet to hear the worst of it. Madame Lavisse is the niece of Louis Darquier de Pellepoix, a descendant of the astronomer, who has just replaced Xavier Vallat, whose incompetence I cannot deny, as Commissioner General for Jewish Questions. That excellent man, one of a great French family, is another victim of your ex-husband, who has written a monstrous little book about him, a tissue of lies and garbage in which he speaks of great personalities of our country in terms that decency forbids me to repeat and that, when I think of them, send a cold shiver down my spine. It is one of those works that attack not only morality but also the security of the state.'

From time to time I let my tongue pass over my open lips, while giving Mespolet approving glances. There aren't many men who can resist a woman's admiration.

'There is even worse,' the inspector went on. 'We know on good authority that your ex-husband is now writing a book of the same kind about the marshal who has done so much for France.'

'This is really terrible!' I said. 'Why does he do these things, for heaven's sake?'

'Because he is perverse – a perverse Jew who lets his vile instincts guide him. In his own interests, he must be prevented from doing any more damage. That is why you must help me to track him down.'

'I promise to do all I can.'

He put out his right hand so that I could tap it to signify agreement, which I did.

'Help me,' he said. 'It is vital. For Marshal Pétain, for France.'

I thought his hand was about to take mine, and left it lying offered to him on the table, but then one of the four police officers came into the kitchen.

'We haven't found anything, sir.'

Claude Mespolet got slowly to his feet, and then sat down again. 'Have you put everything back just as it was before?'

'Well, I mean, well, no... that's not the idea of a search, sir.'

'I want you to leave this apartment in the state in which you found it, understand?'

'We'll do that, sir.'

Inspector Mespolet might be inclined to talk nonsense, but I had got him where I wanted him; after finally taking my hand, he invited me to dinner the next day.

'At six-thirty in my restaurant,' I replied. 'That will be the most practical place. I'm sorry, but I can never dine earlier or later than six-thirty myself; I'm busy in the kitchen then.'

'The time you choose will always be my time.'

He was really beginning to attract me. I liked the prospect of destroying myself by rolling in the mire with him. On the doorstep, I whispered in his ear, 'This has been the nicest conversation I've had with anyone for ages.'

He didn't blush, but he fluttered his eyelids.

When the police had left, I dressed in haste and, checking to make sure I wasn't being followed, I went to warn Gabriel of the risks he was running. When I reached the door of his new apartment at 68 Rue La Fayette, the children were in fits of laughter. He was putting on a puppet show for them.

When I had summed up my conversation with Inspector Mespolet, Gabriel told me not to panic. All the arrangements were made for him and the children to leave for the free zone of the country. He wasn't going to change his plans, he said; he would stay in Paris until my birthday and leave the next day.

When I said goodbye the children clung to me. I had great difficulty in preserving my self-control after Édouard cried, 'Stay a little longer, Mama. We don't want you to go away!'

But when I had closed the door, I began to sob. I think I must have shed my entire weight in tears that day.

33

The Johnny Strategy

PARIS, 1942. On the evening of the next day, Inspector Mespolet arrived at La Petite Provence with an unforthcoming expression. His mouth was dry, his eyes wandered elsewhere. I thought it was love, and did all I could to reassure him, from the aperitif on.

'To us and all we shall achieve together,' I said, clinking my glass of champagne against his.

'To us,' he murmured, his head bent.

'Careful, we must look each other in the eye. Otherwise it means seven years of sexual misery.'

'Do you really think so?'

'I'm a superstitious woman.'

I saw that I would have to begin again.

'*Prost*,' I said provocatively, raising my glass.

He didn't even smile. Inspector Mespolet was not the man he had been the day before. He looked like someone who knows he is wasting his time. His feet were restless, beating a tattoo under the table. He had nervous tics as well, casting furtive glances round the room all the time.

As we were finishing my dish of vegetables baked with parmesan and then chilled, there was such an oppressive silence that I ended up asking him if anything was wrong.

'That's easily answered,' he said at once. 'You've been deceiving me.'

'What?'

'You betrayed my trust in you.'

'But what have I done?'

'As soon as we had left yesterday you chased off to your ex-husband.'

I pretended to be bewildered. 'Excuse me, but you must be out of your mind!'

This is what I call the Johnny strategy. Johnny Hallyday told me he had once used it when all the evidence was against him. It's such a blatant sham that it confounds your accuser – a primal denial, the ultimate negative.

Ten or so years ago the singer had come to dine at my present restaurant in Marseilles, at a late hour after a concert. I liked him at once. A wounded man who has spent decades trying to drink himself to death but hasn't managed it yet. When he arrived he was already rolling drunk, a term that is something of a euphemism in his case. Except when he sings.

In a thick and therefore sincere voice, Johnny Hallyday told me a good story that reminded me of the line I took with Inspector Mespolet all those years ago. One night, when he was just embarking on his career, he came home late, pissed as a newt, with a girl he'd picked up heaven knows where. They had ended up in his marital bedroom and were both undressing in the dark when the light was suddenly switched on. By Johnny's wife. Looking at the half-naked girl, she cried indignantly, 'What are you doing here?'

Whereupon Johnny, sounding equally indignant, had turned to the girl himself, saying, 'She's got a point. What are you doing here?'

I remember that Inspector Mespolet's eyes suddenly alerted me. I saw glints in them like light reflected off a knife blade, and his pale face expressed unrelenting hatred.

My heart began to beat faster. I couldn't control it any more. 'If you know where Gabriel and the children are living, I suppose that means you've arrested them?'

'That's a professional secret.'

'Can't you show a little humanity and answer me?' I cried, shaking.

He got to his feet and left with a little nod of his head, which I hardly had time to register. I was already running, and as soon as I was outside the restaurant I hailed a taxi in the Place Trocadéro. It took me to 68 Rue La Fayette.

On the way we saw a great many Torpedo military cars, tarpaulin-covered trucks, black vans and buses crammed with people. I didn't understand what was going on, I felt terribly tired, and at the same time something inside me was howling.

When I reached the building in the Rue La Fayette, I climbed the stairs four steps at a time. On the fifth floor, trembling, I pushed the doorbell. No reply. Out of breath, I went downstairs to find the concierge and ask her for news of my family.

'Oh dear, madame,' she replied sympathetically, 'the police came to take them away. An inspector told me this is the day when they're picking up the Jews. All the Jews.'

'Children too?'

'Children too, yes, what do you think? The police take everything from the Jews' apartments. Children, old folk, jewellery, but not the cats. They always leave the cats. It's quite a problem. I've already taken in five, so with my own that makes seven, and I can't adopt any more. Luckily your gentleman didn't have a cat, or I'd have been in real trouble.' She sighed deeply, and asked, 'You don't want a cat, do you?'

'I already have one.'

'Two cats are better, three are better still.'

When I asked her whether Gabriel and the children had left with policemen or the militia, she couldn't tell me. 'It comes to the same thing, madame, and the end result is the same too: they leave the cats behind.'

She had a catlike face herself, minus whiskers, so it was her own people she was talking about, although that didn't prevent her feeling sorry for my misfortune. She lowered her eyes. 'You mustn't be under any illusions, they've gone away for a long time. They had baggage with them, and the police told the gentleman to turn off the water, gas and electricity meters.'

She invited me into her lodge for a hot toddy, but I told her I was warm enough already, and I hurried to the police station in the Ninth Arrondissement.

After waiting for three hours without gleaning any information at all, I went to the Prefecture of Police, where I found the doors locked. Then I went back to the restaurant to call Heinrich Himmler at his Berlin headquarters.

Service of the evening meal was over, and I found my second in command, Paul Chassagnon, waiting for me just outside La Petite Provence, sitting on a bench that doesn't exist these days and smoking a cigarette.

'Has something happened to the children?' he asked.

'How did you know?'

'They said you left suddenly and in a great hurry. I thought it must be the children.'

'It was a police raid. I'm going to phone Himmler.'

When I uttered the name of the Reichsführer-SS in a furious voice, as if he owed me an explanation, I didn't see how ridiculous the situation was. But I was in a strange state of mind, reliving the nightmare of my childhood. I was shaking all over, and not in my right mind.

Heinrich Himmler wasn't at his office, and indeed that was the last place in the world where you could have expected to find him. No doubt he was on a tour of inspection in Russia, Bohemia, Moravia or Pomerania, supervising mass executions. I spoke to one of his aides-de-camp, a man called Hans. When I had explained the situation to him, he said in a voice as scandalized as my own, 'This is a terrible mistake. I'll tell the Reichsführer-SS as soon as I get him on the other end of the line. The French authorities mean well, but I have to say they do such stupid things. They make mistakes in the records, they mix names up, they really ought to leave it to us.'

When I had hung up, I fell into the arms of Paul Chassagnon, who told me that the service of the evening meal had gone reasonably well, although there'd been a shortage of almost everything, in particular bread.

'What on earth can I do about that?' I cried, before apologizing and then bursting into tears.

I was dying. I took a long time about it. Everyone who has ever lost children knows that there is still life after death, and I clung to that life so that I could try to find them.

Fearing that Himmler might phone while I was in my apartment, and then not call back at once, I decided to wait for his call in the restaurant. When Paul Chassagnon offered to stay with me, I accepted; I needed to feel his large, hairy arms near me. Anyway I had nothing to fear from him; he was homosexual.

We spent the night on the floor by the cash desk, on a mattress of folded tablecloths. He laid his arm on my stomach, which did me good, but I didn't sleep a wink. I had too many visitors. They filed past behind my eyelids, which were swollen with tears, until the small hours of the morning: Garance, Édouard, Gabriel, my mother, my father, my grandmother, my brothers and sisters, all carried away by the whirlwind of the twentieth century's abominations.

In the morning, Heinrich Himmler still hadn't called me back.

34

Police Raids

PARIS, 1942. On 17 July, the day after the police raid known as the round-up of the Vel' d'Hiv, I got up feeling tired to death, and when I went to the bathroom at home I was horrified to see my reflection in the mirror. I looked like an old papier mâché owl, with large purple bags under my eyes. I'm no make-up expert; up to this point in my life a little rice powder dusted lightly over my cheekbones had been enough for me.

But that day, after drinking some coffee, I applied the full works. I had a round box of tinted Bourjois foundation, dating from before the war and never opened, in my bathroom cupboard, and I put on so much of it that I felt I was hiding behind a mask. After that I painted my mouth bright red with vermilion lipstick, not forgetting to slather my eyelashes with mascara, although I knew it would soon run in the summer heat.

You know how superstitious I am. I felt that I mustn't run the slightest risk: before phoning Heinrich Himmler again I must prettify myself, say an Our Father, put the sea-shell known in Provence as the 'ear of the Madonna' to my own ear, and splash my breasts with holy water in which a sprig of verbena had been steeped.

When I called Himmler's HQ, the aide-de-camp told me

that the Reichsführer-SS was sorry that he hadn't returned my call yet, but he had had 'a very busy evening', was now in a meeting – 'a very important meeting' – and would be in touch at the end of the morning, about midday. I gave Hans the phone number of La Petite Provence, just in case Himmler had lost it.

'Don't worry,' said Hans with a touch of irony. 'Your phone numbers are prominently displayed on the Reichsführer-SS's desk, written on a piece of paper, and I have a copy on my desk as well.'

When I went to work, on my bicycle as usual, I felt as if Paris were in mourning. There was an atmosphere of great sadness in the streets. The more of it I breathed in, the worse I felt. Later, after the arrest of 12,884 Jews, one-third of them children, a report from the Prefecture of Police in Paris would describe the consternation to be seen on all faces that day as follows:

'Although the French people as a whole and in general are anti-Semitic, they have serious reservations about such measures, which seem to them inhuman.'

Something that they could not bear, the report added, was the separation of mothers from their children. Those who heard the children crying that day could never forget it.

As soon as I arrived at the restaurant, Paul Chassagnon made haste to tell me that, more than likely, Gabriel and the children were at the Vélodrome d'Hiver, where a great many Jews had been taken. I decided to go there with him when I had had a chance to speak to the Reichsführer-SS.

With the punctuality that went hand in hand with his

politeness, Himmler called me at twelve noon on the dot.

'You can count on me,' he said, when I had summed up the situation.

'Oh, please,' I begged.

'When you know me better, Rose, you will realize that I am a man who says what he will do and does as he says. I'll call you back very soon.'

Heinrich Himmler called at about six in the evening. He hadn't found out anything.

'There's something that escapes me,' he began, 'and I don't like it when I can't understand these things: the names of your former husband and your children are not on the list of arrest warrants issued for Jews of foreign origin drawn up by the French authorities.'

'What conclusion do you draw from that?'

'None. Everything suggests that they were arrested during Operation Spring Wind, carried out for us by the French. As Jews they are our business.'

'But they aren't Jews!'

'They're considered to be Jews. Those with at least two Jewish grandparents, as in their case, are regarded as *Mischlinge*. Half-Jews, and thus Jews. Normally they ought to be under our control.'

'Then why can't you find them?'

'I'm inclined to put that down to the disorganized French services. They don't do these things on purpose, but they're too unstable, too excitable, if you see what I mean. And too sure of themselves. They are amateurs, not professionals. We have difficulty with them all the time.'

'Do you think they've kept Gabriel and the children?'

'I can believe anything of the French, particularly the worst. They have such a superiority complex; every Frenchman thinks he's a genius. They're always the first to talk, but when it comes to action none of them show up. They just don't bother to concentrate, they botch everything; there's nothing to be done about them. Did your former husband and the children wear the yellow star?'

'No.'

'Did they have "Jew" stamped on their identity papers?'

'No again.'

'If they're Jews who aren't registered as Jews, it could be that the authorities have lost track of them.'

I told Himmler about my conversation with Inspector Mespolet, and suggested that he would have to be questioned. If anyone knew where to find Gabriel and the children, it was Mespolet.

'We'll get what he knows out of him,' said Himmler, 'but I don't think it will be much use. The key to this business, I feel sure, is that names and files have been mixed up. In that case it could take some time to find them. I will see to it myself.'

For fear of missing his call if he phoned back, I slept at the restaurant again with Paul Chassignon, who had spent part of the day in the vicinity of the Vel' d'Hiv in search of information about Gabriel and the children. He told me about the laments, the tears and laughter that he had heard, before bursting into tears himself. To comfort him, I put my arms round him and then kissed him. When our mouths met, I loved the taste of nutmeg in his. As he said he was homosexual, I didn't think there would be any consequences, but in spite of ourselves one thing led to another.

I loved the way he took me, delicately and with circumspection. He was an artist of foreplay, good at caresses, and did nothing without asking first. He had the same tact as Gabriel, something I never found in anyone else afterwards. It is because of Paul Chassagnon that I so often felt drawn to homosexuals later, hoping to find all the pleasure that he gave me with them. But I have never done so with anyone else. It takes a war or a great misfortune for that.

Himmler phoned again the next day in the middle of the afternoon. According to his information, which he told me had yet to be checked, Gabriel and the children had all been deported from Drancy railway station. He was doing his best, he said, to pick them up on the journey, and was putting a plane at my disposal so that I could join him in Berlin, where I could supervise his researches with him.

To reassure myself I took along my salamander Theo in a large biscuit tin, with enough room in it for her to stretch her tail out full length. Theo was now at least quarter of a century old, and was beginning to look an imposing figure. Thank goodness, she could hope to live for several more years yet. I needed her as never before; from now on, she was all the family I had left.

35

A Louse in a Haystack

BERLIN, 1942. Hans was waiting to meet me when the plane touched down. He was standing bolt upright in his SS uniform. I learned later that he had fought with the Panzer Division Wiking on the Russian front, where he had distinguished himself and was one of the fifty-five military men to have been awarded the Knight's Cross of the Order of the Iron Cross.

But for the terrible scar over his right cheek, Hans would have been a handsome man. He was still handsome, but only on the left side. On the other side he was something of a monster; a flame-thrower had destroyed his right cheek and right ear.

When he asked me what my interests were, I said, 'God, love, cooking and literature.'

'How about sport?'

'I'd like to try.'

He advised me to keep fit by practising the martial arts, and said he was ready to initiate me into them. I accepted, and no doubt because he was tormented by pain he kept his teeth gritted until the car stopped outside a handsome grey stone house in the centre of Berlin. This was the Reichsführer-SS's official residence.

I didn't yet know that Himmler had other homes. An

apartment in Berlin-Grunewald to accommodate his mistress Hedwig Potthast, whom he installed later with their two children, thanks to Party funds, near Schönau on the banks of Lake Königssee, while his wife spent her time between a place in Berlin and their property of Gmund in Bavaria, where their daughter Püppi lived.

After taking me round and showing me my room, Hans offered me a light meal: champagne and smoked salmon or marinated gravlax, with blinis and crème fraiche.

'I'd rather wait for the Reichsführer-SS before eating,' I protested.

'The Reichsführer-SS doesn't keep regular hours. He's a glutton for work, he never stops. He could be very late.'

'It would be more polite to wait,' I insisted.

'He told me to give you something to eat when you arrived. He's a man of simple tastes, as you'll find out. People who put on airs aren't in his style, but he likes to be obeyed.'

After complying for the sake of form, I turned my attention to Theo and went to find her some weevils in the garden, with Hans helping me. My salamander ate only one of them.

'What's the matter?' I asked Theo. 'Are you sulking or what?'

'I don't like this place.'

'That's no reason for you to starve yourself.'

'To be honest, these Nazis take my appetite away.'

'Personally I love this planet, Theo, and nothing will stop me from loving it, not men nor even Nazis!'

I shut her biscuit tin and went to sleep on the bed.

'Did you have a good journey?'

It was the virile voice of Himmler that woke me three hours later. He was bending over me, and his sour breath tickled my nostrils.

'I'm pleased to see you,' he murmured.

'And I'm pleased to see you. Do you have any news?'

'Yes,' he said, straightening up. 'We think we know where your children are: on a train that we diverted not far from Stuttgart. At the moment it's being searched.' He looked me straight in the face. 'Be careful, Rose, don't rejoice too soon. It's only a trail.'

'What about Gabriel?'

'We're looking for him.'

He told me that he was hungry, and went to the kitchen to see what there was in the refrigerator. I went too, and suggested making him a plate of smoked salmon pasta.

I asked if I could go to Stuttgart. Himmler replied, with a touch of irritation, 'As soon as we've found your children.'

I knew it would be better to change the subject, but I couldn't help asking, 'Are you optimistic?'

'Pessimism leads nowhere, it's a malady of parasites and the useless. We have the will to find them, that's the main thing, and so we shall do so.'

'What about Gabriel?'

'I can't do more than I'm doing already.'

I was beginning to annoy him. After offering me a beer, Himmler drank two bottles himself one after the other, before letting out a strange little noise; it was like a cat being pestered by a dog or another cat, except that his face was beaming happily.

'Did you think of bringing some of your magic pills with you?' he asked.

'I have stocks to last several months.'

'Thank you, Rose, you're wonderful.'

The Reichsführer-SS came over to me. Thinking that he was going to kiss me, I faltered like a sheep going to the slaughter, but he gave me a friendly little tap on the cheek. I was trembling with fear, but at the same time intoxicated by gratitude.

I knew what he wanted, but he was the kind of man to take his time. He resisted nothing except temptation, but when that was on the horizon he shrank from it; his words and gestures were slow in coming. So much the better.

It was up to me to take the initiative, and of course I had no intention of doing any such thing. Hans had told me that we would be sleeping in two rooms with a party wall between them on the first floor. I knew now that I could sleep easy; I had nothing to fear from Himmler.

He gave a little cough before asking, while I was busy about the stove, whether I had had any adventures since my divorce. Leaving Paul Chassagnon out of it, I lied in a firm voice. 'No, I'd have been ashamed of myself.'

'You're all woman. Goethe summed that up when he said that man is naturally polygamous, woman naturally monogamous.'

He had abstracted three little pieces of the smoked salmon that I was dicing, and relished them and his quotation at the same time.

'We men,' he went on, 'are made for conquest. You women are made for protection of the hearth and home, of your children, of household economics.'

When I told him that I had brought a surprise guest with me, my salamander Theo, Himmler smiled. 'I love animals. Let me see it.'

I brought Theo over, and he said, 'This creature needs water.'

'I'm seeing to that. Theo gets several baths a day.'

'I'll give her an aquarium tomorrow. She's a handsome animal. Francis I of France made a salamander his emblem. It's a pity that they are so often associated with the Jewish people because of their stickiness.'

He held Theo while I went back to the stove. Once the pasta was cooked I drained it, then put it in a casserole to keep warm with the diced smoked salmon, the juice of a lemon, some olive oil, a spoonful of mustard and another of crème fraîche, some grated gruyère cheese and a clove of garlic that I had fried in a pan. I added salt and pepper just before serving the pasta, with some leaves of fresh dill that I had found in a bowl of vegetables in the refrigerator.

After his first mouthful, Himmler let out a sigh of satisfaction, the kind of moan that one utters during love-making. He did the same after the second and third mouthfuls.

After the fourth, Himmler looked me straight in the eye and said, 'I have an idea. Suppose you stay here as my cook? It would be a good cover story; after all, that's your profession, and it would keep people from gossiping while we carry out our research, which could take a long time because of the vast movements of peoples crossing the whole of Europe at this time.'

'But you said just now you thought you had found where my children were.'

'I repeat, it's only a trail, and it concerns only your children. Our search could be a long one. It's like looking for a louse in a haystack.'

Why, I wondered, had he said a louse and not a needle?

36

The Man Who Supped with the Devil without a Long Spoon

BERLIN, 1942. I came down to the kitchen stove very early next morning to make breakfast. The night before, Himmler had told me that he liked crêpes flambéed with rum. Everything was ready, the pancake mixture and the bottle of rum, when he came into the kitchen at about a quarter to six, dressed and shaved, his face pale, as if floury, and with the bewildered expression of a cow giving birth to her calf.

I knew what his reply would be, but all the same I asked, 'Did you sleep well?'

'Not at all, but that doesn't matter. I read and worked. I'll have all the time in the world to sleep once we've won the war. The telephone rang several times in the night. I hope it didn't disturb you?'

'I slept like a log,' I said untruthfully.

Reading my thoughts, he told me, 'There's still no news of your family.'

After that, the Reichsführer-SS complained of his stomach, which had given him terrible trouble during the night. He suffered from repeated cramps which, he said, were regularly treated by his Estonian masseur 'of German descent', who had been trained by a great Tibetan master,

Doctor Ko. The masseur's name was Felix Kersten, and he had treated several members of the Dutch royal family. 'One of the best of men,' I was assured. 'He's coming to dine this evening,' Himmler added. 'I'm sure you and Felix will get on well. You are genuine human beings, two of an increasingly rare kind.'

When I asked him if it was sensible, in view of his stomach trouble, to eat the crêpes I was cooking at that moment, the Reichsführer-SS protested, 'It would be inhuman to deprive me of them.'

He dipped his finger in the pancake mixture, licked it, and then said, 'If they disagree with me, well, I'll ask Felix to repair the damage. Using his hands alone, he can deal with the most atrocious pains when even morphine won't relieve them. They are sometimes so violent that I lose consciousness; you might think it was cancer at its worst, which is what my father had. Cancer of the salivary glands. Do you think your plant lore could help me there too?'

I nodded; there were plenty of plants to help him. For instance, aniseed, dill, coriander and fennel are very effective in getting rid of accumulated wind.

'I don't have wind,' he said.

'Everyone has wind. But if the pain comes from the stomach and intestines...'

'Yes, it does, that's exactly my problem.'

'Well then, lemon balm and peppermint can be very efficacious. I'll make you up some pills.'

And since we were on the subject, I advised him to reconsider his diet as a whole, cutting out fats, raw vegetables, fruit and cheese.

'But what can I eat, then?' he asked in dismay.

'Rice, pasta, purées.'

'I say that I'm vegetarian so as to be like the Führer, but have you seen what it's done to him? There's something in his diet that exhausts his strength. He's at the end of his tether, in great distress. You need iron to feel well, and red meat has iron in it. I eat meat sometimes, but discreetly.'

'Meat isn't good for your health. At least to begin with, I'd recommend you to confine your diet to white fish and cooked vegetables.'

'How about pea soup? I love pea soup!'

'You should avoid dried peas.'

When Himmler had left, I spent the rest of the day preparing the evening meal. I had nothing else to do at the moment, except eat my heart out thinking of Gabriel and the children.

Once I had drawn up a menu, I went to buy my ingredients, escorted by three of the SS soldiers who guarded the house. The streets and shops of Berlin seemed to have been infested by clouds of excited midges buzzing hither and thither. It was as if they hadn't eaten for ages and were now feasting on everything, including the sweat dripping from my face.

'Never seen anything like it,' sighed one of the soldiers.

'Maybe it's a sign,' I said. 'Or a punishment.'

He didn't rise to the bait. At midday I was back in the kitchen, and I didn't leave it until late in the afternoon, when apart from the main dish my menu was ready.

To begin there would be several starters:

Aubergine cake, stuffed artichokes in the Provençal

manner, large prawns with basil.

Then the main dish:

Cod with garlic, milk and dill.

Finally a choice of desserts:

Crustless apple tart, iced Grand Marnier soufflé, and peaches flambéed with kirsch.

I will venture to say that, seeing my dishes on the kitchen table, I felt a surge of entirely unjustified happiness, considering that twenty-four hours after arriving in Berlin I still had no news of Gabriel and the children. When everything is going wrong, nothing does you as much good as cooking, as every woman knows.

*

Felix Kersten arrived at 8 p.m. He began by apologizing for being on time. He was the kind who had to keep excusing himself for mistakes that he hadn't made.

Himmler was very late, as he had been the night before, and we had time to talk while we waited for him. Dr Kersten was a stout man who sweated profusely, yet his clothes still seemed too large for him. Breathing heavily, like an ox, and afflicted with a kind of permanent pruritus, he was always scratching his face, his stomach, his arms and his thighs, unless he had his hands in his jacket pockets, rummaging nervously among the papers in them. If I add that he kept furiously pursuing the midges, you can see that the masseur of the Reichsführer-SS was never still.

'Are you a Nazi?' he suddenly asked me after introducing himself.

'No, I've come to look for my children and my former husband. They've been deported.'

'Delighted to meet you,' he said, pressing my hand. 'Nor am I. I'm not a Nazi either. But you should know that while Himmler is – and a fanatical Nazi at that – you can trust him when you put a personal case to him. I have experience of it myself.' He lowered his voice, and went on, 'I think he's always slightly influenced by the opinion of whoever he last spoke to. It's a nuisance if he comes straight from Hitler's office. But if the last man he saw is me, well, that's different.'

Uncle Alfred Bournissard often used to say that 'heroes are zeroes'. Felix Kersten was the living proof of it. The first time I saw him, agitated and muddle-headed, I would never have thought that later he would be regarded as one of the most extraordinary characters of the Second World War, up to the point of being canonized, so to speak, by one of the great historians of the period, Hugh Trevor-Roper.

Dr Kersten, in fact, was a kind of lay saint, able to sup with the Devil without a long spoon in order to extract human lives from his clutches. Thanks to his masseur's hands, he took control of Himmler's mind and got a great many concessions from his patient, especially when the latter was feeling unwell. After the war, when violent polemics died down, it was established that in 1941 he had saved three million Dutch citizens described by the Nazis as 'irreconcilable' from deportation to Galicia or Ukraine. Furthermore, the World Jewish Congress has officially credited him with saving the lives of 60,000 Jews. Not to mention the many prisoners and people condemned to death whom he managed to extricate from the clutches of the Third Reich.

He advised me not to trust anyone except him and Rudolf Brandt, Himmler's secretary – 'a man devoid of personality,' as he put it, 'but a good fellow. And finally,' he told me, 'there's only one means of surviving all this, and that's drink.'

Whereupon he asked me for a shot of spirits, which I gave him in a large glass, before I took a fly-swatter and set about hunting down midges.

Leaning back in his armchair, he paid me compliments in a soft voice and with an amorous look in his eyes. It wasn't subtle, but it did me good.

He had another three or four glasses of spirits, and by the time the Reichsführer-SS arrived at about eleven in the evening, the doctor was sozzled. It didn't matter. No one had to make conversation with Himmler; he did all the talking. During dinner, for instance, he gave us an instructive lecture on sacrifice and honour, using as an edifying example Frederick William I, king of Prussia from 1713 to 1740, who lived thriftily in two country houses, after drastically cutting the expenses of his court.

Frederick William was a soldier king who reinvented Prussia, reorganized the state and developed the army to the point of doubling the strength at his disposal. When his son, the future Frederick II, known as Frederick the Great, a scholar repelled by his father's total lack of culture, had tried to take flight to England, he did not hesitate to imprison him in a fortress and have his friend Hans Hermann von Katte beheaded before his eyes. 'When it came to his own family and friends,' concluded Himmler, with his mouth full of Grand Marnier soufflé, 'punishments were to be rare, but harsh and just.'

*

Days passed, then weeks. I still had no information about Gabriel and the children. Heinrich Himmler seemed to be very sorry about that, but I think his predominant feeling was humiliation because he, the supreme police officer, couldn't solve my problem.

Now and then Hans, the aide-de-camp, came to the house and made good his promise to teach me the technique of close combat known today as krav maga. He had learned it in his youth from a Jewish university friend, originally from Bratislava, of whom he had heard nothing for a very long time.

Krav maga was a method of self-defence perfected in the 1930s by the Jews of Slovakia, who used it to protect themselves against the Fascist and anti-Semitic leagues of the time. It consisted of moving very fast to attack the most sensitive parts of your opponent – his eyes, the nape of his neck, his throat, knees and genital area – either with your bare hands or using anything within reach, without taking any risks yourself.

'It's like life,' Hans told me. 'Anything is allowed.' I had become used to his double face: one side Adonis, the other Frankenstein's monster. I was fascinated by the wound that had removed a large part of his arm near the elbow. Something attracted me to Hans.

One day, no doubt on Himmler's orders, he stopped coming to the house. I was upset, and when I asked what had become of my disfigured suitor, the Reichsführer-SS seemed annoyed.

'Gone on a mission,' he replied.

I knew that Himmler fancied me, but he hesitated to take matters further. One evening his brother Gebhard came to dine at the house. Himmler seemed very pleased to see him, and I surpassed myself with the menu. My aubergine cake, in particular, won much praise.

Before going upstairs to bed, the Reichsführer-SS suggested that he and I took a walk in the garden, and I realized that he had something important to say to me.

It had rained recently, and Berlin was all green. The air smelled of warm grass, an odour that I loved; it filled me with happiness, but also with nostalgia. I knew it from Sainte-Tulle, when showers had refreshed the earth and brought it back to life.

Himmler invited me to sit down on a stone bench, and then said, with a serious air, 'I am really sorry that our researches are taking so long. If I had to criticize Adolf Hitler and myself, I would say that in trying to draw the demographic map of Europe anew, we acted too fast and on too large a scale. What we have achieved is superhuman, but we did not prepare well enough in advance for these great displacements of the population.'

'But you do think there's still a chance of finding my family all the same, don't you?'

'I hope so.'

Himmler, who was sitting on my left, took my right hand and stroked its palm with his forefinger. This was his first serious approach since the evening of my arrival, and my body was twitching like the carcase of an animal only just slaughtered.

'How do you manage to look so ravishing?' he murmured, leaning a little closer to my face. 'With you, I don't know what's happening to me, but...'

He left his sentence unfinished. I thought it would be a good idea to change the subject.

'You have no new leads, then?'

I could tell that I was annoying him, but he went on caressing the palm of my hand while humming a tune that I didn't know. Trembling but resigned, I told myself that the moment I feared so much had come, but he only raised my hand to his lips and dropped a delicate kiss on it, before letting it go again.

'You keep asking the same question, and I will answer it when I know more. Your former husband and your children must be somewhere on this continent which, by force of circumstance, has become a vast shambles. Think of it: within a few months we have moved huge numbers of persons of German stock to Romania, Bessarabia, Russia, Lithuania and many other countries. The same may be said of the Jews. They are the cross that we have to bear. Ah, the Jews...'

'Nothing can make me think that what you are doing to them is right,' I ventured to murmur, thinking of Theo, who would have been proud of me if she had heard me say that.

Himmler took my hand again and pressed it hard, before saying, 'You talk like Felix, you fall victim to their propaganda. You must understand us. Rather than allowing the Jews to corrupt the European soul, we have decided to deal with the problem. It is no use trying to make Jews more German, you know. Instead, they infect us with their Jewish nature. We can never change them, they will always be in the pay of the Jewish empire that is their one true homeland, and they have undertaken to liquidate our civilization. I know that our policy is cruel, but it is a case of the preservation of the Teutonic race. I would have preferred to let them set up a state of their own, far from us, but under pressure from Goebbels the Führer has decided otherwise, and – I say it in all seriousness – the Führer is always right.'

Himmler was becoming more and more agitated. It may have been love, but it was also the sheer love of talking, his favourite activity. Even in death, the man would have gone on holding forth from the world beyond the grave. The son of a teacher at the famous Wittelsbach grammar school in Munich, he had begun his adult life breeding chickens, but he was a natural teacher, and to please him I became an ardent pupil. He was a murderer, but a pedagogue as well. That evening he gave me a history lesson on Charlemagne.

'From the historical angle I have every reason to disapprove of him. He slaughtered the Saxons, although they were all that is most purely Teutonic in our race. But thanks to that, he built an empire capable of resisting the Asiatic hordes. Never forget this, Rose: in the course of history, good often comes of evil.'

37

Himmler's Kiss

BAVARIA, 1942. It was at Gmund that Himmler kissed me for the first time: a light butterfly kiss, no sooner had he embarked on it than it was over.

Of all the towns I've ever seen, Gmund must be one of the cleanest. It looked almost as if it had been polished. Under the Nazis, and indeed all other governments, from a distance it resembled a well-scrubbed collection of dolls' houses, carefully arranged on the banks of the Tegernsee lake, where mountains overgrown with spruce trees towered above it.

We spent six days in Himmler's chalet with some of his family, most notably his legitimate wife Marga, a vinegary bitch who bore the world a grudge for her husband's infidelity, and their daughter Gudrun, known as Püppi, a little Nazi pest with blonde braids, aged thirteen. Like her father, she suffered from stomach pains.

It was only when I was out walking with Himmler that I wasn't followed by a black-clad guard of SS men in helmets. He valued our privacy, as he told me with a meaning smile. He always had the same thing in mind, but he kept putting it off from day to day.

That evening, after saying goodnight to Püppi, Himmler took me into the woods, and as we walked there by moonlight he talked to me about Frederick II of Prussia, known as Frederick the Great, the philosopher king, the son of Frederick William I, the soldier king of whom he had already told me.

During his long reign, from 1740 to 1786, Frederick the Great had made a small, divided kingdom into a great power, in particular by annexing Silesia and part of Poland. Although he was a cultivated man, he also knew how to talk to his soldiers, for instance when they were in lamentable flight and he asked, 'You dogs, do you want to live for ever?'

'Frederick the Great,' said Himmler, taking my arm, 'had that rigour and constancy of mind that we miss so much in later times. Like me, he left nothing to chance and saw to everything himself, even minor matters. That's Prussia.'

'You mean that's how Prussia became Prussia?' I said, buttering him up.

'But Prussia has a millstone round its neck: Bavaria. The Prussians and the Saxons will always be superior to the Bavarians, you know, and it's a Bavarian telling you this.'

'Why are they superior?'

'Because they have pale eyes and fair hair, while our eyes and hair, I am sorry to say, are black as death. It's a kind of condemnation, and I weigh my words carefully. It means that we Bavarians are obliged to do more than the Teutonic ideal, and not to shrink from the sacrifices that it requires. I would very much have liked to be the Nordic type, as you are. Has anyone told you that you are irresistible?'

Suddenly the Reichsführer-SS took my head in his two hands and kissed my mouth. It was a firmer kiss than the first one. Accepting my fate, I already saw myself being taken in the undergrowth, on a bed of leaves and moss, by one of the leading figures of our time, a man who might perhaps save my children. But Himmler suddenly removed his lips from mine.

'Forgive me, but I don't think we are being sensible.'

'You're quite right.'

I had decided to adopt a policy of always agreeing with him, but this, I thought, was really going too far.

'I am under great pressure at the moment,' he apologized.

On the way back, he took my hand, and I squeezed his. Sixty years later, now that all has been decided, I may say that I felt like shouting at him, 'Go on, seize the moment, this is your opportunity. It's free, it's stupid, it's absurd. It's only love!'

Obsessed by the fate of Gabriel and the children, I was ready to go to the most abject depths if only he would find my family for me. Ignoble as it might be, I couldn't miss the chance.

҉

I was sure that Himmler knew what had happened to Gabriel and the children, but he still pretended to be waiting for the results of his research, and now the falling of the first leaves announced the coming of autumn.

The last time I had broached the subject, he had been a little angry. Since then I had avoided the subject. In the end I realized why: if he had told me the truth, I would have gone back to Paris. And for him, there could be no question of any such thing. He couldn't do without me any more; he was in much better health now that he was taking my pills, even if he still had recourse to the hands of Dr Kersten.

One evening Himmler told me that before I came into his life, he had thought his stomach pains were of psychosomatic origin, but I had given him proof of the contrary. It was partly a matter of diet. However, he did not deny that his anxieties always had repercussions, one way or another, on his stomach, which was his weak point.

'With Dr Kersten,' he said, 'you are my second crutch. I don't know what I would do without you.'

His compliments were not enough. Himmler knew that I wouldn't be happy much longer to go on cooking his dinner in a house where he slept only two or three times a week. I had my mental health to consider.

Consequently, he appointed me adviser to his general staff, with the task of coordinating the work being done at the Centre for Nutritional Research near Salzburg, and the laboratory developing cosmetics and body-care products close to Dachau. That meant I was allowed to travel – under escort, of course.

Himmler also put me in touch with Sturmbannführer Ernst-Günther Schenk, nutritional consultant of the Waffen-SS, and asked me to check that he and the man in charge of administration there, Obergruppenführer Oswald Pohl, were following his instructions in his note to them about the diet of the soldiers.

I knew what the note said, for good reasons; Himmler and I had written it on the night of 11 August 1942. Among its directives were these:

Bread for the soldiers to be toasted, to make it more digestible.

Nuts, pome fruits such as apples, and oatflakes to be added to the rations.

The consumption of meat to be reduced 'slowly and discreetly, in a sensible manner', so as to wean future generations off it.

Himmler had practically written this note to my dictation, although he argued with me over the necessity of eating pome fruits, which in his experience didn't agree with him. But Himmler, the man who put the Final Solution into practice, had no strength of character. He crumbled at the slightest criticism from Hitler and rarely contradicted Dr Kersten or me.

That is why I regretfully differ from my favourite philosopher for bedside reading, Hannah Arendt, who after calling Himmler (wrongly) an uncultivated philistine says that he was 'the most normal' of the Nazi leaders. No doubt the Reichsführer-SS stood out among the paranoiacs, sexual obsessives, hysterics and sadists who populated the higher reaches of the Nazi state, but he was a pathetically needy wimp, weaker in mind and body than almost anyone I've ever met. Is that the definition of a normal man?

38

The Gabriel File

BERLIN, 1942. One evening, Heinrich Himmler came back with a large file that he solemnly handed to me without a word. I was in the kitchen, making him a chocolate fondant. I washed my hands, and then, with my heart beating fast, read the notes it contained, beginning with the longest, which was signed by Claude Mespolet.

Report to the Prefect of Police

Gabriel Beaucaire is a troubled character who, for more than fifteen years, has lived a lie, passing for a patriot attached to the values of our civilization while he was secretly working for the pontiffs of the Twelve Tribes and the diabolical League Against Anti-Semitism. A nephew by marriage of the late lamented Alfred Bournissard, he contrived to profit by his relationship with his uncle in order to infiltrate nationalist circles.

On 11 May 1941, he therefore took part in the inauguration of the Institute for the Study of Jewish Questions, at 21 Rue de la Boétie, where he had no business to be, nor did the publisher Gilbert Baudinière, to whom Captain Paul Sézille, the future President of the Institute, took violent exception, since his hooked nose made him more than suspect.

On 5 September next, Gabriel Beaucaire mingled with the personalities at the opening of the exhibition 'The Jew In France' at the Palais Berlitz, organized by the Institute for the Study of Jewish Questions. This exhibition, let it never be forgotten, attracted 250,000 visitors in Paris and over 100,000 in Bordeaux and Nancy. Under the pseudonym of Francis Aicard, he praised it in *La Gerbe*, to which he contributes regularly claiming that his real name is Frémicourt, which allows him to pass as a relation of Charles Frémicourt, the Marshal's first Keeper of the Seals.

Even if he still, incomprehensibly, has some support in the circles of the Révolution Nationale, he is a recognized Israelite agent, as witness his relationships with the worshippers of Adonaï whom he assiduously frequents or has frequented in the press (which is now undergoing aryanization), notably the Jews Offenstadt, Boris, Berl, Cotnaréanu and Schreiber.

The Jewish origins of Gabriel Beaucaire have been established, both his maternal grandparents having belonged, as the attached document shows, to the Israelite community of Cavaillon. However, this professional impostor brazenly denies everything that confirms his Jewish descent. The great journalist Jean-André Lavisse was the first to unmask him in an article in the newspaper *L'Ami du peuple*, an article against which this shameless person dared to bring legal proceedings.

Those proceedings are being dragged out at length, and so I asked for a thorough expert opinion from

George Montandon, professor of anthropology, who, I would like to point out, with his usual public-spirited attitude does not ask for any fee. I am sending it to you with the file, and you will see that it is conclusive.

After long inquiries, we have finally succeeded in tracking down this dangerous character. I await your instructions. Unless I hear from you, I will have him arrested early tomorrow.

Expert Opinion of Dr George Montandon, Professor at the School of Anthropology

Having examined Gabriel Beaucaire, I confirm that he is of the Judaic type and has its most common characteristics:

— An extremely convex nose with a lower prominence of the nasal septum

— A prominent lower lip

— Moist eyes, not far sunk into their sockets

— A distinct puffiness of the soft parts of the face, more particularly the cheeks

I will add other features that I have enumerated in my work *How to Recognize the Jew*:

— Slightly bowed shoulders

— Wide and fleshy haunches

— Clawlike hands

— An irregular gait

From the anthropological point of view, this person is 100 per cent Jewish.

What on earth did Professor Montadon mean by the word 'Jewified'? Was it a typing error? A new classification? I asked myself those questions while, behind me, the Reichsführer-SS read the sheets of paper over my shoulder, and I felt his breath on my neck. From time to time he heaved a sigh, to express his sympathy for me.

The other documents were not of much interest. Notes by detectives trailing the person concerned. Records of phone conversations. I skimmed it all feverishly and then, with tears blurring my vision, I put the file down on the kitchen table and fell into a chair, where I collapsed in sobs before asking, 'What does all this mean? Don't you think you'll ever find Gabriel?'

'I know no more than you. I haven't been able to get anything else out of the stupid French police.'

'What about the children?' I hiccupped.

'It's the same. I've done all I can, Rose. All trace of them has been lost.' He sat down too, and put his hand on mine. 'Remember, I'm here for you. With all my heart.'

I sobbed more than ever, coughed, and then sneezed. 'I'm sorry, Heinrich. It's too hard.'

These days I was calling him by his first name. So far we had exchanged only two kisses, the first a furtive one, the second a longer kiss on the mouth. But I sensed that we would soon make love: a force attracted me to him, a force full of negative energy like a black hole.

At that time, of course, I did not know what a dreadful character he was. The Final Solution, agreed upon at the Wannsee Conference on 20 January that year, was getting under way on his authority. But even though I am overcome by shame in writing these words, I have to say that his timidity moved me, and so did the lack of spirit that so often led him, like all weak people, to indulge in jeremiads. If he wasn't complaining of overwork, then he was bewailing the humiliations heaped on him by Hitler. The Führer, he said, had no eyes for anyone but Goebbels.

I had my third kiss that evening, an ostentatious kiss mingled with the mucus and tears inundating my swollen face, which had red and purple blotches all over it. It was his way of showing that he loved me in spite of everything. Even ugly. Even ravaged by grief.

After that Heinrich went to the cellar to fetch a bottle of Château Latour 1934, which he proudly presented to me.

'It's the best year I know, along with the vintages of 1928 and 1929. A rather full-bodied wine with a suggestion of fresh walnuts, very well balanced.'

After we had clinked glasses, taking care to look in each other's eyes to spare ourselves the seven years of sexual frustration inflicted on those who fail to do so, Heinrich sighed. 'The one point on which I agree with the Bible is its advice to us to drink wine.'

When we had finished three-quarters of the bottle, he went back down to the cellar and came up with a bottle of white this time, a Chassagne Montrachet, to go with our main dish, a recipe of my own invention: a potato dish, an *hachis parmentier* with truffled crab and garlic cloves.

'Heinrich,' I pointed out, 'I assure you that it's all right to drink red with crab, and with fish too.'

'Not to my way of thinking. There are certain rules in

life, and we have to keep them. If we didn't we'd be no better than animals.'

He ate his first mouthful, and groaned with satisfaction.

'Next week,' he said, 'I leave for a tour of the eastern front. It will take a dozen days.'

'But Heinrich, you're never here!' I protested.

'There are matters that I must supervise there. Very important matters. But I don't think you have to stay here waiting for me. It wouldn't be good for you. I suggest that you set out on a mission to Bavaria, where you will finalize all the pharmocological plans that I've launched there in order to give my SS men more energy, and soothe the anxiety of those we've deported.'

'All right,' I murmured, after a moment's hesitation.

'And then I have great news for you. The Führer has invited us to spend a weekend with him at Berchtesgaden. He's heard of your culinary marvels.'

After dinner Heinrich kissed me again before abruptly removing his lips and hands from me and going to his room, on the pretext that he had an irrepressible need for sleep. As he went upstairs, he stopped after four or five steps and repeated, in the voice of a man inspired, something that he had heard the Führer say a few days earlier. It helped me to understand his behaviour better. 'I'm afraid of bringing women bad luck, so I shrink from forming close relationships.'

39

The Devil's Breath

BERCHTESGADEN, 1942. It was a landscape to take your breath away, and I don't mean that just figuratively; I had difficulty in breathing. On the Bavarian road between Ainring aerodrome, where our three-engined plane, a Ju 52, had landed, and Hitler's retreat of Berchtesgaden, I felt I was in a picture painted in the lofty style of Gustave Doré to illustrate an idea by Richard Wagner. I seemed to hear scraps of the overture to *Tannhäuser* through the wind that beat against the windows of the car.

The Nazi bigwigs must have been blind to remain atheists in the middle of so much natural beauty. Hitler's Eagle's Nest faced the Königssee lake, with its emerald-green waters that threaded their way through mountains over which the peak of the Watzmann, the highest of them all, presided, amidst sheer cliffs, forests, pastures, waterfalls and glaciers.

It was the kind of place where you tell yourself that it's useless expecting to find God in the heavens; He's everywhere. The light piercing through a cloud, a storm casting everything into turmoil, or the golden haze of the starry sky by night tells us more about Him than Holy Scripture. You have only to look at them. It was odd to find myself in this divine place with Heinrich, who was virulently hostile to the clergy; it wouldn't have taken much for him to claim that Hitler and not the Lord had created the universe.

Our luggage was taken away, and while Himmler went to the great hall of the Berghof, Hitler's residence, with its huge window measuring eight metres by four, I was shown the kitchens, where a uniformed brigade consisting mainly of young women was preparing lunch. They greeted me respectfully, sketching curtseys, before turning back to their stoves, heads bent. Contrary to what might have been expected, I met with a friendly welcome from the head of them, a plump girl whose name I forget, but she wasn't either Marlene von Exner or Constanze Manziarly, the two dieticians who worked together for the Führer. I can't swear to it, but I think her name was Traudl.

You might have thought she was a Carmelite nun. There wasn't a trace of vice in her eyes or her expression. She was the kind of woman who turns men's heads; behind that apparent innocence, they imagine (often wrongly), there must be a promising perversity. Although I wasn't one of the opposite sex, I have to admit, with some embarrassment, that she turned me on, just as I learned later she also turned on Martin Bormann, whose fawning flattery had raised him much higher in the hierarchy of the Third Reich than his abilities could ever have done. Bormann made full use of his *droit de seigneur* in the bedrooms of the Berghof, under his wife's nose.

When I asked about Hitler's culinary tastes, Traudl took me aside. 'He loves sweet things. Apart from that it's difficult; cooking for him is a real headache.'

I asked whether Hitler followed a diet, and she murmured, 'He suffers from flatulence and stomach cramps all the time. Just after a meal he often suddenly bends double in pain. It's terrible to see someone suffer like that.'

'Terrible,' I agreed.

'You'd think he'd been hit in the stomach by an arrow, and he starts to sweat profusely. Poor man, you know, he lives a nightmare.'

The words 'Like Heinrich' were on the tip of my tongue, but I was careful not to utter them. I simply told her, 'I've already cooked for people with digestive problems. I know what to do in such cases.'

'We're here to serve you. But you'd better refer everything to Herr Kannenberg.'

She spoke this name with such solemnity that I realized he was a very important person. A former restaurateur of about forty, heavy-jowled and broad in the beam, Kannenberg was Hitler's major-domo. His nickname at the Berghof was Tripe.

When Tripe arrived, preceded by his moustache, there could be no doubt about it: Arthur 'Willi' Kannenberg was indeed important, and looked it. He had the kind of euphoria accompanied by natural authority that you find in great gourmands who, decades after coming into the world, still can't hide their delight in being there. They never get used to it; you'd have thought that misfortune had no hold on them.

'Welcome to paradise,' he said, energetically taking my hand. 'Although it's not paradise for everyone, all the same.

I'm counting on you to soothe the Führer's digestion. His stomach is giving him all kinds of trouble at the moment.'

'What foods can't Herr Hitler tolerate?'

'Well, a great many things, outside of carrots, soft-boiled eggs and potatoes.'

'How sad.'

'Yes, it is. As he follows the Bircher-Benner diet, his only indulgences are walnuts, apples and porridge, think of that. The rest of the time he's condemned to fruit and raw vegetables.'

'Raw vegetables are very bad for him in his present state.'

'Well, you try explaining that to him. At least he's reached the point where he's ready to try anything.'

To help me prepare my dinner menu in full knowledge of the circumstances, Kannenberg took me round the huge glasshouses that provided plentiful supplies of vegetables for Hitler and his guests. There was just about everything growing in them, even late tomatoes with little brown spots at the stem end. It was like an allegory of the Nazi way of life, a dream of autarchy and self-sufficiency.

I pounced on the leeks. At the Berghof, Kannenberg told me, they usually ended up as leek-and-potato soup. I was going to serve them as a starter with a truffle-flavoured vinaigrette dressing.

I had no hesitation in deciding on the main course: in view of this profusion of vegetables, a vegetarian lasagne was an obvious choice. I would present it as multiple layers of pasta interleaved with a variety of fillings, all dominated by carrots, the most easily digested of all vegetables, grated and lightly boiled.

In the fruit store I found plenty of apples. I opted for an apple tart with a finger of rum, a few pinches of crushed vanilla and two small spoonfuls of lemon juice. This recipe, my own invention, was much copied later.

The meal had to be ready an hour before it was served, so that the two women who were Hitler's tasters could eat a little of the dishes intended for him, and then leave time to make sure that they had not partaken of anything poisonous.

It was a huge success. Nazis are sheep to the manner born, so it was enough for Hitler to have enjoyed his dinner, without suffering stomach pains when it came to the dessert course, for me to be the toast of the evening. Heinrich came to find me, and the whole table, led by the Führer, applauded me.

Twenty minutes later, when I was looking out of my bedroom window and watching a storm rip the sky apart, Heinrich hurried in, looking anxious.

'The Führer wants to see you.'

'Yes? What about it?'

'You must promise me not to tell him about your children and your former husband. If he knew you'd been married to a Jew he'd never forgive me for bringing you here.'

'Perhaps he knows already.'

'No, that kind of information reaches him only through me.'

Heinrich took me into Hitler's study. He seemed so strung up that out in the corridor I caressed his arm and then the nape of his neck, to relax him. He smiled at me.

The door was open, and we stood in the doorway for a moment. Hitler must have heard us coming, but he couldn't see us. He was sitting in a large armchair facing the window, with his back to us, one hand petting his dog, a German shepherd, while he held the document he was reading in the other.

'Come in,' he finally said, without turning round.

You don't have to believe me, but I can assure you that at the very moment when I met his eyes a flash of lightning lit up the window, before a thunderbolt struck the mountainside with a crash that was followed by echoes and the sound of falling rocks.

'I laid this on specially to impress you,' Hitler joked. After signalling to Heinrich that he could leave us, he invited me to watch the storm through the window with him. It was a tremendous spectacle.

'I wonder what Pannini would have made of this,' he said, getting to his feet. 'Another masterpiece, I'm sure.'

The Führer went on to tell me that the Italian Renaissance painter Giovanni Paolo Pannini, a lover of grand scenes and monumental effects, was one of his favourite artists. 'I love his work,' he said, 'because nothing frightened him. Real artists are never afraid. Nor are great men. The rest of them are losers.'

Hitler took my arm and led me to the corner of the room where there was comfortable seating. We sat down side by side on the same black leather sofa.

'I have canvases by Pannini here,' he told me. 'Roman ruins. I must show them to you.'

His breath made my nostrils quiver. I don't think I've ever smelled anything so unpleasant, even during the Armenian genocide when I walked along the river in Trebizond, past flotillas of corpses bumping into each other.

I was uneasy. Either to relax me, or to get me talking, Hitler offered me a glass of slivovitz. I drank three shots in quick succession, which explains why I don't remember much of what we said after that.

Joseph Goebbels joined us: a small man with black, brilliantined hair. He had a club foot, and never seemed to keep still. I didn't yet know that he was one of the pillars of the Third Reich, and the man behind the cult of Hitler for whom, anti-Christian fanatic though he was, he said he felt a holy awe. All the same, his hysterical manner that evening remains stamped on my memory.

Goebbels gave me another glass of spirits, kirsch this time. I can't swear to it, because my memories after that are so confused, but I think it was with him that I left Hitler's study.

What did we do together next? Nothing, so far as I remember. I wandered along the corridors for a while, my footsteps unsteady, until I passed a group of men among whom I thought I recognized Martin Bormann, head of the Chancellery. After a certain amount of jostling and laughter, one of them took me into a bedroom where, pushing me up against the window, he took me.

When the man withdrew from me I felt overwhelmed, and stayed where I was for a long time, panting and stupefied as I looked through the window.

A little later, when I put my dress back on, there was no one else in the room. I lay down on the bed and slept for a while.

40

Three Fingers in My Mouth

BERCHTESGADEN, 1942. I didn't see Hitler again. I was put in charge of dinner at the Berghof for three evenings running, and if I am to believe the compliments paid me by the guests I did well, although the Führer was not especially keen on my desserts. He liked large cakes made with butter and decorated with whipped cream, which have never been part of my repertory. Apparently he used to have three helpings of those at a sitting, but he didn't eat a second slice of my apple tart on the first evening, or of my pear charlotte the day after that, or a second *baba au rhum* on the third day.

Hitler proclaimed himself vegetarian in the name of the suffering of animals, and often, especially in front of his mistress Eva Braun, a great meat-eater, he liked to talk about a visit to a Ukrainian abattoir that had traumatized him. However, his chef Willi told me, in strict secrecy, that the Führer did not always despise meat, but liked Bavarian sausages and had been mad about stuffed pigeon for a long time. As a vegetarian myself, after a fashion, I was glad to hear it.

Once dinner was over, the guests at the Berghof often watched a film in the great hall. They did so after drinking their postprandial tea or coffee, sitting back in their armchairs while they listened to the Führer holding forth on the weather or the latest adventures of his German shepherd dog Blondi. Alternatively, his subject might be a forceful little lecture on Wagner, the egg trade, or the advances of science. Everyone listened to him with close attention verging on self-denial. I thought that people able to tolerate such boredom unflinchingly, with smiles on their faces, must indeed be invincible; they had a sense of eternity ahead and were always sizing it up.

That first evening I had the good idea of serving little delicacies after dinner in the form of scones with sesame seeds, raisins and strawberry jam. Since scones are eaten either spread with butter or filled with thick cream, the Führer loved them, until he asked what exactly they were. On hearing of the British origin of my little cakes, he let out a groan that was taken as disapproval.

Heinrich hated the climate of idleness that reigned at Berchtesgaden. In spite of the bracing Alpine air, everything here was relaxing. The days passed in a succession of interminable meals, walks for the sake of the guests' health, and light snacks of sweet things. Nothing is more tiring than leisure; it can make the toughest characters spineless.

When Himmler came to see me in my bedroom at midnight that first evening to hear about my interview with Hitler, I still wasn't sober in spite of the litre and a half of water that I'd imbibed. Dropping heavily on to my bed, Heinrich said, 'You look as if you've been drinking.'

'Well spotted.'

'Not that there's much else to do here. It's so boring! The German people are the only nation who consider boredom a normal state of mind, Rose!' He came closer to me. 'We

Germans would do better to hurry up and win the war, don't you agree?'

The anxiety in his voice delighted me. So not all was lost! Until now, I'd thought that in effect, the Germans had won the war already. I wasn't aware that matters on the Russian front were going far worse than expected.

'We're becoming a nation that no longer inspires fear,' he groaned. 'Hitler has just received your President of the Council, Laval, a kind of bird-turd who annoyed him by refusing to declare war on Great Britain and the United States, on the pretext that Pétain wouldn't like it. I can't think why he was allowed to leave with his life. A weak power is a dead power.'

Suddenly he looked closely at me. 'You stink of spirits. Was it Hitler you were drinking with like that?'

I decided to tell the truth.

'He got you drunk so that you'd talk to him about me, I suppose?'

I told him that we had talked about cookery and the painter Pannini.

Reassured on that point, he got to his feet, took my forearms, led me over to the bed, and when I fell on top of him he kissed me. A kiss with many flavours to it, a strong, greasy kiss, rich in alcohol, with a taste of champagne at first, then of sheep's-milk cheese, rotten wood, fresh hazelnuts, old rum and finally black pepper.

He put three fingers in my mouth. His were the fine fingers of a pianist, and I kissed them with an enthusiasm that I soon saw troubled him. He was struggling with himself, that was obvious from the veiled expression in his eyes; he hated losing control of his feelings.

Suddenly Heinrich got to his feet, cleared his throat, adjusted the collar of his shirt, dusted down his sleeves to smooth them out, said goodbye and left the room.

*

Four days later, two three-engined Ju 52 planes were waiting for us at Ainring airport, some twenty kilometres from Berchtesgaden. One was to take Heinrich to Berlin before he travelled on to the Russian front. The other flew me to Munich, where I was to meet Felix Kersten, Himmler's masseur, and go to visit the Centre for Cosmetic and Homeopathic Studies with him.

Felix Kersten, his expression distracted and his face almost as crumpled as his navy-blue coat, met me with a gravity that did not augur well. He had told me that he would press the general staff of the SS for any news of Gabriel and the children, and as soon as I met his eyes I knew that he had some.

Eyes lowered, he murmured something that I couldn't make out. All that I did catch was the word 'Dachau'. It made me tremble. Set up by Himmler in 1933, the year when the Nazis came to power, Dachau was the only concentration camp I knew about yet. Suddenly everything began hammering away inside me: my heart, my temples, my eardrums. I was nothing but a set of nerves beating in the void.

'Your husband died in Dachau, and the children died on a train.'

Something exploded in me. When I came back to my senses, Felix was patting my cheeks. After helping me to sit upright on the upholstered bench where I had collapsed, he shrugged his shoulders helplessly, and then stroked my forearm with a comforting hand. I sobbed even more than before.

I don't remember what happened after that in the study centre. I came out of it only at the end of the day, when I went back to the hotel near Max-Joseph-Platz to meet Felix Kersten again. He had spent some of the day at Dachau, and confirmed that Gabriel was dead; he had checked it in a register dated 23 August 1942.

'I don't know the details,' he murmured. 'I'm sorry.'

I couldn't get any more out of him, and as for the rest of it, he only wanted to talk about the medical experiments he had seen at Dachau. They had traumatized him. He spoke of healthy prisoners being injected with malaria to test new pharmacological products on them, since quinine to treat the disease was too expensive and too difficult to obtain; he had seen inmates immersed in tubs of icy water, sometimes to the point of death, to study the effects of hypothermia before they were dissected like frogs by opening up their skulls and then chests; he had watched as pus was injected into the thighs of some forty priests, most of them Polish, to induce huge purulent inflammations that could then be studied so as to identify the most efficacious method of treatment. The priestly guinea pigs were divided into groups like laboratory mice and then, depending which group they were in, treated with either sulfamides or biochemical tablets, the latter apparently being Heinrich's preference.

The priests treated with sulfamides recovered fairly quickly, and the stronger of them then immediately received an intravenous injection of their own pus – which would falsify the results of the experiment, but the Reichsführer-SS must not be humiliated. When they were not unconscious, the survivors tossed and turned on their beds, moaning in appalling pain.

'There are no words for what I've seen,' murmured Felix, his voice blank and his head bowed. 'It's a melting pot of abominations. I shall tell Himmler he can't let them do these things.'

'You think he doesn't know about it?'

'I don't care, so long as I can save lives! But I know, not that it's any excuse, Himmler isn't always happy about what goes on.'

And Felix told me that, watching a mass execution at Minsk on 15 August 1941, Himmler had nearly fainted. It was his baptism of bloodshed. Erich von dem Bach-Zelewski, Gruppenführer of Byelorussia and himself responsible for 200,000 deaths, was with him. He said afterwards that his boss Himmler had been 'white as a sheet', looking down at the ground after every salvo of gunfire, and when the SS men had been slow to finish off two girls writhing in agony in the mass grave had shouted, beside himself, 'Stop torturing those women! Kill them!'

To put things in proportion, Felix remarked, one could say that Himmler was like those people who eat red meat but can't bear to think about animals being slaughtered in the abattoir.

Three months later, when his masseur was expecting him for a session, Himmler had come back from the Chancellery devastated. It was 11 November 1941; Felix remembered the date precisely. The Reichsführer-SS had wanted only to 'evacuate' the Jews, but Hitler had just asked him to organize their extermination.

Himmler was depressed, Felix was horrified. When Dr Kersten, as he massaged Himmler, denounced the inhumanity of such a solution, the Reichsführer-SS had objected, 'The Jews dominate the press, the arts, cinema and all the rest of it. They're responsible for the decay and degeneration of the people; they thrive on it. They have prevented the unification of Europe and are always subverting governments with wars and revolutions. They must be called to account for the millions of deaths they have on their consciences over the centuries. When the last Jew has disappeared from the earth, there will be an end to the destruction of nations, and following generations will be spared future massacres on the battlefield in the name of Jewish nihilism. To attain greatness, we must walk over corpses. That is what the Americans did with their Indians. If we want to create a new life, we must cleanse the soil so that, one day, it may bear fruit. That is my mission.'

At that moment in his story, Felix took my hand and pressed it. He passed on to me his sensation of an icy chill.

'A few days later, all the same, Himmler did recognize, before defending the principle of it, that the extermination of peoples was not Teutonic.' He laughed; it was hollow laughter. 'If we are reduced to counting on a man like

247

Himmler to save the Jews,' he added, 'then everything really is past praying for.'

Felix and I felt the same mixture of panic, weariness and sheer prostration. There was nothing we could do about it but drink, and we got methodically drunk in the German fashion, beer chased with schnapps.

Next day we went back to Berlin. In my own room again, I went straight to the aquarium and told Theo my latest news. The SS guards had taken good care of her in my absence. At the end of my story, my salamander said crossly, 'What's your idea, going to bed with Nazis?'

'That's not all I've been doing!'

'But you do it, and it disgusts me!'

'I came to Germany to find out about my children, whatever it cost me.'

'And now you see the result, my poor Rose! You've prostituted yourself for nothing.'

I sighed, looking sadly at Theo's black eyes. 'What did you want me to do?'

'Show some self-respect, you silly woman!'

'How do you expect any woman to respect herself when her children have been taken away from her?'

I spent the night crying into my pillow.

41

The Embryo That Wouldn't Die

BERLIN, 1942. During the week that I spent in the Berlin house, waiting for Heinrich to come back, I passed from terror to exhaustion and back again all the time. Heinrich himself now came top of the list of those I hated.

I saw his failure to tell me the truth about the fate of Gabriel and the children as duplicity, indeed nothing short of betrayal. I had decided to ask him to let me go back to Paris. While I waited, I tried to pass the time by drinking St John's wort tisanes to calm myself, looking after Theo, walking in Berlin's huge park the Tiergarten, and reading the complete works of Shakespeare as translated into German by Georg Müller, published in 1921, which I had found in Heinrich's library. But I was haunted by Gabriel and the children. I could think of nothing else.

While he was away, Heinrich had phoned me several times. His voice sounded hollow, which meant that he had been drinking a lot and not getting much sleep, and his conversation was tedious; he sounded like someone dutifully delivering a report. If I wasn't much mistaken, I must be the fourth woman on his list, coming after his wife, his daughter and his mistress.

As for Dr Felix Kersten, who had gone back to the Netherlands after his visit to Bavaria, he phoned me every evening, always anxiously asking the same questions. 'How are you? Are you sure that you're all right? Is there anything I can do for you?' They didn't really call for an answer.

It was on the day of Heinrich's return from his visit to the Eastern Front that everything was turned upside down. As I weighed myself in the morning, I noticed that my breasts had grown larger. I don't want to boast, but I had always been well endowed in that area – this, however, was too much.

I went to look at myself in the bathroom mirror. Feeling my large, full breasts I realized that my Montgomery tubercles had also grown, and the areolas themselves were darker. I took advantage of my self-examination to caress my breasts, and they quivered with arousal several times.

The day before, I had seen traces of blood in the lavatory bowl after I had urinated. I hadn't paid much attention to that, but now there was no doubt about it. I uttered a cry of horror, which swiftly brought the two SS guards who protected the house up to the bathroom.

'Leave me alone,' I told them. 'It's nothing. I jammed my finger in the door, that's all.'

I couldn't bear the thought of letting the seed of a Nazi grow inside me. I felt like the cicada in which a wasp has laid its egg after imprisoning it at the bottom of a hole sealed by a pebble. As soon as the egg hatches, the malignant larva eats its host alive, right down to the last scrap of its flesh.

I was ready to do anything to get rid of the intruder. I took spoonfuls of castor oil. I drank infusions of parsley, absinthe, wormwood, bay and white willow. I injected soapy water and introduced abortifacient plants into the neck of the uterus. I tried running, exercising with a skipping rope, punching my stomach.

Given the terrible possibility that whatever I did, the foetus would stay where it was, I would have to find it a substitute father, and I couldn't see that I had any alternative to Heinrich. I had to arrange that with him if and when it turned out that my attempts to miscarry were doomed to fail.

That evening, when Heinrich got home after his visit to the east, he sat on the sofa, sighing, and after asking me to come over to him he took a little box out of his pocket. It contained an engagement ring; the setting contained a large Burmese ruby surrounded by diamonds.

Once my ring was on, I knelt down in front of him, unbuttoned and opened his flies, took out his prick, and taking it between my lips I pleasured him, as only a woman can, with the best I had to offer – my life, my dignity, my skill – until he came in my mouth and I felt it run down my throat.

When I got up again, Heinrich was lying there with his arms flung open along the back of the sofa, his head tilted slightly back and a wide smile of satisfaction on his face. And in telling me, 'You're the woman I have always dreamed of,' he used the familiar *tu* pronoun to me for the first time.

I wasn't about to return the compliment. I acted as I did because I needed a father for the child I was carrying, and it would have to be Heinrich. I urgently needed him to penetrate me, or I was going to be in terrible trouble.

Furthermore, it seemed to me that passing on to full

sexual intercourse was the best way to get him to leave me alone; the loves that people claim are eternal are often also impossible. As long as ours lasted, I could hope that Heinrich would get tired of me and let me leave within the next few days. That would mean I could go back to Paris and get an abortion.

I detected a certain charm in the contradiction between his calm expression and the question indicated by his raised eyebrows. Not to mention the fact that his lips sometimes had an ironical twist. If it hadn't been for his moustache, which was too well groomed, and his lips, which were too thin, he would have been attractive. But now that I knew the fate of Gabriel and the children I longed more than anything to kill him.

At the end of dinner, when I told him that I wanted to go back to France, he said in a toneless voice, and with an ominous expression, 'Certainly not.'

*

On those evenings when Heinrich came back to sleep at the house, I spoiled him in the same way: once the Reichsführer-SS was sitting on the sofa, I brought him a glass of port on a platter, and as he began to sip it I knelt down in front of him.

I did not dislike feeling his hand on top of my head, guiding me. Nor did I fail to gasp with pleasure when he took hold of my jaws so as to plunge his prick between them, or when he put his fingers into my nostrils to prevent me from breathing.

But I was beginning to panic. Day followed day, and I still couldn't get him to indulge in full intercourse. My devoted efforts failed; all he would do was to spill his seed in my mouth, and no more. To ensure that Heinrich truly believed he was the father of my child I had to get him into bed, and there was no time to be lost.

I was beginning to think that my embryo, tenacious of life as it was, would refuse to be nipped in the bud. I had been trying to rid myself of it for the last five weeks, and nothing had worked. Not jumping three steps at a time down the stairs. Not all the furniture-moving I did, hoping to make myself miscarry.

One evening Felix Kersten came to dine at the house. On the same day, he had negotiated the liberation of several Dutch Jews while he was massaging the Reichsführer-SS. If I remember correctly, the date was 19 December 1942, Emma Lempereur's birthday. I had been to pray for her that morning at St Hedwig's Cathedral. One of the canons of the cathedral chapter had died on his way to Dachau, where he had been sent for taking the side of the Jews on Kristallnacht.

In his usual way, Felix arrived an hour early, so there had been time for us to exchange news over a bottle of schnapps. When I told him that I was pregnant he sighed, and asked, 'Who's the father?'

'I've no idea.'

'Why not?'

'I was so drunk at the time that I don't recollect much about it.'

He got up from his chair and came over to me. 'I strongly advise you not to lie to Himmler,' he said in an undertone.

'Telling him the truth is the best way to get your freedom of movement back.'

'You mean I'll disgust him, is that it?'

'More than you may think. He's obsessed by ideas of venereal disease. He has a phobia about it, and for good reason.' Felix hesitated for a moment before going on, still in a low voice, 'It's an established fact that Hitler contracted syphilis about twenty years ago.' He stopped abruptly, pointed to the ceiling as if it had ears, and then whispered, 'You won't tell anyone, will you? Swear you won't.'

'I won't tell a soul. I'm listening.'

'For the last five years Hitler has suffered from all kinds of symptoms showing that even though his syphilis was treated at the time, it is still ravaging his body.' And he lowered his voice yet further, to a tiny thread of sound, as he enumerated the Führer's ailments. 'There's no appeal against that sentence: Hitler is suffering from progressive paralysis of the limbs, trembling hands, chronic insomnia and headaches. I must also add fits of dementia and megalomania. All of those are signs that he's still racked by syphilis. The only symptoms he doesn't yet show are fixed vision and verbal confusion, although his speeches seem to me more incoherent than they used to be.'

'Do you think Hitler is going to die?' I whispered.

'Himmler is extremely anxious. You only have to hear him talk about Hitler's disease. He is so keen on hygiene that the mere thought of venereal disease fills him with disgust.'

'Then he'll leave me alone.'

'You have nothing more to fear. Himmler already thinks

the whole Nazi hierarchy are infected with syphilis. He may quarantine you.'

During dinner, while we were enjoying my truffled artichoke soup, Felix delivered a tirade against the Reich's anti-Jewish stance. In particular, he warned Heinrich of the poor opinion posterity would have of him.

'But I'm not responsible for any of that,' replied Heinrich. 'Goebbels is in charge of the Jewish question.'

'No,' Felix said firmly. 'You are.'

'Unlike Goebbels, I never wanted to kill all the Jews. I just wanted to expel them from Germany. With all their goods, too, but I wanted them to leave the country and never be heard of again. We tried the diplomatic route, asking Roosevelt to help us by taking them in – there's plenty of room in the United States, any amount of virgin territory. He didn't even condescend to reply to us. Then, in 1934, wishing to avoid a massacre, I went to the Führer and suggested founding an independent state to take all the Jews. Somewhere a long way from us.'

'In Palestine?' I asked.

'No, that's too close. I was thinking of Madagascar, which has the kind of hot climate that Jews love. Not to mention its many natural resources: graphite, chromite, bauxite. But there you are: everyone was against my idea.'

I couldn't stand his plaintive tone, and went off to the kitchen for a little while, leaving Felix to continue his attack. I was so exasperated that I broke a Moustiers faience plate.

Felix himself was also infuriated; he describes this conversation in almost the same terms in his memoirs.

After dinner, when I had told Heinrich how I had been raped and impregnated at Berchtesgaden, it all turned out just as Felix had foreseen. Heinrich went off to the drinks cupboard in a terrible temper, got out a bottle of schnapps, and drank a good quarter of it before saying, 'What a way to behave! Göring, Bormann, Goebbels, they're all the same. Syphilitic swine. Setting such a shocking example!'

'Wouldn't it be better for me to have an abortion?'

'Don't even think about it, Rose! We need new blood in the Reich.' He drank again, at length, and then said, 'Now, you're going to let me look after you, and you must promise not to say a word about this to anyone.'

I promised. When the time came to say goodnight, he didn't kiss me on the mouth. He merely patted my shoulder, as if I were an animal under his protection and must be encouraged to take advantage of it.

42

The Cheeping of a Sick Chicken

BERLIN, 1942. So far as Heinrich was concerned, everything turned out just as Felix had said. He kept his distance from me throughout the rest of our conversation, and his disgust never once got the upper hand of his usual irony. Finally, after patting me on the shoulder, he did not go up to his room but went to sleep somewhere else. He was as horrified by me as if I had been syphilitic myself.

I never saw Heinrich again, and he never gave me any other sign of life. I didn't regret it; I hadn't had much dignity left when I met him, and I had none at all at the end of our story. From then on I could feel no love in him for me, or even indulgence. It is thanks to him that I believe the human propensity to narcissism and infatuation is a terrible thing, always dragging us down. He created a void in me, and it has made me a survivor.

I was assigned a residence permit, and was secretly accommodated in our former love nest until the birth of my child seven and a half months later. The Nazis seemed to think of my huge excrescence as something sacred. I was under the care of an SS doctor who came to examine me every week, and had twenty-four hour care from an auxiliary nurse who slept in what had been Heinrich's room.

Her name was Gertraud, and she was a little scrap of a woman with a curvature of the spine, who seemed to be afraid of everything. I understood why when she told me, one day, that she was a distant cousin of the carpenter Johann Georg Elser, who had tried to assassinate Hitler on 8 November 1939 in the Bürgerbräukeller, the restaurant in Munich where the Führer was celebrating the anniversary of his failed putsch in 1923.

Elser had timed his bomb to go off at 9.20 p.m., but Hitler left the restaurant with his entire retinue earlier than expected, at seven minutes past the hour, thus escaping assassination. All the same, eight people were killed.

It was obvious that Gertraud did not think well of the Third Reich, but she gritted her teeth and put up with it. Her kindly glance was a great support to me throughout this time of trial.

Every day I prayed to Christ, the Virgin Mary and the saints for the thing inside me to die. I made promises and lit candles. In the third month I even tried aborting myself with a knitting needle.

All the evidence showed that Felix had been instructed not to phone me or come and see me. I expect that the telephone number of the house had been changed. For the time being I was not permitted to get in touch with anyone, or to go out except for a ritual walk in the Wannsee district, well guarded, so that my foetus could get the benefit of fresh air.

I liked walking on the banks of the Wannsee lake, with the frost crackling underfoot. I used to pass the handsome white villa where, as I learned later, the Wannsee Conference was held on 20 January 1942. It was on that occasion that several Nazi dignitaries, under the chairmanship of Heinrich's right-hand man Reinhard Heydrich, decided on the methods to be used in exterminating the Jews.

I also liked walking beside the smaller lake, the Little Wannsee, where the poet Heinrich von Kleist committed suicide in 1811, after shooting his companion Henriette Vogel, who had cancer. I often stopped to meditate in front of their tombs, a large stone slab for the writer and a small plaque for his lover. It seemed to me that they would have felt so much better together under the same tombstone.

In spring we sometimes went to Peacock Island, where the birds from which it takes its name walked, uttering their raucous mating cries, around the romantic palace built for his mistress by King Frederick William II.

I saw landscapes that reminded me of Trebizond round the lake, particularly in the morning when mist lay over the water, rising in a gentle, milky curve above the ground until a light wind opened windows in it, giving wider and wider views of the pale blue sky as the hours passed. To me, it was an image of a lost paradise.

What upset me most, during these walks, was the sight of children. I immediately thought of my own, and burst into tears. Accordingly, whenever my SS guards saw children coming they led me in another direction. I have never felt so close to Édouard and Garance as I did then. I had only to close my eyes, and they would appear in my head.

During one of my last walks beside the Wannsee, I set Theo free. We had not been on good terms for several weeks. One day my salamander told me, after I had fed her, that she wanted to be at liberty again. 'There's no more I can do for you,' she said.

'You're wrong, Theo. Living is hard, but surviving is even harder.'

'I'm only your guilty conscience, that's all. You'll manage very well without me. I'm nearly thirty years old, the natural life span of a salamander, and I don't fancy dying in an aquarium in a Nazi grandee's house.'

As I approached the lake my salamander was quivering with joy. She plunged into the water without a backward glance.

*

Heinrich had decided that once my baby was born, it would be placed in the care of a Lebensborn home, one of those nurseries where the state, acting on behalf of the SS, brought up children born to 'racially worthy' mothers who had passed the test of racial purity.

Several thousand children were born in these homes, but it is sometimes estimated that about 250,000 more were kidnapped in the occupied countries to be 'Germanized' in such Nazi institutions. They were chosen on racial criteria to become the aristocracy of the Nordic Germans whose number, according to the Reichsführer-SS, would rise to 120 million individuals in 1980.

As I was a blue-eyed blonde, not too long in the body, with shapely calves and straight legs, I was the ideal breeding female.

I may say in passing that I had difficulty in understanding the Nazi hierarchy's obsession with fair hair, when none of its leaders, except Göring, had a blond hair on his head. Almost always brown if not black-haired, they were the antithesis of the people whom Hitler had once conjured up in a speech. 'We all suffer from the degeneration of our mingled, corrupt blood. What can we do to make amends and purify ourselves? [...] Eternal life, as conferred by the Holy Grail, is granted only to those who are truly pure and noble.'

With his dull complexion, slight shoulders, receding chin, almond eyes and drooping eyelids, Heinrich was far from the ideal. His enemies sometimes said that he looked like the description of a Jew in the Nazi pamphlets. Perhaps that was why I hadn't found him so repulsive.

On the evening of our last conversation, Heinrich had explained the philosophy of the Lebensborn organization to me. First, thinking he was consoling me, he had said that he would never be content with a single woman. 'In sanctifying marriage,' he went on, 'the Church and its satanic principles have dramatically lowered our birth rate. That's easily explained; as soon as they're married women let themselves go, husband and wife become indifferent to each other, and that's why we are short of millions of children in our population.'

'Are you suggesting that men should have more than one wife?' I asked, scandalized.

'Exactly. The first wife, to be known as the Domina, will retain special status, but we must put an end to the stupidity of Christian marriage and let men reproduce in their own way. The Lebensborn movement is the first stage of our family policy; an illegitimate child will no longer be considered a disgrace, indeed, such children will become the elite of the Germanic people. Your child will be happy, Rose.'

I didn't tell him how little I cared about that. I was in a hurry to get rid forever of the monster growing inside me, and at last it came into the world on 14 August 1943.

'Do you want to see the baby?' asked the midwife.

'Definitely not,' I replied, closing my eyes.

I do remember the baby's cry. I had never heard anything like it. A kind of cheeping, like the sound of a sick chicken, with something heart-rending about it. That is the only memory I have of the child, who left immediately for the nearest Lebensborn nursery.

Over the next few days, I stayed at the house alone, until two SS guards took me to the airport and put me on a plane bound for Paris, just as Heinrich had promised.

43

Signing My Name to My Crime

PARIS, 1943. A year since I was last there, nothing had changed except that my cat Sultan was dead, run over by a military truck in the Place du Trocadéro. During my absence Paul Chassagnon, my right-hand man at La Petite Provence, had taken over, and the restaurant was still getting by somehow. He had paid the bills that came to my apartment, where to my great surprise there wasn't a speck of dust in the air or on the furniture; at Paul's request, my cleaning lady, a virtuoso performer with the broom, had gone on coming in twice a week.

On my return to Paris, I suffered from stomach cramps for several weeks. Judging by the symptoms, the cramps were the same kind as those that tormented Hitler and Himmler. I felt bilious and was prone to belching, sometimes in the middle of a sentence that I had to break off, and these attacks left brown marks at the corners of my lips in the small hours. My herbal pills had no effect on them. It was a psychosomatic malady.

I tried to shake it off by sheer hard work in the restaurant and by visiting the graves of Gabriel's parents in Cavaillon graveyard; they had died while I was in Germany. I had not recovered from the summer of forty-two; I was fenced in by my past, and like a mad old woman I kept talking to my dead – Gabriel, Édouard and Garance.

'I know what you want,' I told them. 'You don't have to go on telling me all the time. I'll do it anyway.'

'Don't forget us,' Gabriel begged me.

'I think of no one but you!'

At this point Paul Chassagnon turned up, eyebrows raised, ladle in hand. 'What's the matter, Rose? Is there a problem?'

'No, of course not,' I replied, blushing with confusion.

One of the restaurant's customers was also worried about my state of mind: Jean-Paul Sartre, who had come to dine at La Petite Provence with Simone de Beauvoir. The philosopher had raised his face to mine and whispered, giving off a strong aroma of tobacco, coffee and alcohol, 'You must rest, my child. You're exhausted, you look as if you'd just risen from the grave. Is there anything I can do for you?'

I had shaken my head, although I would have liked to make love with him, despite the fact that much about him repelled me, beginning with his voice, which seemed to come from a knife-making factory. I had melted before his large, moist, globular eyes; he was the first person since my return, other than Paul Chassagnon, to read my heart.

Sartre himself was in a melancholy mood; his play *The Flies*, directed by Charles Dullin and performed a few weeks earlier at the former Théâtre Sarah Bernhardt, now aryanized under the name of the Théâtre de la Cité, had been a flop.

After the war, the orthodox attitude was to say that Sartre's play, although authorized by the punctilious German censorship organ, was an act of resistance, which has never been proved, while it has been confirmed that Dullin was on good terms with the occupying power, and such Nazi newspapers as *La Gerbe* and the *Pariser Zeitung* were in favour of it. Then there was the little party at which, after the performance of the play, the author and Simone de Beauvoir drank healths with several German officers holding the rank of Sonderführer – Baumann, Lucht and Rademacher by name.

As it happened, there was no photographer present to immortalize the scene of Jean-Paul Sartre drinking champagne with the Nazis. That fact did not prevent the philosopher from sitting on the denazification committee after the Liberation, while Sacha Guitry, a staunch supporter of Pétain, went to prison for drinking with the occupying forces.

Sartre was both better and worse than he was thought. I will forgive him everything, his libertine conduct, his lies, his condemnation of others, for placing his hand on my arm that day and saying, with such humanity, 'You must think of something else.'

He was right. The loss of my children was spoiling my love of live, not that life itself was worth much at the time. A song by Charles Trenet kept going round and round in my head. It summed up the general state of mind in those days.

Que reste-t-il de nos amours?
Que reste-t-il de ces beaux jours?
Une photo, vieille photo de ma jeunesse.
Que reste-t-il des billets doux,
Des mois d'Avril, des rendezvous?

What indeed was left of our days of love, our love letters, our tender meetings? There were three lines of the song in particular, that I sang to myself, for it was as if they had been written for me.

Bonheur fané, cheveux au vent,
Baisers volés, rêves mouvants
Que reste-t-il de tout cela?

Faded happiness, stolen kisses, yes, what was left of them?

*

I am sure that I was still humming Trenet's song on the autumn morning when I went to see Jean-André Lavisse in the Rue August-Comte, near the Jardin du Luxembourg. The sky was like a waterfall that day, crushing us under grey rain and dead leaves.

I went to that meeting light at heart with anticipation. After much hesitation, I had finally concluded that only vengeance could cure my stomach pains. After all, it cured everything else.

Vengeance is certainly a type of violence made to suit the civil code and religious precepts, but it is also a pleasure, and it seems to me stupid to deprive oneself of it. Like love, when it has been consummated it brings a sense of relaxation. To have done justice is the best way of finding that you are at peace with yourself and the rest of the world.

Far be it from me to argue with those who claim that forgiveness is the finest kind of vengeance, but it is an idea that partakes too much of morality and philosophy for my taste. It is only a kind of abstract vengeance; it doesn't put anything right.

If it is to do you any good, vengeance must be physical and concrete. When it is cruel, it allows our wounds to close and it alleviates pain for a long time.

Contrary to what most people think, the wish for vengeance does not die down in the course of time. Indeed, it gets more and more inviting. So when I rang Jean-André Lavisse's doorbell, I was in a state of great excitement. The door was opened not by the writer himself but by a pathetic young girl with a curved spine who, judging by her rustic accent, had only recently come to Paris. I gave a false name, Justine Fourmont, and she led me through a labyrinth of corridors to her master's study.

I had not imagined him as he really was. He had an almost adolescent figure, with a suggestion of the hermaphrodite about him, united with the face of an old goat and a rebellious quiff of hair, and he looked as if he were drunk on vinegar. He was in his dressing gown, working at his desk, surrounded by thousands of books. There were books everywhere – on his bookshelves, of course, but also piled into unsteady towers on the floor. Some of these towers had already crumbled and fallen.

Having invited me to sit down, Jean-André Lavisse asked why I wanted to write his biography, which was the excuse I had given for calling on him.

'Oh, because I admire you so much,' I replied without hesitation.

'A biography is the worst thing that can happen to a man.

I call them worms from on high, to distinguish them from the worms from below that will eat us in our coffins.'

He gave a silly smile, and I smiled back in the same way before going on. 'I just love your novels. They are far better than anything else to be found in contemporary literature. I am only sorry that you have written so few of them.'

'My journalism takes up too much of my time; it detracts from my work as a whole.'

Getting to know writers had shown me what you have to say to them, especially when they are also journalists. They don't come down to earth until you talk about their books. I claimed to think particularly highly of his *An Uncertain Love* and *The Rising Morn*, two romantic novellas that had been quite successful.

'Only you write so well about love,' I told him. 'You and Stendhal.'

'I'll accept the comparison.'

The vanity of writers conveys a good idea of infinity. Sitting as rigid as a statue, Jean-André Lavisse basked in my compliment until I came up with the next one, which had him preening with his high opinion of himself.

'All your work shows that you know women, and how to love them.'

'Allow me to say that they repay me in kind.'

I looked at him with fascinated eyes and open lips, assuming the expression of the Virgin praying to the Almighty, and my manoeuvre worked at once. Jean-André Lavisse rose to his feet, picked up one of his books from the shelves and then, having chosen a page, came over to me, reading aloud several maxims from his great success,

Pensées d'amour, published five years earlier.

'Love kills men and brings women to life.'

'The only possible way to resist love is flight.'

'Love is a disease, and only death can cure us.'

'Even when old age comes, there is something that love never understands – that it is not eternal.'

He had adopted a peculiar stance, with his hips tilted forward and his head back, in the pose of a great writer with his gaze bent on posterity. When he was within my reach, I stood up and struck him smartly across the windpipe, using my knowledge of the rudiments of krav maga as taught to me in Berlin by my SS friend Hans. I could have rammed my fingers in his eyes or hit his genitals, but being only a weak woman I preferred the most expeditious and least risky method.

Jean-André Lavisse fell full length and began writhing about on the floor like an animal in its death throes. He was having difficulty in breathing, and was clutching his throat with both hands. His face was the colour of red brick. He was choking.

I didn't want to kill Jean-André Lavisse, or anyway not yet. I knelt down and bent over him in a compassionate manner. 'Are you all right, monsieur?'

By way of an answer he gave vent to a mixture of words and bubbles that told me nothing.

'You have taken all that I held most dear from me,' I murmured to him, 'my husband Gabriel Beaucaire and my children. Nothing can ever bring them back to me. I can't feel any better about it unless I make you suffer. That is my only way of relieving my own suffering a little.'

I took a Bible out of my handbag and read him several lines from the Book of Deuteronomy.

'The Lord shall smite thee with the boils of Egypt, and with the emerods, and with the scab, and with the itch, whereof thou canst not be healed.'

I got up, commenting, 'And there are plenty of other curses like that in the Bible. I find them fascinating.'

His face had turned purple; he was hardly breathing, but his mouth was wide open, like the mouth of a fish taken out of the water.

'Don't worry,' I said, kneeling down. 'I won't be as cruel as the Lord.'

I had intended to empty a bottle of hydrochloric acid over his nether parts, to respect the letter of the word of God concerning haemorrhoids, but no – that was too stupid, and would be complicated. I struck him a second and then a third blow on the throat with the edge of my hand, and Jean-André Lavisse died.

Suddenly I heard a mighty, ridiculous cry behind me. It came from the servant girl.

'Help! Help! Murder!'

She flung herself on me, barking, slavering and biting. It was like dealing with a mad dog. The noise she made roused the whole neighbourhood, and when I heard footsteps in the corridor leading to the study, I got to my feet and ran, as I did so knocking down a young man, no doubt Lavisse's son, who came running towards me. Next I collided with a woman who had a face like a bulldog – as I learned later, Lavisse's second wife, whom he had married a month after her predecessor's death.

She clung to my legs. I kicked her full in the face several times, and she finally let go, uttering a sound like a death rattle.

Quickening my pace, I made off in the direction of the Jardin du Luxembourg. I felt stifled. This wasn't a normal reaction to my vengeance, which ought to have lifted a weight from my mind. I put the sensation down to the trees, whose bare branches formed tall hedges with the wind whistling through them. The right setting for an assassination.

Once in the Rue Vaugirard, I began perspiring. I understood why when I drew level with the Church of St Sulpice; I had left my Bible in Jean-André Lavisse's apartment, thereby putting my signature to the crime.

The fly-leaf bore the inscription:

To my darling Rose
on her fifteenth birthday,
with all the love in the world.
Emma Lempereur

I decided to set off at once for the free zone of the country. I would go to Marseilles, and travel on from there to the United States. I had already lived through a great deal, but I was only thirty-six years old. There was no reason why I shouldn't embark on a new life.

44

A Trip to Trier

MARSEILLES, 2012. As I was finishing the last chapter, Samir the Mouse rang my doorbell long and hard.

'Rose, you're a grandmother!' he announced.

'What on earth are you talking about?'

'Your daughter Renate Fröll had a son. I got on his track at the primary school he used to attend in Aschaffenburg.'

'You're off your rocker!'

'You must stop denying everything, Rose, you're getting ridiculous.'

'Don't you talk to me like that. I'm not standing for it. Show a little respect, arsehole!'

At that word, lightning flashed in his eyes and he started trembling all over. Samir was a very sensitive soul. He seized my arm and shook it, crying, 'You'll apologize for that, you daft old biddy!'

'I'm too old for that sort of thing.'

'Apologize!'

He was twisting my arm, which was painful. 'Sorry,' I muttered.

He immediately came off his high horse. 'I managed to dig up all the basics; you had a daughter in Germany and she had a son. His name is Erwin.'

And Samir showed me a photo of Erwin Fröll at the age

of eighteen, when he failed his *Abitur*, the German school-leaving examination that tells you if your secondary-school education marks you out as a success or a failure.

Samir was lounging on my sofa, and I stayed on my feet to look at the photograph of my grandson by the light of the standard lamp. It showed a boy with black curly hair, and a face that immediately reminded me of Gabriel. That was absurd, but it's the truth. He had the same imperious nose, the same brow like Beethoven's, the same self-willed expression, the same irritating smile. I couldn't refrain from shedding a few tears, which made Samir smile. Suddenly I wanted to take Erwin in my arms as soon as possible.

'Where can I see him?' I asked.

'Well, I know where he is. In 2004 he went into an institution in Trier for people with neuronal problems.'

'Is he sick?'

'I don't know. I couldn't get access to his medical records, but he's very tired. That's what the girl on the switchboard told me when I asked to speak to him. I didn't understand a lot of what she was telling me, because we were talking in English, and hers was as bad as mine.'

I asked Samir for the phone number of the institution in Trier, which he had stored in his Contacts, and after tapping it in he handed me his mobile. The switchboard girl told me she couldn't put Erwin on the line because he was no longer in a fit state to talk.

'What's the matter with him?'

There was silence, and then she said, 'If you're a friend, or a member of the family, I advise you to come and see him soon.'

'You mean he's going to die?'

'I didn't say that. We're not authorized to give information on the health of our patients over the phone. On the other hand, if you come here you can see how he is for yourself.'

At the end of this conversation I had made my decision; I would close the restaurant for four days and we would leave for Trier the following evening: Samir, Mamadou and me.

*

Mamadou's car, an old Peugeot with 220,000 km on the clock, was very slow. We reached Trier early in the morning after a drive of almost fifteen hours, whereas according to the Internet it shouldn't have taken more than eight.

I knew that Trier, the oldest city in Germany, often called the second Rome, is also one of the most beautiful, but we hadn't come as tourists. I couldn't wait to see my grandson.

On the way, passing the vineyards protected from frost by the schist rock that keeps the Mosel valley warm, I felt like a glass of Riesling, but that could wait until later. I asked Mamadou to go and buy some, while Samir and I were visiting Erwin. When we got out of the car I was ashamed of the stale smell that came out of it with us, and at the same time sorry for the flowers and birds that had to put up with it until the wind blew it away.

The same stuffy atmosphere reigned in the hospital of the Peter Lambert Foundation, named after the famous local rose-grower, where Erwin was a patient. All the TV sets were on at full blast, as so often in such establishments. If you spend all your time watching television it means you're going to die. I don't know whether it's a case of cause and effect, but experience has taught me that this was the waiting-room for death.

Erwin Fröll was forty-nine years old, but I'd have taken him for over sixty. Apart from his nose and forehead, he had lost all resemblance to Gabriel. He had gone bald and was clean-shaven. The handsome boy in the photo was nothing but a wreck now, propped up on his bed with cushions under his arms, his hips and his legs to support his joints.

Like all the patients, he seemed to be watching television, but the film being shown went too fast for him. I turned the volume down, and he didn't object.

'Oh, there you are at last,' he said in a hesitant voice. 'Have you brought me my smile back?'

'What smile?' I asked.

'Mine. They say I don't have it any more.'

'Who said so?'

'Everyone.'

'Everyone can be wrong.'

'Someone keeps stealing my things. My smile. My car. My cat. My toothbrush. Lots of my things are disappearing.' He raised a reproachful forefinger. 'I want to know who took my smile away.'

Erwin was looking at me intently, and then, as if in a sudden moment of lucidity, he muttered, 'I like it when you're here, Mama. Why don't I see you more often?'

'Your mother's dead. I'm not your mother, I'm your grandmother.'

'Oh yes, like Waltraud.'

He gravely nodded his head, and commented in the tone of an oracle who has had a revelation, 'Grandmothers are like mothers but nicer, they're the only ones who really understand us. You've been a real grandmother to me, Mama. Like Waltraud.'

This exchange seemed to have exhausted him for the rest of the day. He went to sleep at once, and I told myself I was never going to get any more out of him, which the aforesaid Waltraud confirmed. She was the head nurse on this floor of the hospital. She told me in confidence that Erwin had already passed the average duration of the terminal stage of Alzheimer's disease by several months, and that after ten years spent developing the illness, patients seldom survive more than another two years.

Erwin had arrived at the Peter Lambert Foundation hospital eight years earlier, and hadn't had any visits since, except one from his mother, who had died from cancer of the stomach several weeks ago, just after her research had come up with the name of her own mother, me. But her pathological timidity had kept her from getting in touch.

Waltraud also told me that Erwin had had various jobs – as a pork butcher, a plasterer, a grocer, a warehouseman, a house painter – before becoming one of the professionally unemployed in his late thirties. 'Society hasn't lost much,' she summed him up. 'He was very lazy and glib.'

Next day, as the car was approaching Marseilles with its boot full of Mosel wine made from the Riesling grape, Samir the Mouse, sitting in the front passenger seat, turned to me. I was lying on the back seat with my legs in the air and my head on a pillow.

'I picked up some souvenirs in Erwin's room,' he said.
'You didn't!'

He smiled, and brought out of his travelling bag a plastic figurine of Karl Marx, born in Trier at 10 Brückenstrasse, a fan and an eggshell with his picture on them, his *Manifesto of the Communist Party*, and two books by Rosa Luxembourg, *Reform or Revolution* and *The Crisis of Social Democracy*.

Relieved to find that Samir hadn't been stealing money, I smiled too, and then I burped, a Riesling-scented burp dating from yesterday evening. Everyone burst out laughing, me first of all.

'There's still one thing I don't know,' I said. 'Who sent me Renate Fröll's death notice?'

'There's no magic about that,' he replied. 'It just takes a little common sense. Since the Red Cross opened its archives a few years ago, anyone can get access to the Lebensborn files to find out the names of their parents. Your daughter Renate found your name, but for some reason that I don't know – maybe her illness, maybe something else – she didn't look for your address.'

'How do you know?'

'If she had, she'd have been in touch. She did give your name to someone before she died, I should think that head nurse, who found you on the Internet.'

'I'll go back to Trier to talk to that Waltraud.'

'I don't think that would be a good idea. Contrary to what I thought, this journey hasn't done you any good, Rose. You should rest.'

'He's right,' agreed Mamadou behind the wheel, without turning his head.

'I was glad to see my grandson,' I said. 'But I'm sorry to have arrived too late.'

'Don't indulge in regrets,' Samir interrupted me. 'When you don't much like your past, it's best to avoid looking back. Better just continue on your way.'

'Especially when I only leave dead people behind me,' I said in a low voice.

For once, the look that Samir gave me was so kind that I almost burst into tears. I felt helpless.

Now that my grandson was on the point of death, Samir and Mamadou were my only family. I wanted to tell them so, but the words wouldn't come.

I still hadn't found them when we arrived in Marseilles just as night had fallen. The horizon was covered with blood-coloured splashes, like a slaughterhouse. I don't like dusk. It's as if it drew my life out of my mouth. The world is not well made; the sun always goes down when we need it most.

45

Simone, Nelson and Me

NEW YORK, 1943. Paul Chassagnon bought the business of La Petite Provence from me, using the savings he had built up while I was away, so I arrived in the United States with a nice little nest egg. I had sewn the banknotes into the lining of my coat.

Thanks to an Armenian mutual-aid association, I immediately found work cooking in a little restaurant on 44th Street, near the Algonquin Hotel and not far from Times Square. I slept there too, in the basement. I don't think I ever worked so hard in my life.

It wasn't so much the work that bothered me as the mingled smells of sugar, meat, onions and hot oil, the four typical odours of New York. I lived in them all day and took them to my sleeping bag with me at night. I often felt like vomiting myself up.

Since the restaurant closed only on Sunday afternoons, there wasn't much going on in my personal life. My one weekly outing was to Mass on Sunday at St Patrick's Cathedral on Fifth Avenue, a building that was all marble and gold.

After several months, I changed my place of worship to St Thomas's Church, a little further down the same avenue. The atmosphere there was so sombre and cheerless that, but for its magnificent altarpiece featuring the twelve apostles as well as such figures as George Washington and the former British prime minister William Gladstone, it would have depressed the most sanguine of Catholics, but I prefer the Christian tradition that dwells on suffering to the worship of the Golden Calf, as symbolized to the point of caricature by St Patrick's.

I had come back from Germany more of a believer than ever before. I regularly went to church to ask Jesus and the Virgin Mary for news of my family, who were now in heaven with them. Apparently that news was good. If the dead aren't necessarily happier up there, they don't get as tired as the living here below. They don't have to struggle, they have time to themselves.

In fine weather I used to go and eat a sandwich in Central Park after Mass and before getting back to work. I liked to watch the squirrels running about on the grass, before searching it for an acorn. They shelled the acorns with their childlike little paws, happily waving their feather dusters of tails.

It was in Central Park that I met the man who was going to give me a new chance. He was a business rep for a company that made toothpaste and shaving foam. He was about fifty, with a paunch, a tiny moustache and an air of bovine melancholy. His name was Frankie Robarts, and he wanted to open a restaurant in Chicago.

I decided to throw in my lot with his that same day when, after trying out my cookery at the greasy spoon on 44th Street, he suggested going into business together. America is a country where you never stop embarking on a new life until you die. That's why it has come to think itself eternal, which is the nation's weakness but also its strength.

*

Frankie and I called our restaurant in Chicago Frenchy's. The first few months were difficult; my Provençal cuisine didn't go down well with the customers, and we lived from hand to mouth. However, once I began specializing in hamburgers our little establishment looking out on the lake took off.

Customers came flocking to Frenchy's as soon as it began smelling of death, by which I mean grilled meat. My vegetarianism didn't go well with that dreadful odour. As I couldn't get used to it, I realized that I could never become an American.

The Americans are a carnivorous society, and need to eat their fill of rare, red meat. They are fuelled by ground steak just as others are fuelled by hope or sex. I felt I was living in sin the whole time. I even stank of sin.

At Frenchy's the customer could order the ingredients for his own hamburger: with herbs, spices, pine kernels, oat flakes, mozzarella, grated gruyère, onions, peppers, tomato, aubergines, spinach, diced pineapple, you could have anything you liked. As accompaniments I had devised several sauces – mustard, blue cheese, garlic or dill – all of them heavily sweetened.

I also made the best strawberry shortcake in Chicago. I had rechristened it in French on the menu, as *Tarte aux fraises à l'américaine*, and it was even more popular than my famous caramel flan, which I couldn't bring myself to sweeten even more in conformity with the local taste.

I liked to have a man in my bed in those days. Frankie Robarts wasn't much of a performer, and he snored into the bargain. Not to mention that his belly, behind and thighs seemed to be made of some gelatinous substance, which gave me the feeling that I was swimming in porridge when we made love.

We had just one thing in common, the restaurant, and that was enough to provide us with material for conversation. When we changed the subject, Frankie soon became tedious, resorting to empty phrases as if he feared to take risks by showing what he was really like.

He was always in control of himself, and if I put up with Frankie in spite of everything, it was because he admired my culinary skills and adored my breasts and my bottom. Boring as he was, he was a good antidote to my troubles. He was always saying that I was the only family he had, and the same was true the other way around. At the end of a year living together, I agreed to marry him.

All the same, I looked elsewhere. I had resumed my habit of going round the dining room at the end of service, and from time to time I met customers whom I liked, but I never ventured to cross the line by responding to their advances. I was like those people who look for a chance to leave the conjugal hearth but take to flight when they find one.

I told myself that I was dead to love. Two years passed before, one winter evening in 1946, I stopped, fascinated, in front of a man with a saturnine expression; you couldn't tell, from looking at him, whether he was an artist or a manual labourer. Such men are found only in America and Russia: writers with the shoulders of woodcutters who seem to have only just emerged from cutting down trees in the forest.

His name was Nelson Algren, he was a boxer, a gambler, a drunk, a communist and in addition a novelist, already the author of a book that had attracted a lot of attention, *Never Come Morning*. I knew at once that he was both violent and romantic; there was an anger that I couldn't wait to taste in this man who had plumbed the depths. He would be the storm and I the earth that nourished him. I longed for him to ravage me, and felt the urgency of it like an insect bite that was assuaged only on the day when we consummated our attraction.

The first time I saw him, he was dining with a self-styled actress whose hair was done like Vivien Leigh's in *Gone with the Wind*, which had gone on release in the States four years earlier. She was unable to string two sentences together, whether from stupidity or shyness I don't know, but the result was the same. When he heard that I was French, Nelson Algren asked how I could have left France for a rat-hole like Chicago.

'The war,' I said. 'The war was like an air raid, with the blast sending bodies and inanimate objects flying through the air to unforeseen places.'

I saw that he thought my reply interesting, and that for a moment he considered continuing our conversation along those lines, but instead he asked what I most regretted after leaving France.

'Nothing,' I said.

'That's impossible!'

'If I go back to Paris I know that I'll never stop shedding tears.'

'I don't believe you.'

'I don't want to go back to where the dead people in my life once lived. I could never live again myself among them.'

'And you don't want to try?'

'I like life too much. Why spoil it?'

He repeated what I had said, and then remarked, 'That's good. Everything you say is good. Will you let me put you into a novel some day?'

'I'd be extremely flattered.'

I wasn't stupid, and was able to check later that he often used that line with women. Unlike many writers, he was a professional seducer.

He came back to dine at Frenchy's the next day with a different girl, a floozy with bleached hair, and left me his phone number on a scrap of yellow paper. I called him the following morning, and went to visit him in his two-roomed apartment in the north of Chicago. I was thirty-nine years old, and I was anxious to waste no time.

When he opened the door I planted my mouth on his so firmly that he almost fell over backwards. After getting his balance back, and as we went on kissing, he led me to his bed, where we made love.

After that we lay there side by side for quarter of an hour, before I decided to clean out Nelson's lair, which was repulsively dirty and full of corpses in the form of empty bottles.

I went to his place two or three times a week, always after giving him notice of my arrival. Under the influence of love, my looks were visibly improving. I told my husband that I was going to see a supplier for the restaurant, or I had a dentist's appointment, and he was completely fooled. His credulity made my guilty conscience so much worse that it preyed on my mind, particularly when we were in action, and if I took my eyes off Nelson's glazed expression in mid-orgasm I imagined that I saw Frankie's devastated look in the dim light. By concentrating hard, I am sure that behind Frankie I could also have seen the faces of Gabriel, Édouard, Garance, Papa, Mama and all the others.

What were they doing here? Why, whenever I allowed myself pleasure, did I always have to see those who were dead and gone from my life? After all, I wasn't doing harm to anyone else by doing some good to myself.

One afternoon early in 1947 I phoned to let Nelson know I was on my way, but he asked me not to come to his place this time. 'I have someone here.'

It was Simone de Beauvoir, who was on a lecture tour of the States. When Nelson brought her to dine at the restaurant on the following evening, she and I fell into one another's arms. She smelled of alcohol, cigarettes and other odours that I will not describe, but that I had known in her before.

Nelson had given her pleasure too, or at least more of it than Sartre. I had never seen her so beautiful and radiant.

I stayed at their table until closing time. At a certain moment, the conversation turned to the United States, where according to the two of them the situation was becoming 'revolutionary' because of the impoverishment of the working class. The tone became increasingly heated as they egged each other on, and I thought it was dreadful. Only cultivated and talented people can say such silly things with the authority of conviction.

'The Americans don't seem so very unhappy in spite of those difficulties,' I protested. 'I don't see why they would want a different form of government.'

'Surely you won't deny that great changes are taking place in Russia and China?' said Nelson indignantly. 'You can't remain blind to the future of humanity!'

'That kind of government can't bring happiness. I shall never believe in such trifles.'

'Well, what can bring happiness, then?'

'It comes from ourselves. What's more, I like the life here.'

'Because you don't take the time to think,' sighed Nelson scornfully. 'You've been alienated by the capitalist system, totally alienated!'

Simone was drinking in Nelson's words; speaking of alienation, Sartre would have said, so much love is what comes of it. In spite of all that has been said of Simone, she never merely lent, but gave herself fully. I often wondered, later, whether it wasn't the men in her life who made her always see the world askew.

That evening her pupils were dilated. You only had to see the look in them to know that my former lover had dethroned Sartre and was going to be the man of her life, at least for a while.

I may as well tell you that long afterwards, I was not surprised to hear that yes, she wanted to be buried beside Sartre, but wearing the ring that Nelson had given her. After the break between them, they hated each other so much that I am sure they were still in love.

The two lovers fell into the habit of eating at Frenchy's over the following days. I liked their love; it didn't take anything away from me. On the contrary, my own relationship with Frankie, which had to some extent been shaken by my adventure with Nelson, came out of it stronger than before.

When Simone returned to the other side of the Atlantic, Nelson went on visiting the restaurant, but not so often and always with girls. I feared for the love between him and Simone, which seemed beyond human measure, and I feared for it even more when, on a day when he was alone and wanted to talk, he took a letter dated 14 January 1950 out of his wallet, and I read:

'Oh, Nelson, I will be good, I will be wise, just wait and see. I'll scrub the floor, I'll cook all your meals, I'll write your book at the same time as my own, I'll make love to you ten times a night and as many times again in the day, even though I may find it a little tiring...'

I still remember Nelson's smile when I gave him back the letter. It was the smile of an animal-tamer who has got the better of a wild beast.

'Being a feminist makes her no less of a woman,' he said, stroking his arms.

Some time later, after dining at Frenchy's with two journalists who had a conspiratorial air about them, Nelson stayed behind for a little while and opened his heart to me. He thought that Simone de Beauvoir was two women at the same time, the lover and the feminist. The woman in love and the woman of intellect. He wasn't asking her to tear up her roots and commit spiritual suicide. He only wanted to build something with her: surely to want a home and a child together wasn't too much to ask? But apparently she wouldn't hear of it.

I didn't resume my relationship with Nelson. It certainly was not that I didn't want to, but he didn't share my feelings. No doubt I had broadened out too much for him, particularly my pelvis and my legs. Perhaps, too, he was afraid I would talk to Simone about us some day. In the years that followed my conduct was exemplary, as if I were in search of forgiveness for the sins of which my husband had hardly any idea. I didn't have to force myself to behave well; I was getting a taste for the routine of our lives as successful restaurateurs. It was reassuring. Our future was the past that kept beginning again.

Frankie had grown very fat. At that time, such was the effect of success. He weighed well above a hundred kilos now, and we hadn't been able to make love in the missionary position for a long time; I'd have lost my life in the attempt.

Chicago is a city of extremes. Sometimes it's like Greenland, sometimes like the tropics. 'The climate here goes too far,' Frankie liked to say. It was always either too cold or too hot. Sometimes everything seemed to be simmering as if in one of my pans, and the fish rose ready-cooked to the surface of Lake Michigan before rotting on the fine sand of the beaches.

'Welcome to the Dead Fish Sea,' was a local joke. But it wasn't as funny as all that; there were days when the smell was a nuisance to our customers.

My husband didn't stand up to a heatwave any better than the fish of Lake Michigan. When such weather descended on us, he was soaked like a sponge and running with sweat. I dreaded those times, which could condemn me to two months of sexual abstinence. Every night a terrible thing happened... to wit, nothing.

On 2 July 1955, as the sun was beginning to beat savagely down on the earth, Frankie Robarts finally breathed his last. He died on duty in the restaurant, of a heart attack set off by a cerebrovascular accident while he was serving a hamburger to a female customer. As he fell, he knocked her over on the banquette where she was sitting, and she emerged with tomato sauce all over her face.

A few days later, I received a letter of condolences from Simone de Beauvoir. Nelson Algren had told her the news of my husband's death. She suggested, as a change of scene for me, that I should join her and Jean-Paul Sartre when they set off on a journey to China in the autumn. 'All expenses paid,' she added. They would tell the Chinese authorities that I was their secretary.

I sold the restaurant, and found out how to join them in Peking going by way of Moscow. I didn't want to set foot on French soil again.

46

The Second Man in My Life

PEKING, 1955. When I reached Peking I immediately liked the Chinese, down-to-earth people who will go to endless trouble for you. They are like Americans, but without the big, toothy smile, or the tendency to putting on weight through excessive consumption of sugar and animal fats; in my humble opinion, since they walk faster they will inevitably go a great deal further.

I was forty-eight, it was time for me to find a sister soul, one who could relight the sun that had always, even at night, illuminated my inner being, until the last spark of it had gone out with the death of Frankie Robarts.

The Sartre–Beauvoir couple being what they were, I could have let him tempt me, as he did a dozen years earlier in La Petite Provence. I even had an idea that Simone would not have been averse to that. But fascinating as he was, Sartre the intellectual, with his toadlike head and gap teeth, was not my type. I couldn't stand his forced smile – you'd have thought he was positively pushing it out. Moreover, his steely voice always reminded me of a pebble screeching on glass. Finally, he often suffered from the venomous nastiness that is characteristic of certain ungainly people, and is expressed in their breath; his smelled of bitterness as well as tobacco and alcohol.

It was ages since Simone had had anything to do with him physically, and I will say in passing that I understood her. After her liaison with Nelson Algren, she spent a lot of time in the company of Claude Lanzmann, a very handsome young man – not that I ever saw him, but she spoke of him with emotion, and when she did so her face wore the transfigured look of a woman who is loved.

The best thing about Sartre was Beauvoir. What would he have been without her? A peremptory weathervane, a poor writer; in fact, nothing much. It was she who created his legend.

We went all over China for six weeks, from Peking to Shanghai and from Canton to Nankin, but as Sartre said much later, when he had recovered his lucidity, 'We saw a great many things, but nothing that really mattered.' It was all official, even the asides, and I shall never forget the migraines I suffered when the apparatchiks inflicted on us those speeches in which they took the utmost care to say nothing at all. I felt sorry for them.

Sartre and Beauvoir noticed none of this. So long as their hosts bowed and scraped, they were perfectly happy. You might have thought them a couple of blind and deaf peacocks strutting about in a poultry yard.

I shall never tire of repeating what, for me, has been one of the great lessons of my life: no one is as stupid as the intelligentsia. You have only to flatter their egos and you can manipulate them as you like. Since credulity and vanity go hand in hand, they feed on each other, even in the greatest minds, as I had plenty of chances to see throughout this trip.

While Simone took notes for what was to be her worst book, *The Long March*, an essay on China that she published in 1957, I was scribbling phrases that inspired me during our travels in an exercise book.

'Man works, Chinese men work even harder.'

'You can caress an intellectual with your hand but not a poor man. He is too battered; caresses hurt him.'

'Communism is a system which fails to understand that, to make others happy, all you have to do is leave them alone in front of a fine landscape.'

It was on the eve of our departure that I fell in love with a Chinese Communist. I felt much the same as when I met Gabriel: a seismic tremor going down my back, a kind of faintness and a strong wish to urinate. The first time we exchanged glances, I knew I would live with him for the rest of my life, or at least as long as my love lasted.

His name was Liu Zhongling. He was a widower and twelve years younger than me. When I try to decode what I loved most about him I don't know where to begin; he was so perfect, from head to foot, with his almond eyes, his lips that were good enough to eat, his clever, muscular tongue, all the way to his shapely toes, which I never tired of sucking. He was a delicious man, and when I think of him I'm not ashamed to say that my mouth still waters.

I must also mention the smell of him in the evening, when we met. It was slightly musky, with the scent of autumn flowers, moist wood and marc, the spirit distilled from grape must.

His mind was as good as the rest. Liu was a guide, a translator, a political commissioner, all of that. On our return from a mission to the north of the country, he had been assigned to us for our last day in Peking, in particular to explain to Sartre and Beauvoir that President Mao couldn't receive them. They were very sorry about that.

Commandeering me after the farewell reception, Liu declared his love for me in perfect French. 'I don't know how to say this to you, I don't understand what's happening to me and you will think me a fool, but forgive me if I say that I can't imagine my life without you.'

'I feel the same about you,' I replied without hesitation.

Our conversation concluded in my bedroom where, without more ado, Liu wreaked such havoc with me that at the end of an hour I felt as if I had been ravaged by a whole army of ardent lovers. He was both exhausting and inexhaustible in bed.

With him, I could do nothing but abandon myself as if I were adrift in a storm-tossed sea. During all the years I spent with him I was covered with bruises, pinches and love-bites, which I proudly displayed like badges of honour. Not to mention the aches that I suffered.

After making love, Liu talked to me about literature, more particularly about Stendhal, whose work he seemed to know inside out. Although he was far from being pedantically proud of his knowledge, I realized the full extent of my ignorance.

I remember how he quoted a phrase that, he said, was typical of Stendhal, and occurred in *The Life of Henry Brulard*, which to this day I haven't read:

'To me, love has always been the main if not the only business of life.'

After making love to me for a second time, he told me that he had found the solution that would allow us to live together in spite of the difficulty of the situation. He would ask the Albanian ambassador to China, who was a friend of his, to engage me as a cook.

Next day I saw Sartre and Beauvoir off on their return to Paris. Simone understood why I was staying behind. At the airport, to which I had accompanied them, she came close to me and whispered in my ear, 'Liu?'

I nodded.

'I understand you,' she said quietly. 'A very handsome man. When love is in the air, it's no use hesitating and waiting until it comes your way again. Take it when it offers itself, and don't let it go.' Simone lowered her voice even further. 'If I may give you some advice, you should never put yourself in a position where you make a decision only to regret it to the end of your days. I think there can be nothing worse.'

Simone's advice on the emotional aspects of life was good, as I could tell much later from those books of hers that I devoured, and would like to re-read one last time before I die: *The Second Sex, The Mandarins* and *Memoirs of a Dutiful Daughter*. When she wrote on other subjects, notably politics, she got them exceptionally wrong. Moving straight from the constraints of the bourgeoisie to those of the world of intellectuals, her mind was too rigid to let her think straight. Her rigidity accounted for her attitude.

As for Sartre, her evil genius, he had no such excuse apart from the extraordinary intelligence that induced him to indulge in the most idiotic actions; such was his self-confidence in believing, for instance, that he would always fall on his feet, which as a matter of fact he did when you think how wrong he was about everything. Short-sighted in the case of the Nazi regime, since he failed to see its satanic aspect during his visit to Germany during the academic year of 1933–1934. Craven towards the Vichy government, which he opposed only at the last minute, although when the Liberation came, that didn't prevent him making himself out a member of the Resistance from the first. Blind to the nature of Communism, which he praised under Stalin, of the revolutions of the Third World, which he supported frenetically, and of the Left itself – he wallowed in left-wing ideas to the end of his life.

Never mind if he was always getting things wrong, so long as he featured in the photograph, preferably with Simone de Beauvoir, who was distinction itself. It didn't matter that his political line regularly led him in the wrong direction; he went the opposite way at once, and his followers went after him, cackling like so many chickens. His status authorized him to go astray. If you wanted permission to do that in those days, all you needed was to be on the right side – his side.

47

The Homing Pigeon

PEKING, 1958. Liu Zhongling often met Mao Tse-tung (height 1.80 metres) and Deng Xiaoping (height 1.50 metres), but it took me months to work out his precise function in the structure of the Chinese Communist Party. With his height of 1.65 metres, he came somewhere between the two of them.

At the beginning of our relationship he would change the subject whenever I tried to talk politics with him. I soon realized that one of his concerns was not to let too deep a rift appear between us.

For a long time, the new man in my life kept everything in separate compartments. He never gave himself away. No doubt he even avoided thinking in my presence, for fear that I might read his thoughts, and our relationship was so close – I was him, he was me – that in fact I would have been able to do so.

I could suffer agonies when Liu had toothache; I could howl in pain when he burned his hand on the lid of a pan. If we had a cold or flu we always did so together. From morning to evening we were the same person, before changing ourselves into the beast with two backs at night.

He travelled around a great deal. When Liu was in Peking, he seldom spent a whole day with me; he was too busy. Today, I have only to close my eyes to recall our occasional walks in the Peking parks, or in the *hutongs*, the old parts of the city with their narrow streets, where you had to walk between hedges of linen hung out to dry.

I liked Peking in all weathers, including those times when the sky seemed to have fallen to earth, and we walked in the midst of clouds through a pea-souper of a fog. But I feel nostalgia mainly when I remember our nights in my attic room at the Albanian Embassy. I feel a kind of internal bleeding in my body as I write these lines.

We never spent a whole night together without making love at least once. I can tell you, it made a change from Frankie Robarts. I wrote it all down in a little notebook that I carried round with me; in thirteen years, he gave me 4,263 orgasms. His vitality went together with an acute sense of hearing and close attention that would have reconciled the most anti-phallocratic of feminists to the masculine sex.

It is true that Liu never banished Gabriel from my memory, or even ousted him from it, but he has his place in it, and a large one. Even now, when my dear departed loved ones crowd into my head, where there isn't room for all of them at once, I think of him several times a day. When I open the window to let in fresh air, I remember how that was the first thing he did in the morning. When I dip my hard-boiled egg, cut in half, in soy sauce, I remember how he liked to do that at breakfast.

The Albanian embassy was short of money, and my work there was both thankless and tiresome. Matters didn't improve even when Albania fell into line behind China after Nikita Khrushchev's report on the crimes of Stalin at the Twenty-second Congress of the Communist Party of the Soviet Union in 1956.

His Excellency Mehmet Artor was an old bachelor, formerly a teacher of French in Tirana and a distant cousin of Enver Hoxha, the pocket Stalin of Albania. He always wanted to eat Albanian food, particularly goulash, chicken with walnuts, vegetable pie and vine-leaves stuffed with rice. He was irritable if I didn't have his buttermilk ready, or I hadn't prepared *boza*, a fermented and slightly alcoholic beverage based on wheat, maize and sugar, to which powdered vanilla might be added. I was in his bad books if there wasn't a plate of baklava with honey and almonds ready for him at the end of his lunch or dinner. He consumed immoderate quantities of these pastries, as witness the size of his belly.

Getting hold of the ingredients for these dishes was a nightmare, and it wasn't unusual for me to have no honey, cereals or vegetables in stock for weeks on end, whereupon His Excellency would take his bad temper out on me before blaming the malfunctioning of the Chinese government. His faith in Maoism seemed to vary according to what he found on his plate.

Just now that wasn't much. The reason was the policy of the Great Leap Forward, launched by Mao Tse-tung in 1958 to speed up progress towards Communism, particularly in the countryside, which was subjected to a crazy programme of collectivization going hand in hand with a struggle against right-wing deviation. The result was to starve the rural areas down to the most remote villages, bleeding them dry. 'Permanent revolution' was Mao Tse-tung's way of mounting a counter-attack against his critics at home, after several political grandees such as Zhou Enlai and Liu Shaoqi had called the left-wing 'adventurism' of his policy into question. So they claimed that the president was going too fast, did they? Too bad; he would go even faster.

As I never left the Albanian embassy on my own except to go shopping, I had no idea of the disaster being perpetuated by Mao Tse-tung's policies. All the same, it soon struck me that something was wrong; however often I went the rounds of the markets, the stalls were all but empty. I often came back with sweet potatoes or pak choi, Chinese cabbage, sometimes with dog cutlets, but I found less and less to put in His Excellency's soup, and he cut a sorry figure as he sat down to dine.

The more drastic the situation became, the more Mehmet Artor clung to the doctrines of Marxism–Leninism that the Chinese Communists had been unable to implement. The ambassador put the food shortages down to obscure conspiracies on the part of the bourgeoisie and capitalism.

'They're starving us to turn us against Communism,' grumbled Mehmet Artor as he tapped the table with the handle of his knife. 'They only have to be eliminated and everything would be so much better. My cousin Enver would do it in no time.'

It was now that Liu began talking to me about his activities and expressing his doubts. Formerly the best friend of Mao's eldest son, Anying, who had died under fire in 1950 during the Korean War, he had access to the presidency. But above all, he was one of the right-hand men of Deng Xiaoping, General Secretary of the Communist Party, who was more and more hostile to the folly of the Great Leap Forward, even if he didn't say so in public. Liu carried his messages and warned him of the plots being hatched against him. He called himself a 'homing pigeon'.

The disorganization of the agricultural sector led to famines that, for three years running, ravaged most of the provinces, from Sichuan to Henan, from Anhui to Gansu. It was the same as in Stalin's time; Mao's Communism was wiping out the peasants by cutting off their provisions, in a kind of genocide that according to experts rose to 33–70 million dead.

There was no getting away from it: if capitalism was the exploitation of man by man, communism was the other way round but worse.

The people of the Chinese countryside had been eating anything and everything for several seasons. Leaves, weeds, the corpses of human beings who had died of starvation, in particular children, who could end up in their parents' digestive systems. As for the local wildlife, it had almost disappeared from the country.

I had a beautiful Chinese cat, whose fine features and piercing eyes reminded me of Liu, so much so that I called him Liu the Second. He often went exploring the neighbouring gardens. One day he disappeared, and must have ended up as meatballs or in soup. Even sparrows were beginning to be a rare sight in the sky above Peking, and the silence of death reigned in the city. The flesh of small birds featured in all meat dishes, including my goulash once I had removed the bones from their small carcasses in case they stuck in His Excellency's throat, but they were not nourishing fare.

I often think of all those Western intellectuals, writers and ministers who were so enthusiastic at that time about Maoism, and whom Liu showed around so that they could admire the achievements of the regime. All they saw was fire. During all those years they filled newspapers and books with the stupid things they said and their abject servility. I know some who are still full of it as they hold forth on other subjects, having swallowed their shame.

I accuse all those outspoken arse-lickers of moral corruption, complicity in murder, failing to assist persons in danger and, at the best, of blindness and stupidity leading to death, if without actually intending to deliver it.

'President Mao is sleeping very poorly,' Liu told me one day in the serious tone one usually reserves for important news.

'Listen, Liu, that's the least of it after all the bad things he's done. It shows he still has a conscience.'

'Mao has never been a sound sleeper. That's why he often gets up very late, but this time it gives real cause for concern, and he has severe headaches more and more often. What's more, he refuses to eat meat out of solidarity with his people. That will make him weaker than ever.'

'Far from it,' I protested. 'He'll be in better health, and that will allow him to digest his food and the misfortunes of his people better.'

Liu did not react to this. After I had asked him whether Mao had terrible bad breath like Hitler's, I could not have the slightest faith in his reply, which seemed to come from an official bulletin.

'The general opinion is that President Mao's breath smells very good.'

'Wonderful,' I said. 'And does he smell good all over?'

'All over.'

I laughed, and so did Liu. He never lost his sense of humour, even when the ground was giving way beneath his feet.

*

One night when we were pleasuring each other, Liu almost strangled me. It was my fault; I had asked him to squeeze my neck while he was fucking me, and he had followed my instructions so well that my eyes began turning up.

I had hardly recovered before he asked me to marry him. I was now fifty-nine years old, and he was still twelve years younger than me. If I wanted to change my name again, it was now or never. I preferred his to Robarts, the surname I still bore.

Liu, who could go anywhere he liked, managed to get special permission. That is why my surname has been Zhongling ever since. Marriage changed nothing between Liu and me. We went on working like Trojans, and enjoying ourselves when we had time for it. His Excellency's state of health was gradually deteriorating, and I had become his nurse as well as his cook.

Mehmet Artor, who suffered from a paralysingly painful slipped disc, could no longer move around except in a wheelchair, and for want of staff it was I who pushed him about in it. He was grateful, and thanks to his connections he got me a diplomatic passport. I hadn't asked him for it, but it was soon to be very useful to me, when the Great Leap Forward was followed by disaster.

It was always when you thought Mao Tse-tung was done for that he rose from his ashes again. Always on the move, this master of political tactics never forgot to answer the discontent of the country by blaming his rivals in the Party for his own setbacks. To draw a veil over the failure of the Great Leap Forward and bring his team to heel, for once again there were latent protests, the President of China thought up the Great Cultural Revolution. It was a kind of popular coup d'état aimed at, among others, Deng Xiaoping, my husband's spiritual godfather, although he was a very prudent man, and once again he outmanoeuvred the fault-finders and protestors among the elite.

On 16 May 1966, in a text that Liu translated for me, adding comments – his hands were trembling – an enlarged meeting of the Politburo was held, at which Mao attacked the representatives of the bourgeoisie who, he said, had hypocritically infiltrated the Party, the government and the army. When the conditions were right, said the Chinese president, these 'counter-revolutionary revisionists' had meant to seize power and 'replace dictatorship by the proletariat with dictatorship by the bourgeoisie.' That was why he was calling on the people to pass judgment on them without delay, beginning with his intended successor Liu Shaoqi, who according to my husband was 'a good and just man... a humane specimen of humanity,' he added, proud of his phrasing.

'I don't know what will happen now,' Liu told me, 'but

I think we shouldn't see each other so often, or perhaps at all. I don't want to expose you to misfortune or compromise you.'

'But I am your wife,' I replied. 'I want to share everything with you.'

'From now on, I shall be fighting a life-or-death battle for my ideas. I am sorry, Rose, but this isn't your battle or your story. If anything unfortunate happens to me, I shall need you to survive me so that, after my death, something of our love will be left in the world. Can you understand that?'

My husband had a good way with words. With tears in my eyes and swallowing my sobs, I made him promise to call at the embassy from time to time bringing news, and for another purpose on which I need not dwell. He said he would, but nothing came of it. I did not see him for a year and a half.

Deng Xiaoping was exiled, Liu Shaoqi was imprisoned; the ex-future successor of Mao died of neglect long afterwards in 1969, in his prison in Kaifeng. As for my husband, he was killed in Canton by Red Guards wielding iron bars. It seems that he fought like a lion, injuring several of his assailants.

On 2 February 1968, when Mehmet Artor told me the news of Liu's death, of which he had learnt from someone high up in the state, I was in despair. I immediately thought of leaving the embassy at once to kill one or more Red Guards in the street. I had no doubt of my skill at krav maga, but I was afraid I would be arrested as soon as I had achieved my purpose. Fortunately the Albanian ambassador nipped my foolhardy idea in the bud.

'This country is going mad,' said Mehmet Artor. 'We must leave.'

'I want to see Liu's body. I want to see him, kiss him and bury him.'

'You mustn't even think of it. Your husband died over three weeks ago and is already underground, no one knows where. There's no time to lose. We must go as fast as possible.'

We flew to Albania next day.

In the plane I began to devise another project: I would avenge Liu's death with the blood of some great French intellectual who had shown sympathy with the ideas of Mao Tse-tung. Jean-Paul Sartre seemed to be a prime candidate, but I rejected that notion for fear of causing Simone de Beauvoir pain. A few weeks later, when I was back in France, I realized that I had a very wide choice.

48

A Ghost from the Past

MARSEILLES, 1969. All roads, for me, lead to Marseilles. Just as it was in 1917 when I was first there, the city was extraordinarily dirty. Criss-crossed in all directions by rats, beggars, pickpockets and people gleaning from dustbins, it was still cheerful, putting all and sundry in their places, and amidst all this confusion I immediately felt at home. I rented a two-roomed apartment in the shade of the Cathedral of St Victor.

I had added the names of several intellectuals to the list of my hates, and my choice finally fell on Louis Althusser, one of the bigwigs of Saint-Germain-des-Prés, whose career had followed a perfectly logical course: a Stalinist, a Maoist and then a lunatic. He didn't have the courage to kill himself, but later he strangled his wife.

It was lucky for Louis Althusser that I was in Marseilles, where I soon abandoned my plan, carried away by the laughter of the city, which has the right idea about everything. With the proceeds from the sale of Frenchy's, which I had kept in reserve while I was in China, I had bought a restaurant on the Quai des Belges in the Vieux-Port district. It could seat twenty-four, and had a little terrace. I stupidly called it La Petite Provence, like its predecessor in Paris – stupidly because I didn't stop to think what trouble that might make for me some day.

My restaurant soon became very popular. I did everything except the housework, for which I had hired Kady, a young woman of twenty-three from Mali, who had no papers, no complexes and no underclothes. As soon as I set eyes on her, I dreamed of undressing her, which I did that very evening before we got between the sheets together. After knowing so many men I had decided, once past sixty, to change to women, and this one suited me nicely.

I was her first woman, and her last too. In the small hours she said, with a wide smile, 'Better fantastic than never.'

That was her kind of humour. She had an Afro hairstyle like Angela Davis, the famous activist whom all the boys loved, and she said her ancestors had been princes in Africa. Kady liked telling lies, but I didn't mind that so long as it didn't interfere with her work. And she was so graceful that I could forgive her anything. I wanted to kiss her all the time, and I did too, before or after we served the customers. When it came to using my skills to make her wriggle with pleasure, I waited until we were in my apartment and between four walls so that her chuckles and yells were muffled, discretion not being up her street. I was bowled over by her temperament.

She had me in a spin. I was carried away by her sensual voice, tinged with irony, her throat dancing against my neck; the way that her breasts quivered when she spoke, and her full lips that always seemed to be in search of something to bite or eat. I tried to give her what she wanted. Love, of course, but also warmth, security, protection, understanding and constant attention. All that a woman needs.

However, there was one thing she lacked. One day, when we were buying live sea bream from our usual fisherman, a bearded neurasthenic with greasy hair who had his stall on the quay opposite the restaurant, Kady told me in a firm voice, 'I want a baby.'

I didn't see what that had to do with the poor fish who were flailing about pathetically in the bag where I had just put them. After a moment of stunned amazement, the fisherman assumed a half-surprised, half-ribald expression as his eyes went from Kady to me and back again.

I didn't know what to say. Kady repeated, raising her voice even more, 'I want a baby.'

'Yes, all right, all right,' I replied with an embarrassed grimace, to close the incident. When we got back to the restaurant we hadn't opened our mouths. It's true that I had my hands occupied with my bag full of fish gasping and trembling in their death agony. I never liked to ask the fisherman to kill the fish, in case he accused me of misplaced sensitivity, so I was in a hurry to put an end to their suffering myself on my work surface in the kitchen, bashing them on the head with my rolling pin.

So it was around midnight, when we got back from work, before Kady and I returned to the subject of the baby. We were sitting side by side on the sofa, nestling close, and caressing and kissing as we listened to Kady's favourite song, performed by Scott McKenzie, which I had put on the record player:

If you're going to San Francisco
Be sure to wear some flowers in your hair.

If you're going to San Francisco
You're gonna meet some gentle people there.

I haven't mentioned Kady's tongue yet, a grave omission. That organ was a fleshy instrument that often changed colour, sometimes turning purplish, and she made virtuoso use of it. It was a kind of male organ, only more mobile. After a kiss that left me dazed, Kady told me, while I was returning to my senses, 'I want a baby because I've found the right father for it.'

'Who is he?'

'You don't know him.'

'Black?'

'Of course. I'm not about to sully my line of descent with blood from the white race, am I? If you can call it a race at all these days, considering how it's degenerated.'

'Whatever you say.'

The masculine half of this reproductive deal washed dishes in the brasserie next door. Like Kady, he was from Mali. Tall and handsome, long-necked, with a proud look in his eyes. His gait was like hers, slow and royal. On the day that we thought most propitious for conception, we took him to the apartment, where he applied himself without great enthusiasm, indeed reluctantly, to the task that we had given him to perform.

He didn't know that he and his prick were there to make a baby. He thought he was simply there for a voyeuristic session which I was supposed to be relishing while they sprawled before my eyes. I wasn't exactly enjoying myself, especially as I thought I saw Kady's eyes shining in orgasm when he came inside her.

Thank goodness there was no need for a replay. Mamadou was born nine months later, weighing 3.7 kilos, father unknown, so he took his mother's surname, Diakité.

Mamadou set the seal on our happiness and made us more of a couple than ever. Until the day when, as I made the rounds of my customers after turning off the stoves, I found myself facing a ghost from the past. He hadn't changed. Faces full of hatred always seem to have been preserved in formalin. They stay the same. His hair had hardly gone grey at all. As for his teeth, they had never had the tartar removed, which did nothing for their appearance and suggested that there was no one in his life who cared for him. They were disappearing into a viscous gunk of brown deposits, and I was just studying them with disgust when, melodramatically rising from the table, he made his way towards me, large nose first, with a wide smile.

'Madame Beaucaire?' he inquired, shaking my hand.

'No,' I told him. 'Madame Zhongling.'

'I can't believe my eyes. Aren't you Madame Beaucaire, née Lempereur?'

'I'm afraid you're mistaken,' I insisted. I shook my head and shrugged my shoulders, breathing deeply to relieve the constriction squeezing the blood of my brain.

'Fancy that!' said the man. 'Forgive me, my mind must be straying. Let me introduce myself: Claude Mespolet, Marseilles's new Prefect of Police. I knew a lady in Paris who had a restaurant serving the same dishes as this place of yours, as well as bearing the same name, La Petite Provence. Foolishly, I thought you must be the same person. I do apologize for the confusion.'

He introduced me to his two lunchtime companions, a couple of fat, red-faced parliamentary deputies, one of them much smaller than the other. Their mouths shone with grease, like the muzzles of dogs coming straight from their bowl.

'All the same, you really do resemble the lady I mentioned,' persisted Claude Mespolet, scrutinizing me from head to foot. 'Only stronger, because she was rather slim, but one always gains weight with age, and it's quarter of a century ago that I knew her. How time flies!'

'It does indeed,' I agreed.

When the time came for Mespolet to pay the bill, I asked him to stay behind for a moment when the two politicians had left.

'Congratulations on your parmesan dish,' he said as I sat down with him. 'You've certainly kept your hand in.'

'I don't suggest that we discuss gastronomy,' I replied, 'but something that directly concerns you.'

And with the smile of a practised blackmailer, I indicated that I had in my hands compromising documents relating to him, more particularly a note dated 1942, signed by himself, in which he dilated on the Jewish origins of my first husband. I had drawn a bow at a venture, because Himmler hadn't left the document with me after letting me read it, but Mespolet's superior little smile was instantly wiped off his face. However, he was not the sort to be easily thrown off balance.

'What are you suggesting?' he asked in a casual tone.

'I'm suggesting that you leave me alone.'

He thought, and then murmured through his teeth,

'You committed a crime when you murdered Jean-André Lavisse in a very shocking way.'

'He was a collaborator,' I said in a low voice.

'Not really. He did the Gaullists of the Free France movement such good service that after the Liberation they awarded him the Resistance medal posthumously.'

'What, they gave it to that heap of shit?'

'People are never all black or all white. Hasn't life taught you that?'

'No, it's taught me the opposite.'

'In any case, your crime isn't subject to any statute of limitations. I've made sure of that with the examining magistrate who was on the case. He's a friend of mine.'

'And yet it was all more than twenty-five years ago.'

'Justice has its codes of which the penal code knows nothing.'

He repeated this remark, puffing himself up with pride at his own wit. He made me think of a gargoyle with a peacock's feather stuck up its bum by some joker.

'If you move to get the case reopened,' I concluded, 'then I will move by making the document in my hands public. This is what's known as dissuasion or the balance of terror. I think it would be best to leave things at that, don't you?'

'Yes, to be sure.'

When Claude Mespolet had left the restaurant I felt an apprehensive twinge from my chest to my stomach, and in spite of the joy that Kady and Mamadou gave me, it was only going to grow in the following years.

49

The Last Death

MARSEILLES, 1970. That twinge of pain never left me. I woke and fell asleep with it. Sometimes it dug so deep into my flesh, spreading pain that left me weak through my breast, that I stopped breathing.

Although for lack of time I put off going for the examinations prescribed by my doctor, I told myself that I was developing cancer. But it was Kady who contracted that disease. It carried her off in a year and a half, after she had lost first one breast to it, then the other, then half a lung, and a tumour developed in her bladder before a glioma in her brain was diagnosed.

Kady didn't want to die in hospital, but at home in our apartment. Wishing to be with her to the end, I closed the restaurant on the pretext of annual holidays. They went on for six weeks.

Courage gives way to nothing except death. It was her refusal to capitulate as she faced her cancer that led my wife to suffer so much, up to the very limits of what was reasonable, that in her last days I sometimes wanted to cut her torments short.

But Kady would spare herself nothing, not even a second, to the very end pretending to savour every drop of life, with a wry little smile that I see before me as I write these lines.

She had asked me to find her some good last words to say when she felt she was about to die. I had suggested Alfred de Musset's: 'Sleep, I am going to sleep at last.'

Kady didn't think that was amusing enough. Most of all she liked the famous last words of Auguste de Villiers de L'Isle-Adam, an unappreciated writer who at least made a good exit: 'Well, I shall remember this planet.'

However, her choice was a phrase that I had thought up myself: 'Is there anyone there?' Yet at the moment when she was breathing her last, holding my hand while Mamadou slept in his cradle, she whispered something else. I couldn't make it out properly and had to ask her to repeat it.

'See you soon,' she said.

From then on she featured in the graveyard of my mind as one of the dead whom I thought of several times a day: my children, my parents, my grandmother, all the men in my life – Gabriel, Liu, even Frankie. With Kady as well they came to quite a number; my personal plot in that graveyard was brimming over.

On the intellectual plane I had lost a good deal. That's the problem with old age; a time comes when you have such a shambles of people and things in the lumber room of your mind that you can't lay hands on anything.

On the sexual plane, I made do with myself from then on. What I like about masturbation is the absence of any prelude leading up to it, and the fact that you don't have to talk to anyone when you've finished. There's nothing like it for saving time and giving the mind a rest.

After Kady's death, I had sometimes felt that I still had life ahead of me. I owe thanks to Mamadou, whose mere smile helped me to patch myself up again. But I had lost the ability to bounce back that had always brought me to my feet again after every blow of fate. I had a tendency to stay in a heaven of my own, viewing the world from above. At sixty-three I felt that wasn't right for my age. At least, not yet.

Something prevented me from letting my vital spark keep me going, as it had always done before. I suffered from that twinge of pain, accompanied by nausea that tormented me to the point where I was waking several times in the night. I underwent all kinds of examinations, and the doctors could find nothing. I knew what I might still try.

*

When I made inquiries about Claude Mespolet, I learned that he had a second home at Lourmarin in the Luberon area, and went there regularly, particularly in summer. He was divorced, without children, and usually visited it on his own, generally on Saturday evenings.

His teeth were so clogged up with tartar that it would have been a miracle for any woman in good condition to agree to share his bed, even for a single night. At the Prefecture of Police, his subordinates said he spent his Sundays gardening, which ought to have convinced me that he wasn't such a bad person after all.

I had come to think that he was impotent, or at least not very good at masturbation. In which case it was something that we had in common, and we could have discussed its advantages; practised in that way love is no longer dangerous, and autarchy allows you to escape the pain of final separation.

One Saturday afternoon I closed the restaurant, left little Mamadou with a neighbour and went to wait for Mespolet at his property in a pine wood. It was August, and the air was alive with midges dancing and swallows flying above the song of cicadas, while the ground was covered with threads of gold.

Claude Mespolet's chauffeur dropped him off at the end of the day. The Prefect of Police was accompanied by a dog, a Jack Russell, the most egotistic and infernal animal in all creation after man. I wasn't expecting the presence of this minor character, but I had the means of putting him out of action, in the shape of a bottle of chloroform in the pocket of my safari jacket.

The prefect walked round the property with his dog, stopping to caress certain trees. Twisted olive trees with black eyes and silver hair. Trees ready to go to war, they seemed to have resisted so much: intense heat, frost, floods. Although I was too far away to be sure, I think he talked to some of them.

When Mespolet had gone into his house, the dog stayed outside, running all over the place and barking at everything in sight. Cicadas, butterflies, birds. He suddenly charged up to me, yapping, and I put out a friendly hand which he licked at once. Having tamed him, I suddenly immobilized him by turning him over on his back, and then I wiped his muzzle with a cloth on which I had poured quarter of the chloroform in the bottle.

'Castro! Castro!'

Claude Mespolet called to his dog for part of the evening from the steps of the house, and he also walked round the garden several times shouting his name. He had no chance of finding him; Castro was lying some way off in the scrubland with his paws tied together and a roll of adhesive tape round his muzzle.

When Mespolet went up to bed, he left the front door ajar in case the dog thought of coming back to sleep in the house. I waited for an hour.

When I went in and faced him, he was sleeping soundly, to judge by his gentle, regular breathing. I watched him for some time in the dim light, in a state of terrible ecstasy. All these years later, I still feel ashamed of that.

I didn't want to hear what Mespolet had to say. He would tell me, plaintively, what such people always say, and in fact it is true enough. There was nothing else he could do, he was only a functionary, he was obeying orders. It made no difference whether the orders came from Marshal Pétain or General de Gaulle; they had to be obeyed, and he didn't know how to do anything else. He had been adept at changing masters throughout his career, passing from Pétainism during the Occupation to the Soviet sentiments of the Liberation when he had to escape being purged – there was nothing else to be done about it – and then reconverting to Gaullism at the end of the 1950s. I already knew what he would say; that's life, it consists of ringing the changes. For one Camus who really resisted, how many were there like Sartre or Gide who were caught in the winds of change and went round like so many weathervanes?

Nor did I want to meet Mespolet's eyes. My friend Jacky in Marseilles has often told me that crooks avoid meeting the eyes of their intended victims, for fear of softening before they pull the trigger. So I did not put on the light before lodging seven bullets in the body of the Prefect of Police with my Walther PPK, which I had equipped for the purpose with a silencer.

After that I set the dog free, before driving back to Marseilles light at heart, listening to Beethoven's Ninth Symphony, which I was playing to celebrate my last death, with the volume turned up high.

50

Ite, missa est

MARSEILLES, 2012. The heat is heavy, falling to the ground like rain. The city stinks of fish and dustbins. Everything is rotting, and all you want to do is throw yourself into the water, but I don't want to make an exhibition of myself. I feel too old for that.

It's my birthday. I've decided to celebrate the day I am a hundred and five years old in small company, at my restaurant, privatized for the occasion. The party consists of Mamadou, Leila, Jacky and his wife, Samir the Mouse and Madame Mandonato, my bookseller friend, who can't hide her delight at having sold her shop yesterday to an organic wine merchant. A very handsome man, she says, and she's made a killing. I'll check up on that when he opens.

I don't know what idiot invented Christmas parties, but if he's still alive I could sort him out. It's at that time, particularly on the evening of 24 December, that I always feel great nostalgia when I think of my dead, beginning with my children and not forgetting my grandson in Trier who was carried off by Alzheimer's.

The feeble-minded narcissist who had the idea of the first birthday party in history is even more criminal. From the age of forty onwards, it's a torture that social convention says you have to inflict on yourself to give other people pleasure. At my age it's even worse; you tell yourself, every time, that this is your last birthday.

If it weren't for the birthday ritual to which I must submit, everything would be all for the best. Since the death of Mespolet the Prefect of Police I have felt happy and relieved; the twinge in my breast went away that very night, never to return. But I notice that all of them round the table seem incredulous when I tell them happily how much I am enjoying life.

'I'd like to believe you,' said Jacky, 'but it can't be easy to feel like that every day, after all that you've lived through.'

'In spite of all, that I'm in the seventh heaven.'

'Or one of the lower ones anyway,' said Samir with his usual scoffing attitude.

I told Jacky that I had indeed, I felt it in the marrow of my bones, lived through what may be considered, without fear of contradiction, one of the most terrible periods in the history of humanity: the century of murderers.

'There have been so many deaths,' I said, 'that people haven't even bothered to keep count.'

The Clingendael Institute in the Netherlands, which specializes in international relations, puts the number of deaths attributable to conflicts, wars and genocides in the twentieth century, always pushing back the boundaries of appalling behaviour as it did, at 231 million.

What animal species kills so many of its own members, and with such ferocity? Not monkeys, anyway, not pigs, and we are close to both of those, nor dolphins or elephants. Even ants behave more humanely than humans.

The twentieth century has seen the extermination of Jews, Armenians and Tutsis. Not to speak of the killings by communists, anti-communists, fascists and anti-fascists. The famines that, for political reasons, have taken place in the Soviet Union, the People's Republic of China and North Korea have decimated the allegedly rebellious peasant populations. There were the 60 or 70 million victims of the Second World War, the brainchild of Adolf Hitler, who invented methods of slaughter on an industrial scale. And we must add all the other infamous incidents in the Belgian Congo, Biafra and Cambodia.

Hitler, Stalin and Mao top the lists of horror, with dozens of millions of deaths to their discredit. With the complicity of their intellectual and political sycophants, they have quenched their thirst for blood and sacrificed non-stop on the altar of their vanity.

'And I'm the one who's the target of abuse!' joked Jacky, setting off laughter. 'After this, don't you think that the police, instead of hounding me, would have done better to call all those criminals and their licensed toadies to account?'

'But then they'd have had to put most of the country in prison,' objected Samir the Mouse. And he turned to me. 'I have a feeling that you've shaken off all these horrors without really being affected by them. How did you manage it?'

I told him that, to be perfectly honest, for a long time I had no idea what allowed me to bear such things, even if I always felt a natural repugnance for adding my own mite to the chorus of humanity's lamentations. If hell is history, then paradise is life.

Happiness isn't given to us; it makes and invents itself. I learned that recently in reading, on the advice of Madame Maldonato, the philosophers of joy who had set down in black and white what I thought, without being able to put it into words. Epicurus, who spoke so well of the happiness of contemplation, died of urine retention after suffering the malady of the stone. Spinoza, who celebrated happiness, was proscribed and cursed by his community. Nietzsche, finally, celebrated life and claimed to know nameless happiness when his body was suffering torments, eaten away by a huge genital sore and third-stage syphilis, together with progressive blindness and auditory hyperaesthesia. Not to mention severe attacks of migraines and vomiting.

'Nietzsche called his pain "my bitch",' said Jacky, a well-read man. 'He said it was as faithful as a dog and he could take out his bad temper on it.'

At the end of dinner, when I was tipsy, I rose to my feet and made a little speech.

'A speech is like a woman's dress. It must be long enough to cover the subject and short enough to be interesting. Mine can be summed up in a single sentence: you only ever get the life you deserve.'

After which I distributed photocopies of my seven commandments to them:

Live each day on this planet as if it were your last.
Forget everything but forgive nothing.
Don't trust love; it's easy to see how to get into it, but not how to get out again.
Leave nothing in your glass, on your plate, or behind you.

Don't hesitate to swim against the current. Only dead fish follow it.

Die alive.

I was just finishing my glass of champagne when I remembered another precept that I'd always made sure to follow: 'Rid yourself of self-esteem or you will never know love.' I cried it out loud, repeating it twice so that everyone could have the benefit of it. Then Jacky connected his mobile phone to the loudspeakers, and conducted us to the music it played while we sang my favourite operatic aria, 'E lucevan le stelle', from *Tosca*, before striking up 'Il Mondo', performed by Il Volo, a trio of Italian tenors, adorable adolescents who had only just flown the nest:

Iiiiil moooooooondo
Non si è fermato mai un momento
La notte insegue sempre il giorno
Ed il giorno verrá ·

Oh yes, day will come, dear little tenors, never fear. It's there to meet you every morning; you have only to open your eyes.

After dinner, while I was saying goodbye to Jacky and his wife on the doorstep of La Petite Provence, I heard a lot of shouting. Bleats, interrupted by squealing. On the corner of the Avenue de la Canebière, a woman in a floaty dress was on the ground grappling with a hooligan who was trying to tear off her necklace. I immediately recognized the Cheetah I mentioned at the beginning of this book.

By the time we reached the scene of the crime, he had made off. Jacky helped the lady, a young slip of a Botoxed octogenarian, to her feet. She was shedding tears and sniffling, 'That was the necklace my husband gave me the year he died. It's so long ago now! The necklace isn't worth anything, but it's the sentimental value, you see.'

I asked Jacky if he could use his contacts to find the name and address of the hooligan, because I had a couple of things to say to him.

Epilogue

The Cheetah's first name was Ryan, and he lived with his mother on the coastal road, in a little Baroque house with a view of the sea. Madame Ravare, who was a respected psychotherapist and a widow aged forty-six, saw her clients at home, except on Wednesday and Thursday afternoons, which she spent in the Timone Hospital where she treated other patients.

I had this and other information from Jacky Valtamore, who had insisted on going with me. I agreed, with a bad grace, but at the age of 105, as he bluntly pointed out, you can't be too careful. It was true that the heatwave of the last few days had not done me any good, even though I observed the instructions of the Ministry of Health to the letter when they recommended the elderly, who were threatened by dehydration, to drink plenty of water. I also felt as if I had butter in my trainers. At every step I took, it was as if I might slip and fall.

After greeting his henchman, a large, lethargic character on watch in the alley, Jacky told me to wait for him at the door. He climbed over a low wall to go round behind Madame Ravare's house on the side facing the sea, before opening the door to me a few minutes later. I smiled; at the age of eighty-two, Jacky hadn't lost his touch.

'Is he there?' I asked.

'I told you he would be,' Jacky murmured in some irritation. 'I've been having him watched from morning to evening for the last three days. If he wasn't here we wouldn't have come.'

I followed Jacky up the little spiral staircase leading to the Cheetah's room. The boy was lying on his bed with his eyes closed, and the headphones of his MP3 player in his ears. Whether he was asleep or not didn't make much difference; he was cut off from the world of the living.

'Are you asleep?' shouted Jacky.

Ryan Ravare opened one eye and then the other before sitting up straight, with a horrified expression. I was pleased with the effect I'd had on him; he recognized me.

'Yes, you're right, punk. I'm the mad old biddy who scared you so much one day on the Vieux-Port.'

I took my pistol, a Glock 17, out of the pocket of my safari jacket.

'I did warn you,' I went on, 'what would happen if you did the same thing again. Well, laddie, the Day of Judgement has come.'

Jacky took me by the sleeve, frowning, and whispered in my ear, 'What do you think you're doing, Rose? We talked about teaching him a little lesson, that's all.'

'We'll see about that,' I whispered. 'I'm improvising.'

Sensing discord in the enemy ranks, Ryan tried to turn

it to his own advantage. 'Let me tell you, madame, you are very aggressive.'

'And you're not aggressive with the people you steal from, punk?'

'I don't know what you're talking about. I haven't done anything, and there you go accusing me in my own home. What's the world coming to?'

Whereupon he adopted the whining tone peculiar to the younger generation. 'In case you haven't noticed, I'm suffering from severe depression at the moment. I can't sleep, I can't eat, my mother is very worried. You can check if you like; I'm on a course of medical treatment.'

He showed us a quantity of medications assembled to form a kind of small Provençal village, perched on his bedside table as if it were on a mountain peak.

'I'm terribly tired,' he went on. 'I've been suffering from profound depression for years, that's what they diagnosed at the hospital. My life is no fun, believe me. I can't bring myself to go out, and recently it's been even worse. I've had thoughts of suicide.'

He seemed to be talking to me, but all the time he was looking at Jacky, the weak link. I coughed to attract his attention, and said, 'I'll offer you a deal. If you hand yourself in to the police with all your loot, your life will be saved. If not I'll finish you off here and now.'

'Take it easy,' Jacky whispered between his teeth. 'Talking would be a better idea.'

Ryan seemed to be hesitating. I stuck to my point.

'If you won't pay your debt to society, you'd better know that I shall find it a real pleasure to kill you. It's only because of my friend here that I'm restraining myself instead of firing this gun at once, so as to give you a chance.'

'I don't fancy going to prison.'

'You have no option.'

To this Ryan replied that his priority was to get out of the bad patch he was in, and detention didn't seem to him ideal for doing that. I told him to face his responsibilities, before adding that if he felt like denouncing us once he was behind bars, he wouldn't make old bones; Jacky and I had many contacts in the prisons. Vicious and nasty characters who loved taking it out on minor thugs of his kind.

After we had escorted Ryan to Canebière police station, I went to drink my first pastis of the year with Jacky at the brasserie on the Quai des Belges. When I ordered us a second round, Jacky shook his head.

'Another one, just one,' I protested. 'You have to drink fast before they take the glass away.'

'Promise me it will be the last.'

'We must always drink as if it was the last, Jacky. I'm sure I don't have to tell you that we die from not having lived, and if we haven't then we die just the same.'

'If it comes to dying, Rose, you might as well do it fully conscious and in good health. Not bruised like a quince.'

'Excuse me, but that's the kind of idea a drunk would get. The one thing that life hasn't taught me is how to die. And guess what, I don't intend to leave you just yet.'

*

Life is like a favourite book, a story, a novel, a work of history. You get used to the characters, you let the incidents carry you away. In the end, whether you're writing the story or reading it, you never want to finish it. That's the case with me. Especially as I still have so much else to do and say.

I know that my lips will always go on moving, even when they are mingled with the earth, and that they will go on saying yes to life – yes, yes, yes...

Recipes from
La Petite Provence

MY GRANDMOTHER'S PLAKI

For six or more

Ingredients
2 kg white haricot beans, shelled
1 large onion
2 carrots sliced into rounds
1 bunch of parsley, chopped
1 head of garlic, the cloves peeled but not sliced
2 large ripe tomatoes, chopped
the leaves of 2 large celery stalks
a bunch of parsley for flavouring

Preparation
Chop the onion and brown it in a casserole dish.

Add the carrots, tomatoes, garlic and celery leaves.

Add the haricot beans and bunch of parsley, cover with water.

Simmer over gentle heat for an hour.

At the end of cooking time, add salt and pepper to taste and the chopped parsley.

Allow to cool. Eat warm or well chilled, adding a little olive oil.

MAMIE JO'S PARMESAN DISH

For eight or more

Ingredients
1 kg tomatoes
1 kg aubergines
1 kg courgettes
5 onions
5 cloves of garlic, thyme, a bay leaf, parsley
3 eggs
100 g grated parmesan

Preparation
Brown 3 of the onions in olive oil, with the skinned and deseeded tomatoes. Allow to simmer for 45 minutes with 3 cloves of garlic, thyme, the bay leaf and some parsley. Take the lid off the pan towards the end of cooking time to let liquid evaporate, intensifying the flavour. Put the onion and tomato sauce through a sieve or liquidize in an electric mixer.

Slice the aubergines, salt them, then drain the liquid that comes out of them. Brown the aubergine slices, put them on kitchen paper to absorb the fat.

Brown the chopped courgettes with the two remaining onions. Let them soften over gentle heat until you can crush them with a spoon. Add the garlic, crushed, the parmesan and the beaten eggs.

Line an ovenproof dish with the aubergine slices, making sure they come well up the sides. Put the courgette and egg mixture into the dish on top of the aubergines.

Place the dish in water in a bain-marie in the oven at 180° C, leave for 20 minutes. Let it rest, and then chill it in the fridge. Take the dish out an hour before the meal, turn the vegetable mixture out and serve with the tomato sauce.

EMMA LEMPEREUR'S CARAMEL FLAN

For six

Ingredients
7 eggs
1 litre milk
1 vanilla pod
1 sachet of vanilla sugar
200 g caster sugar
7 sugar lumps and two spoonfuls of water for the caramel, to be added directly to the pan. Boil together to make the caramel, pour into a charlotte mould or non-stick cake pan 20 centimetres in diameter, allow the caramel to chill.

Preparation
Mix the milk, the caster sugar, vanilla sugar and vanilla pod together and bring to the boil. Allow the mixture to chill.
   Add the beaten eggs.
   Pour the mixture into the mould or pan on top of the chilled caramel.
   Put the pan or mould into a bain-marie in the oven at a temperature of 180° C for 45 minutes.
   Chill the flan again, putting it in the fridge with cling film over it to keep out any other odours.
   Turn out of the mould or pan just before serving it.

FRENCHY'S *TARTE AUX FRAISES À L'AMÉRICAINE,* OR STRAWBERRY SHORTCAKE

For eight

Ingredients for the pastry case and filling
1 sachet of dried yeast
250 g of finely sieved flour
150 g double cream
A pinch of salt
115 g unsalted butter
5 soup spoons caster sugar

Ingredients and preparation for the strawberry topping
1kg fresh strawberries. Choose them carefully; if possible they should come from local soft-fruit farms.
Cut them into two or three each, depending on size.
Add 100 g white sugar and mix gently.
Leave the fruit to rest. If you have any doubt of the freshness of the fruit, add a little lemon juice.

Preparation
Preheat the oven to 210° C.

Mix together the flour, dried yeast, sugar and pinch of salt.

Add the butter cut into small pieces, but handle the mixture lightly.

Add the cream to moisten the pastry dough.

Roll out the pastry, cut it into eight rectangles about 2 cm thick.

Place the pastry rectangles on a greased or non-stick baking sheet. Sprinkle with a little icing sugar.

Bake in the oven for about 12 minutes, until the pastry is golden brown. When it is cold, cut each rectangle in two lengthwise.

Arrange the strawberries between two layers of pastry. Add sweetened whipped cream flavoured with vanilla. Place three strawberries on each slice for decoration.

This is the traditional recipe. At Frenchy's I took a shortcut with the pastry. After mixing the baked pastry slices and strawberries, I served the strawberry shortcake in a large glass salad bowl, covering it all with vanilla-flavoured whipped cream to which I added a finger of whisky.

*A Little Library
of the Century*

The Armenian Genocide

ARNOLD J. TOYNBEE: *Armenian Atrocities: The Murder of a Nation*, Hodder & Stoughton, 1915.
RAYMOND KÉVORKIAN: *Le Génocide des Arméniens*, Odile Jacob, 2006.

Stalinism

VASILY GROSSMAN, trans. Robert Chandler: *Life and Fate,* New York Review Books Classics, 2006.
ALEXANDR SOLZHENITSYN, trans. Thomas P. Whitney: *The Gulag Archipelago,* Harvill Press Editions, 2007.
SIMON SEBAG MONTEFIORE: *Stalin, The Court of the Red Tsar,* Weidenfeld & Nicolson, 2003.
TIMOTHY SNYDER: *Bloodlands: Europe Between Hitler and Stalin*, Basic Books, 2010.

Nazism

HANNAH ARENDT: *The Origins of Totalitarianism*, Schocken Books, 1951.
HANNAH ARENDT: *Eichmann in Jerusalem*, Viking Press, 1963.
JOACHIM FEST, trans. Richard and Clara Winston:, *Hitler. A Biography,* Harcourt, 1974.
JOACHIM FEST, trans. Michael Bullock: *The Face of the Third Reich,* Ace Books, 1963.

Saul Friedländer: *Nazi Germany and the Jews*, Harper Collins, 1997.

Günter Grass, trans. Ralph Manheim: *The Tin Drum,* Harcourt, 1961; fiftieth-anniversary ed., trans. Breon Mitchell, Harvill Secker, 2009.

Ian Kershaw: *Hitler*, 2 vols., Allen Lane, 1998, 2000.

Felix Kersten, trans. Constantine Fitzgibbon and James Oliver: *The Kersten Memoirs* (1940–45), Doubleday, 1957.

Peter Longerich, trans. Jeremy Noakes and Lesley Sharpe: *Himmler, A Life*, OUP, 2012.

Michaël Prazan: *Einsatzgruppen*, Seuil, 2010.

Michel Tournier, trans. Barbara Bray: *The Erl-King*, Collins, 1972.

Stanislav Zámečník, trans. Peter Heumos and Gitta Grossman, *That Was Dachau*, publications of Dachau memorial site, 2004.

Maoism

Jung Chang and Jon Halliday: *Mao: The Unknown Story*, Jonathan Cape, 2005.

Jean-Luc Domenach: *Mao, sa cour et ses complots*. Fayard, 2012.

Yang Jisheng, trans. Stacy Mosher and Guo Jiang: *Tombstone: The Great Chinese Famine*, Macmillan, 2012.

Alexander V . Pantsov with Steven I. Levine: *Mao, the Real Story*, Simon & Schuster, 2012.

Jean Pasqualini: *Prisonnier de Mao*, Gallimard, 1976.

The Death Camps

ROBERT ANTELME, trans. Jeffrey Haight: *The Human Race*,
Northwestern University, 1992.

RAUL HILBERG: *The Destruction of the European Jews*, Yale
University Press, 3 vols., 1961.

PRIMO LEVI, trans. Stuart Woolf: *If This Is a Man*, Orion,
1959.

DAVID ROUSSET, trans. Ramon Guthrie: *The Other Kingdom,*
Reynal & Hitchcock 1947.

ELIE WIESEL, trans. Stella Rodway: *Night*, MacGibbon and
Kee, 1960; new trans. Marion Wiesel, 2006.

The German Occupation of France

SIMONE DE BEAUVOIR, trans. Peter Green: *The Prime of Life,*
Lancer Books, 1966.

GILBERT JOSEPH: *Une si douce occupation, Simone de Beauvoir
et Jean-Paul Sartre, 1940–1944*, Albin Michel, 1991.

IRÈNE NÉMIROVSKY, trans. Sandra Smith: *Suite française*,
Chatto & Windus, 2006.

The Twentieth Century in General

SIMONE DE BEAUVOIR, trans. H. M. Parshley: *The Second
Sex,* Vintage Books NY, 1989.

SAUL BELLOW: *Herzog,* Viking Press, 1964.

ALBERT CAMUS, trans. Anthony Bower: *The Rebel* (new
ed.), Penguin Modern Classics, 2000.

MARGUERITE DURAS, trans. Herma Briffault: *The Sea Wall,*

Farrar, Straus, 1967.

WINSTON GROOM: *Forrest Gump,* Knopf Doubleday, Black Swan 1986.

JONAS JONASSON, trans. Rod Bradbury: *The Hundred-Year-Old Man Who Climbed Out of the Window and Disappeared*, Hyperion Books US, Hesperus Press UK, 2012.

JACK KEROUAC: *On The Road*, 1957, new ed. Penguin Modern Classics, 2000.

J.M.G. LE CLÉZIO, trans. Daphne Woodward: *The Interrogation*, Atheneum 1964, new ed. Simon & Schuster 2009.

NORMAN MAILER: *An American Dream,* Dial Press, 1969.

TIERNO MONÉNEMBO: *L'Aîné des orphelins*, Points-Seuil, 2000.

J. D. SALINGER: *The Catcher In The Rye*, Little, Brown, 1951.

GAÉTAN SOUCY, trans. Sheila Fischman: *The Little Girl Who Was Too Fond of Matches*, Arcade Publishing NY, HarperCollins UK, 2002.

JOHN STEINBECK, *Tortilla Flat*, Covici-Friede, 1935, new ed. Penguin Modern Classics, 2000.

KURT VONNEGUT: *Slaughterhouse-Five*, Delacorte 1969.

SIMONE WEIL, trans. Arthur Wills: *Gravity and Grace,* Routledge & Kegan Paul, 1952.